Geoff Hollister
Out of Nowhere

OUT OF NOWHERE

THE INSIDE STORY OF HOW NIKE MARKETED
THE CULTURE OF RUNNING

Geoff Hollister

MEYER & MEYER SPORTS

British Library Cataloguing in Publication Data
A catalogue record for this book is available from the British Library

Geoff Hollister
Out of Nowhere
Maidenhead: Meyer & Meyer Sport (UK) Ltd., 2008
ISBN: 978-1-84126-234-5

© 2008 by Meyer & Meyer Sport (UK) Ltd.
Aachen, Adelaide, Auckland, Budapest, Cape Town, Graz, Indianapolis,
Maidenhead, New York, Olten (CH), Singapore, Toronto
 Member of the World
Sport Publishers' Association (WSPA)
www.w-s-p-a.org
Printed and bound by: B.O.S.S Druck und Medien GmbH
ISBN: 978-1-84126-234-5
E-Mail: verlag@m-m-sports.com
www.m-m-sports.com

Events that seem so inconsequential at the time, history changes all of that.

—Homer Hickam, author of *The Rocket Boys*

If you are going to tell the truth, you better make them laugh: otherwise, they'll kill you.

—George Bernard Shaw

ACKNOWLEDGEMENTS

It started with a story—so many stories. These were verbal presentations I delivered to high school athletes, Nike employees and University of Oregon and Lehigh University business students. The latter changed everything.

Of course I wrote the stories down. Lehigh business professor Karen Collins said my stories deserve a wider audience than just her students. "You should write a book." She kept the pressure on me for two more years. Finally, in 2004, I began to write. Then I had a major disruption.

I rededicated myself and attacked the project with discipline and a sense of urgency in January 2007. My thanks to Karen for never giving up on me.

Another pivotal influence was Homer Hickam. I'm laughing out loud to myself on a flight to Melbourne while reading Hickam's *The Rocket Boys*. My daughter Kaili is an actor and landed the part opposite Jake Gyllenhaal in the feature film version *October Sky*. I wrote to Homer asking for advice. His wonderful and truthful quote deserves a page by itself within this book. In addition he supplied me with another key. Homer insisted that such a task would be much easier if I kept a diary or good notes. I did. I kept all my trip reports and daytimers. My story had good bones.

I have an incredible list of real characters I am indebted to. They pushed me, inspired me, worked with me and competed with and against me. In addition, I am thankful for the many teams I've been a member of—from my childhood to college athletic teams, my Navy teams, many Nike teams and medical teams.

Unfortunately, between the covers, many have failed to make the final edit. That does not mean I forgot you. My friend Laura Houston, a creative writing instructor and consultant to Nike, encouraged me to participate in a writer's workshop on the Oregon coast. I was somewhat reluctant to read my work in front of total strangers. It had been over 40 years since I had taken an English class. I took the leap of faith, and there I was reading my stories. At the end of the workshop, instructors Stevan Allred and Joanna Rose approached me saying, "We would be interested in shepherding you through the remainder of your project."

I remember that at the end of each day of the workshop, I could not wait to return to my laptop. I had better work to do. As at the coast, I jumped at the chance to continue to work with Stevan and Joanna. They helped shape the arc of the story, did the heavy editing and elevated my work with their thoughtful questions. They wanted to know more. In the process, they took me from a rough draft to a readable story.

I am thankful that my lifetime friend Jeff Galloway introduced me to his publisher, Hans Jurgen Meyer. Hans embraced the story early. With the goal of delivery prior to the 2008 Olympic Trials in Eugene, an ambitious deadline was set.

Nike archivists moved swiftly and electronically for images that help bring the story to life. I powered through my boxes of prints and slides for additional work I had shot over the years. This took days in what became a visual trip down memory lane. Thank you Dan Long and Pete Montagne.

Nike's first employee is still with us—at least he was with me on this project. Jeff Johnson never takes anything at face value and had the most critical eye in reading the manuscript. He corrected errors that only an insider would know and he pushed me. This is an improved work because of his effort.

Lastly, thanks to Lenee Cobb who took on the task of transcribing my handwritten journals into print. When I left architecture, my handwriting degenerated from legible printing to a semi-scroll that some identify as "Greek." Not an easy job.

My story is just one of many thousands at Nike. While I focused primarily on Nike's running culture, which gave us our start, Nike today is multi-sport and global. There have been many players of importance. My life happened to take place at a unique time where the stars converged. Thank you to the many who contributed to bringing my rollercoaster ride of a life to print.

CONTENTS

PREFACE

As I write this, I am fighting cancer, but I've had an extraordinary life. I had the good fortune to meet Phil "Buck" Knight when I was still in college, becoming Buck's first salesman in the state of Oregon. Like Buck, I was one of "The Men of Oregon" coached and mentored by the incomparable Bill Bowerman. Call it luck and timing, but Bill and Buck formed a partnership that became Nike. Running brought us together, and running has remained a part of my life ever since.

Athletics impart the values of teamwork, discipline, loyalty and giving your all, and these same values are at the heart of Nike's corporate culture. On the field of athletic rivalry being competitive means winning. In the corporate world, Nike has won with innovative design, and by being sensitive to its customers' needs in an ever-changing environment. But in my personal and professional life, something greater has been built—a community. It started small. But that community of athletes is now global and extends from the elite to all of us who participate in gyms, on courts, on roads and trails. Anyone can belong.

Looking back, I am blessed, proud and humbled. I started selling shoes out of the trunk of a modest Sunbeam Talbot 90. I was part of a small team that's become much larger. We came out of the Pacific Northwest where there was no shoe industry. We came "out of nowhere."

CHAPTER 1: THE ROAD TO EUGENE

The last of the dew has melted off the grass on a late summer morning. I run out to my distant position after members of the Kiwanis Club lime the base lines. Center field is partially occupied by the large wood-sided roller rink. Perfectly placed broad leafed maple trees ring the entire field. In another month, the sap from the leaves will dot the waxed bodies of the Desotos, Packards and Studebakers parked beneath as the Canby faithful come to watch their team. Just like the Dodgers, I'm wearing a white uniform with blue cap and socks, but proudly have a blue "C" on my chest.

I turn and face the opposing batter at home plate. It seems so far away. I am Duke Snyder, just as I had seen him on the little black & white television set Mr. Miller brought into our classroom. "This is big stuff—the World Series, the Dodgers against the Yankees at Ebbets Field."

I stand in center, waiting for something to happen. I wonder if Duke ever got this bored. Or Jackie Robinson or Maury Wills. It didn't matter to me whether those guys were black or white, I just wanted to be like them. In my mind, Wills sprints to second, stealing another base to lead the big leagues.

Mike Masterson is our catcher. The biggest guy in our class, Mike can hit the long ball and damage a windshield beyond left field. He has hair in places I didn't know I would. He also isn't afraid of Mike Stone's stinger fast ball. They are "the two Mikes." With Mike Stone on the mound, we have a good chance of winning.

Harry Eilers plays first. Lanky and bespectacled early in life, Harry reminds me of Goofy in the cartoons. In our warm-up, he threw a mean sidearm, occasionally missing the intended target, sending the ball into left field. But the two Mikes, those guys were special, the guys who had the gift, that something extra to give at game time when it counted the most.

Dad is the head wrestling coach at Canby High School. Baseball along with wrestling are my first sports. This is a big thing to him. On a Saturday, Mom is busy making banana splits at the Parson's Drug Store soda fountain two blocks away. My sisters will have to oblige me and stick with Dad through every inning.

Our coaches are parents who know something about the game. They are smart enough to put the two Mikes near the front of the batting order. "Hairy Mike" is positioned to get two or three runners batted in with a hit of Babe Ruth proportions. "Hit it a city block, Mike! Com'on, Babe!" Don't know where the "com'on, Babe" came from, but we all say it anyway. I am well down the batters' lineup. Often I don't get my chance until another inning. Our side is retired and I run back out to center field, turn and wait. Crouched with mitt on the left knee, hand on the right, if a ball ever is hit anywhere close to center field, it is mine.

We retire the side from Lone Elder. I'm finally on deck. I run the neck of my Louisville Slugger through my hands with a little fine dust from the dugout. Harry Eilers bobs up and down in his batter's stance. I know Harry is giggling within, thinking he's confusing the pitcher with the height of the strike zone. I have never seen pitching like this before. I look back at the pitcher, then Harry, and then the catcher. "Whop!!" The ball is in the catcher's mitt, Harry strikes out, and I am up.

I remove my cap and put on the plastic batter's helmet. I stare out at the pitcher, and try to see the ball. I wonder how I could fear such a small object. With no one on base, he only has me to look at. Even without a distraction, the first ball hits the dust in front of the plate—"BEall!" the umpire screams, which I think is overkill for little Canby, Oregon. I follow with a wild swing at a pitch that doesn't merit the effort. Then I just stand in my stance and let him come to me. Finally, "ball four," and with a huge smile, I carry my bat halfway down the first baseline. I don't exactly know what to do with it.

I stomp my metal cleats on the first base bag. The caked white lime from the bottom of my Spalding black leather spikes covers the dirt. John Plant is up next. I take a few steps away from the bag, gauging the 50-60 feet to second. A "righty," the pitcher turns on the mound. I am off in a mad sprint. The infielders yell and the ball is lost in the catcher's glove. But I only see one thing—the bag. Two strides out, I pull my right leg back, point my left toe and go airborne. I slide in a dust cloud until my foot stops at the bag—just like Maury Wills. I stand up untouched and look down with pride at my dirty uniform. I am in the game.

John Plant strikes out and strands me, and I am back out in center field. At least now, I feel like a real player. Under the cotton candy cloud sky, I think of my heroes Robinson, Snyder, Hodges, Campanella, but mostly Wills. This must be what it's like to be a baseball player.

It takes another inning, but I get another at bat. This time, I am leading off. Hurrying to get the helmet, and with only a few practice swings, I am into my stance. "Zing!" The first pitch comes right at me. I turn and duck. The ball must have hit the numbers on my back. There's a hot sting in my back that makes me grimace and hop a little as I make my way to first base. I swing my left shoulder to loosen up, then take a couple steps off the bag. As soon as the first pitch is on its way, I pivot and dig in my cleats. I am running upright with the crunching sound of fresh dirt beneath my cleats and then I'm down in a swoop of dust. The ball flies over the second baseman, landing in center field. I know I can't make the throw from center to third, and it's a safe bet their fielder can't either. I'm up and off to third, and this time I don't even have to slide. The errant ball hits on the third base line and clanks loudly into the chain link fence in front of the bench. There isn't an infielder near. I race to home plate standing up.

The whole summer, I never get a hit. With the opposing pitchers often missing the strike zone, I lead the team in stolen bases after being walked. Sometimes I am even lucky enough to get hit by the ball.

The stage is set. I know what I can do. I can run.

Fast forward a few years to high school, and I was starting to run more, which on weekends included a trip on the Canby ferry and a run around Pete's Mountain. It seemed like it took all day, but I got my letter as a freshman, mostly in the sprints. I can remember running the quarter mile on a grass track at Gervais, pushing their star senior football player all the way to the tape. Then he came up to me afterward and said, "Kid, stick with it—you could be good at this."

I kept wrestling and playing football to keep my options open. On the track, I decided to display my new talent and sprinted all out on the turn. I thought I'd breeze the hurdle in my lane but I crashed through it with my lead leg, sending me to the cinders with a forward somersault. The only thing that got damaged that day was my ego.

If I owe my parents anything during my childhood, it would be that they let me play. There was no immediacy to my future, and no great expectations. And play, I did. The old Cozy Corner house had a barn next door, perfect for Cowboys and Indians with cap guns blazing away and plenty of hay to soften the blows of the fallen. I don't know how Mom tolerated the "whop-whop" on the south side of the house as I wound up my pitch with a tennis ball from across the driveway. I was Sandy Koufax, except I was right handed. When the ball returned I shifted to second for the stop, completing the double play with a midair sidearm play to first. The laurel hedge in the front yard became the opposing line as I'd run a slant or dive on a muddy day. Heisman Trophy winner Terry Baker was in charge of the Beaver offense now, and all 5-foot-8-inches of me duplicated his moves.

My dad was gone for the whole summer of '60, working on his doctorate at the University of Oregon, and he asked me to join him for a week. The Men's U.S. Olympic Track and Field Team would be training there, at Hayward Field.

I had read about Hayward Field in the newspapers. It was home to the University of Oregon and the Emerald Empire Athletic Association, and in my mind, it had to be a very green place. When I walked on the northwest corner for the first time, I couldn't believe it. It was just as I had imagined, with a manicured green infield, surrounded with green wooden grandstands built in 1918, and beyond that, a dark green ribbon of conifer trees.

For a track athlete, this was nirvana. It was enough just to see it, but once I could focus on the athletes using it, I scrambled to put film in my Brownie camera and readied the pages of my scrapbook. World record holder John Thomas was on the high jump apron and Ralph Boston was landing in the long jump pit. Dave Sime was putting his sweats back on. Then there was my favorite, Olympic gold medal hurdler, Glenn Davis. I bet he never hit a hurdle.

I'd take their picture, say hello, and ask for their autograph. I still have the scrapbook, and decades later I would recognize one particular picture I took. I knew the athletes congregating around a bench on the infield. They were Oregon distance runners—Dyrol Burleson and Bill Dellinger. There was a man sitting on the bench with his back turned to me, arms stretched out, broad brimmed hat on, in the epicenter of the discussion. I had no idea who he was, but he would become the most influential person in my life. He was Bill Bowerman, coach of the University of Oregon track team.

Dave Sime won a silver medal in the 100 at the 1960 Olympics with a time of 10.35 seconds. Glenn Davis won back-to-back gold medals in the 400 hurdles, first in the 1956 Melbourne Olympics, and then in the 1960 Rome Olympics, where he added a gold medal in the 4x400 relay.

In 1960 and 1961, Burleson set American Records for both the 1500 and the mile. His best times were 3:40.9 and 3:57.6, respectively. Dellinger set American Records in the 1500, 5000, 2 mile (indoors) and 3 mile (indoors) in 1956, 1958, and 1959. In 1959, he set world records in the 2 mile (indoors: 8:49.9) and the 3 mile (indoors: 13:37:0).

Dad was finding that the pressure of paying a mortgage on a school administrator's salary could strain the budget. I did my part, and from the time we lived in the old Cozy Corner house, I bought my own clothes and Christmas presents, mowing neighbor's yards for $1 and selling bows of holly and spruce from our trees. In the summer, all three of us kids would pick berries, cherries, and beans. I always credited Mom for inspiring the work ethic, but once, when I walked my two sisters all the way home from the berry fields because I thought it was too hot to pick, Dad smacked me so hard across the face I could see stars.

Two years later, on an early summer morning, outside Eugene, here was Dad joining us in the fields, picking berries and beans. Teachers don't get paid in the summer, so while Dad was working on his doctorate, he toiled to provide a little more for the family table.

Life was good, then Dad dropped the bomb. He'd been offered the position as Vice Principal and Dean of Boys at North Eugene High School and was taking it. Mom was in tears over the decision. When I got home from school and saw her sobbing endlessly over a chair, Dad was on his way to the mailbox. I ran out to the drive and picked up rocks, launching one after another at him in my best Sandy Koufax fastball motion. Dad didn't move. He knew it wasn't a popular decision and just stood there and took it. What I didn't know was that this was the best move we ever made, and my life would change forever.

My parents bought a house at 1462 Hilyard, just two blocks from the University of Oregon campus. One of the advantages of living on Hilyard Street was that I could walk or run up to Hayward Field anytime I wanted and watch the Oregon team work out. Coach Bill Bowerman had built a powerhouse that had balance. The sprinters were led by Canadian world record holder Harry Jerome, joined by football stars Mel Renfro and

Mike Gaechter (both of whom would later play for the Dallas Cowboys) and the world's top hurdler, Jerry Tarr. They would set the world record in the 440-relay. As much as I marveled at their talent, I knew I'd never be like them.

I was hanging on the chain link fence on the north end of the track the Thursday afternoon that Dyrol Burleson outran Stanford's Ernie Cunliffe to the first sub-4 mile at Hayward Field. Following Cal's Don Bowden, he was only the second American to do what many thought was humanly impossible. "Burly" anchored Bowerman's 4-mile relay team, along with Keith Forman, Archie San Romani and Vic Reeve. Together they set a new world record, and they received an invitation to travel "down under" during the Christmas break. The trip followed a raucous week of competition at Hayward Field where Oregon won the NCAA team title in front of a home crowd. This was the moment when Eugene fell in love with the U of O track & field team, and I was there. The sense of pride was inspiring, and I wanted to be like them.

> The 1962 world record time set by Forman,
> San Romani, Reeve, and Burleson was 16:08:9.

I had learned that a favorite weekend run for the university runners was around Spencer Butte, a tall volcanic projection that stood guard over the south end of Eugene. I could head right out Hilyard, start the climb on the east slope, follow the dips and turns on the backside, then fly almost out of control down Willamette Street, zigzag to the right past South High and then slow for a few blocks until I was home. It became a ritual. As a result, I ate more food and went through shoes.

The only place in Eugene to buy a track shoe was John Warren Hardware. There was Luby's, but Luby was a retired stick and ball guy, and the attitude there was that running was for sissies. I didn't know it, but Warren was also a stick and ball guy, and a good one. But between the death of the legendary

Bill Hayward and the arrival of Bowerman, John Warren filled in as the Oregon track coach.

At John Warren's, you could buy running shoes made by Puma, Adidas and Converse. Training shoes were called flats. Adidas made training flats with either a hard outsole or a soft. With the pounding I was taking on the road, I went for the soft outsole that sported a white leather upper and green stripes. The soft sole wore like butter, and it didn't help that I'd wear them to school with my lettermen's sweater.

CHAPTER 2: CALL ME BILL

As a senior in high school, I had decisions to make about my future. The Vietnam War was on, and I would be subject to the draft if I didn't go to college. My parents had both gone to Oregon State and would have been pleased if I'd chosen to follow their lead, but the University of Oregon had the better track team. Still, I hadn't heard from Bill Bowerman and had never met him. Burleson had run for coach Sam Bell at Cottage Grove High School, but when Bell got the Oregon State job "Burly" went to Oregon to run for Bowerman and was getting ready for a summer showdown with the world record holder Herb Elliot in the Tokyo Olympics. Bowerman was also preparing his team for the NCAA championships. I knew he had plenty on his mind, but I should at least show my interest. So I walked over to his office to meet him.

The walls were bare. There were no plaques nor mementos, no reminders of two national championships, not even a framed diploma like you'd see in your doctor's office. Nearly 40 years later on my final visit to the Bowerman house perched like an eagle's nest on the hill above the McKenzie River, I would find the plaques piled in a dirt basement, covered with dust and mouse droppings. So little was this man consumed with self-importance.

Bowerman stood up when I came in and just seemed to keep rising, outstretching a large hand that engulfed mine. He was six-foot-two, with a military crew cut and short sleeve white shirt. "Have a seat."

I sat down, and then there was silence. There always seemed to be silence when his crystal blue eyes searched you like a lighthouse protecting you from a damaging rock in your near future. I was a graduating senior in high school, and a lot of that future was in front of me. I did not know then that this molder of men would have such a profound impact on me. Somehow I found the courage to speak to him.

"Coach Bowerman, I am interested in coming to Oregon."

"Why do you want to come to Oregon?"

"To be the best miler I can be."

"Why do you want to come to Oregon?"

Repeating the question surprised me—it was something my German teacher, Herr Webking, would do when you gave an incomplete answer. Bowerman could obviously read the confusion on my face without a word from me.

"You're going to Oregon to get an education," he said. "You can't run for the rest of your life."

My dad's office was next door to one of Bowerman's closest friends, Bob Newland, and I knew Dad had a high regard for both Newland and Bowerman. What I didn't know was that Bob Newland and the North Eugene Principal Ray Hendrickson were two of Bowerman's closest friends. Hendrickson, sporting his red coat, was the starter for all the meets. Newland was the event manager and would coordinate three Olympic trials at Hayward Field. Together, they would be the backbone in the formation of the Emerald Empire Association, which would become the Oregon Track Club. Little did I know that through these family connections Bowerman already knew about me.

It was time for me to leave, so I said, "Thanks, Coach," and stood up. He got up as I left and shook my hand. "Son, don't call me Coach. Call me Bill or Mr. Bowerman."

Walking across the campus to my parents' house I was filled with excitement. I'd finally met "The Man." Although he was already a legend in Eugene, the sport and beyond, there was so little I knew about him, and it seemed he preferred it that way. Yet, he didn't confuse you. Direct and to the point, you knew what he expected. If there was a difference of opinion, there would be little question whose path you would take.

By the time I opened the front door, Dad was home. I shared with him my conversation with Bowerman, and then I told him, "I'm going to Oregon." I thought this might bother Dad, as he initially stood there without expression. Then he said something I've never forgotten, "Son, I raised you to give you to Bill."

What Dad meant was, "I love you, but at 18, you're becoming a handful, and I have all the confidence Bill will take you the rest of the way." I think a lot of parents felt that way. You do your best, but sometimes the person who will really make a difference has been places, shared experiences and met people that you, as a parent, have not. It all becomes part of the molding process, and Bowerman had a mold in mind that he called "The Men of Oregon."

CHAPTER 3: HE MARKED ME

My favorite instructor at the University of Oregon was a short, portly lady with a Cheshire cat grin. She wore knit hats in bright colors adorned with fabric flowers on the hat band. Already recognized as one of Oregon's great print makers and watercolorists, her grin belied a strong discipline. You did not waste Laverne Krause's time, and she did not waste ours. In the evening, she'd invite you to Maxie's Tavern off campus, where she'd hold court, learning more about her students in a verbal free-for-all of art and politics. It was the Vietnam era, and the debates were lively. There was the draft, and I had to decide what I was going to do.

A letter arrived soon after my 19th birthday. I was told to report for my physical downtown. After standing in line for over an hour, I was asked to fill out a medical form, then my blood pressure and pulse rate were checked. This left the person checking my pulse confused. He repeated the procedure again and asked me, "What do you do?"

"What do you mean?"

"Well, you have a resting pulse of 38— we don't see that around here."

"I'm a distance runner for the University." And I was suddenly "1A," eligible for the draft.

So what was I going to do? As long as I was in school, I wouldn't be drafted. But if the war was still going when I graduated, I was fair game. I knew the Army wasn't for me. My friend John Plant had gone to Vietnam, and he'd told me stories. As much as I liked to run, I didn't want to go running through rice paddies, dodging bullets. But I loved boats, so I paid a visit to the local Naval Reserve Office. The Navy had a program called the ROC—the Reserve Officer Candidate program. After two summers in Newport, Rhode Island, and a weekend drill each month throughout my college career, you got a commission as an officer upon graduation and entered one pay grade higher. I jumped at it.

For Laverne Krause, athletes like Neal Steinhauer, the track team's nationally ranked shot putter, and I were an oddity. She seldom had athletes in art classes. Eugene was a liberal town to start with. Ken Kesey, Ken Babbs and The Merry Pranksters, The Grateful Dead, and anti-war activists would find safe haven in a community that mixed education with timber and agriculture into one thick pot of political soup. You often had the school administrators and police on one side and a wall of long hair, peace symbols, and tie-dye on the other.

In 1967, Steinhauer set the indoor world record for the shot put with a distance of 67'10".

A lot of people like me were in-between. As athletes, Neal and I had to have a reasonable level of discipline. Our workouts took time that had to fit into the same number of hours everyone else had. There was also an order and structure to our training with goals, dates and methods. Yet, in Laverne's world, you had to stretch the creative envelope. You had to detach your mind from repetitive action. Once, when I broke all the rules of print making, Laverne gave me an A+. My classmates argued that I had cheated, because rather than print from the zinc plates exactly the same, I arranged a different collage of plates between each printing. But Laverne said, "Novel," and rewarded me.

It was an unspoken, unwritten rule that as a Frosh, you didn't speak to Bowerman, and he didn't speak to you. We were to report to our freshman coach Charlie Bowles if we had any questions. If you went to Bowerman, he'd point to Charlie without saying a word and continue with what was currently occupying him. We thought he wasn't even paying attention, but we were wrong. Bowerman was constantly sizing up what he was going to have to work with in the future. At 18 or 19, our future was today.

By the time the cross country runners completed their long run and headed to the locker room, the football players were already changing into their street clothes. They had drained the undersized hot water system of old MacArthur Court. We skinny guys had a small corner with our name on a piece of athletic tape to identify our stall.

Nothing could beat a temperate fall day run with your shoes rustling through dry leaves as you crossed Laurelwood Golf Course. But that was a good day. What hardened you was a rain-laden southwesterly blowing over Spencer Butte. In an effort to protect us, Bowerman had dyed men's long johns that went under our cotton training shorts and matched our hooded green sweatshirts. When you went out, you were warm and dry. When you returned, you felt 20 pounds heavier and the skin rubbed between your thighs.

All this before a cold shower. And you knew it would be cold. So there I am, tiptoeing across the painted, cold, concrete floor to the community shower. I soaped quickly to get it over. Then inexplicably warm water lands on my calf and runs down my ankle. How can there be warm water when I have none?

I turn around straight into the stare of Bowerman who is smiling as a stream of pee continues to land on my lower leg. His eyes record my sense of shock. The upperclassmen who failed to run out of the shower the very second Bowerman entered, laugh all around me, "Today is your day, Geoff."

I've thought about it often. Bill led by example and didn't do anything without purpose. I can't say for sure why Bill peed on the legs of his athletes, but I am sure that each time he learned something—"Is this young man going to attack me, run, or simply return the favor and pee back?"

Bowerman strode down the hall, toweling with each stride on his way to the sauna. At my stall, I smiled and pulled my clothes on, thinking "He marked me."

It was the summer of '65 and the Navy gave me options for my summer in Newport, Rhode Island. I decided to go now, and for the first time I was on a plane, heading east for ROC school. I can't even tell you how I arrived at the Navy base in Newport, but I do remember being totally disoriented. Gone were the mountain ranges of the West that always framed my sense of direction. East became west, and north had become south. The sun now rose over the Atlantic, and although the coastline could give you a bearing, the edge meandered to where you could be standing on an eastern shore looking west. You had to follow the sun.

On base, you were divided by class number and company. Each company divided up for intramural competition. My choice was simple. I was on the relay, and following a few workouts around the base, I was selected as anchor. We were pretty good and I figured once I got the stick in my hand, no one could touch a collegiate trackman. In our first competition, I was even with the anchor for another company; I figured I'd lose him right away, but he was there. Two blocks, still there. We were stride by stride. On the straightaway, I went to another gear, only to have this shadow move with me and we came into a gasping dive to the tape, where a hand extended from a frame with the same build and body fat as mine. With a southern twang, he said, "Good run buddy— my name's Jeff Galloway."

With that handshake we would begin a lifelong friendship. Jeff and Geoff. Each of us still claims to have won that race.

One of Jeff's teammates on the Wesleyan track team, Amby Burfoot, would drive to the base in an old station wagon and haul us off to a local road race. This was a new experience for me. I was stunned to see how many people of all ages would line up to beat themselves to death for a 10k race on asphalt roads. I warned Jeff and Amby at a race that started at the Buzzard's Bay

Amby Burfoot is now the executive editor of Runner's World.

VFW Post that I was not in great shape nor probably capable of 6-minute pace at that distance. Jeff pointed to an old, white-haired man in worn singlet and shorts, "Then run with him. He'll be right on 6-minutes." He was pointing to old Johnny Kelly, winner of the Boston Marathon decades before. I thought Jeff was kidding as he introduced us. The course was one loop through the country, finishing at the same place we started, so I warmed up running from the finish to a mile point that had a hill in front of me as I turned on a small bridge and jogged back to the finish. That's where I would pick up the pace for my finish.

The gun went off, and I stayed right on old Johnny's shoulder as an official yelled out splits, "5:58, 5:59, 6 minutes." I was impressed. At two, the splits were "11:58, 11:59, 12 minutes," and I quit thinking about what I was doing as I glanced over, admiring this remarkable man shuffling effortlessly with barely a notice of breath. Before I knew it, we were heading down hill with a bridge at the bottom, and I took off. Crossing the bridge, the course hooked right and there was a hill I didn't remember, then another downhill with a bridge at the bottom. I had slowed back down— in fact, I was feeling winded and found it was difficult to maintain any rhythm to my stride. Old Johnny Kelly went floating by, again, seemingly without effort. Finally, I came down a hill with a bridge at the bottom and the VFW Post in the distance. With a smile, greeting me at the bottom, Johnny grabbed my arm and walked me over to his wife. "Honey, I want you to meet one of Bill Bowerman's boys!"

It was embarrassing to be called one of Bill Bowerman's boys at that moment, because as a freshman, all my training had been handed down to me by Charlie Bowles. I'd barely spoken to Bowerman for a year. But Galloway had become a sponge as to what Bill actually had us doing out in Oregon. The fact that he'd rest us with light runs for a day after a high mileage workout had escaped the Wesleyan team, a team that, in addition to Jeff and Amby included a then unknown Billy Rodgers. They hammered all the time. Bowerman would indulge endurance only with a long Sunday run.

> Bill Rodgers went on to win the Boston Marathon and the New York Marathon four times each.

CHAPTER 4: UNIVERSITY OF OREGON

I returned to the University of Oregon in the fall. Bowerman was in charge of me now, and taking a more active role in everything I did as a sophomore. He could watch our every move for a week as we shared cabins at a resort on Odell Lake in the central Cascade Mountains. Already at 4000 feet, we climbed snow-laden trails higher to test our capacity. As a team, we had to cook, do the dishes, and clean the cabins owned by a Bowerman friend, timber baron Nils Hult. We had been joined by a Canadian, Cedric Wedemeier, a guy from Chicago, Steve Bukeida, and Hawaiian-born Brian Clarke. It was obvious that making the top seven just got more difficult. But Bowerman combined discipline with an allowance for fun, and in charge of fun was none other than Dave Wilborn.

Loud and gregarious, Wilborn challenged the rules of decorum. The highlight came when Bowerman instructed the team, "Today I want you to run light, and get in twenty 200's." He didn't say how or where. As a group, we jogged up to the railroad tracks a few miles from camp where a trail followed the north side and became a 2-track service road. Wilborn said, "Down to our shoes, men," and dropped his shorts. One at a time, we followed, and off we accelerated, 15 sets of bare buns on what became known as the "Totem Scrotum 200's."

At Hayward Field, Bowerman had formed jogging classes for the Eugene-Springfield community. Ten members of the community would be assigned to each distance runner Bill had selected for the program. Wade Bell, steeplechaser Bob Williams, and I would meet our aging charges at the track either at 6 a.m. or after work in the evening to lead them on a watered down version of our own hard/light Oregon training program. Working with cardiologist Waldo Harris, Bowerman ensured they each received a physical first. It was a good thing, as some could not jog one lap around the track without walking.

Bowerman felt that 1965's cross country team had promise and that the season goal would be to be competitive in the local championships. We were led by Kenny Moore. Moore, under Bowerman, had risen from a gangly North Eugene runner who never won a race to the only guy in the conference who could challenge Washington's star sensation Gerry Lindgren. Not far behind were Bob Williams and Bruce Mortenson, both tough and always consistent. To help determine the make-up of the team, Bowerman would rely on five run-offs prior to the Northern Division Championship.

With the income from the jogging classes and work at the mill, I had moved into the SAE fraternity house, but I was out the door by 5:30 getting in my morning run prior to meeting my joggers at Hayward Field. Having achieved a good base of training mileage, I was consistently finishing in the top 5 in Bowerman's trials.

Bowerman arranged a loan that allowed Aaron Jones to start his plywood mill. Jones reciprocated by offering Bowerman's athletes jobs at Jones Veneer and Plywood.

Bill had been experimenting with shoes for his runners for years. This season, he delivered a new training shoe for the team to test. Arriving in plastic bags with drawstrings, they were called Tigers, from the Onitsuka Company in Japan. Bill had complained to them about the outsole and mid-sole density and advised them to marry the soft and the hard, to combine cushion with durability. Called the Tiger Cortez, the difference in this shoe was noticeable with the first step, and you had to try them.

I got mine just before Bowerman sent us out on a country road with a long downhill. When I finished, I could feel a throbbing in my big toe on my left foot. I looked down, and there was blood showing where the leather upper met the mid-sole.

I complained about it, and Bill had me remove my shoe. Never a man to waste words, he took a pair of shears out of a toolbox, cut the toe out, and handed them back, "Here," he said. Bill had an intolerance for anyone asking too many questions. He always chose action over words.

I was going to lose that toenail. Another annoying feature of the Cortez was the top line of the shoe's heel cutting straight across your calcaneus. Normally referred to as "the heel," the calcaneus has often been the bane of the distance runner. Devoid of fatty tissue, and the foundation where both the Achilles tendon and the plantar fascia root into the bone, the calcaneus is critical to proper foot function. Once the calcaneus is disturbed, a runner's career can abruptly come to an end. In the Cortez, the top line crossed the bone, and after two months in the shoes, I was getting a sharp, concentrated pain in the middle of my heel. I slit the back of the Cortez topline with a razor blade to relieve the stress. I didn't complain about it and kept my training a priority.

Bowerman surprised me at the track, pulling me aside. "I've had requests from women to join the jogging classes. I want you to conduct them over at South Eugene. If they need to change, they can use the YMCA across the street."

There I stood the first morning, as one after another showed up, some wives of our Hayward Field joggers, hair in curlers, plastic rain caps, three quarter length raincoats and white canvas Keds with no cushioning. Few could complete a lap, yet they were determined and filled with hope.

That wasn't the only surprise from Bill. He pulled out of his green Melbourne Olympic bag a pair of handmade spikes with a white nylon mesh upper. My mouth dropped open. Few coaches in the world had ever taken the time and challenge to master the pattern making and assembly of custom shoes for track athletes. As a boy I had watched Jerome, Burleson, and Tarr compete in Bowerman prototypes, but these were for me, just in time for Northern Divisions. "Try them on. Let's see how they fit."

Although the mesh felt abrasive around my toes, the length was right. I laced them up snugly and pranced around putting my full weight on the plastic spike plate. Then I could feel the sharp pain in my right heel where the top line crossed the tendon. After finally explaining what I had kept from Bill, he rubbed his mouth and chin, looking down after touching the hot spot. "I can do one of two things—either I lower the top line, or I put a heel pad inside."

I elected for the heel pad and Bill had them back to me for practice the next day.

That weekend, we traveled to Mary's Park for the contest against Oregon State, the University of Washington, and Washington State. It had rained heavily during the week, but this was a clear day and I felt ready as I jogged with my teammates passing Gerry Lindgren and his fellow Cougars heading the opposite direction. Typical of Gerry, he waved.

The race course headed off at the end of a grass field, and all four teams started bunching for the first turn onto the trail that wound along the south bank of Mary's River. I was up where I should be with my teammates; led by Kenny, who was matching Lindgren, stride for stride, although Kenny had a lope and Gerry a chop. I had carefully pulled my new spikes snug and tied the double knot just as Bill had advised us to. The course was muddy in spots, and there were numerous turns. I felt light and my knees were lifting effortlessly, but then my right foot stepped right down to crushed gravel under the mud without protection. The shoe was gone. I turned, and circled behind the pack to find it stuck in the mud.

Madly untying the knot, I knelt down and laced it back up, and was off, catching the rear of the pack at the mile mark and confident I could regain my position by staying cool. Within a quarter mile, I lost the shoe again. Rather than lose time again, I ran barefoot. Only then did I fully appreciate the need for spikes. The trail sloped down on the right side to the river, and I did not have spikes on my right foot. Underneath the mud there was crushed rock that stung with each step and broke my stride as the pack disappeared ahead. With tears washing through the mud splattered on my face and down my lemon colored singlet, I finished next to last.

After showering in the basement under Gill Coliseum, Bowerman sat us down and announced that Athletic Director Leo Harris had informed Bill that only five would get to nationals. He didn't have the budget for seven. Bowerman decided the team would be as they ran today—the time trials would not be a factor. Kenny Moore, Dave Wilborn, Brian Clarke, Bruce Mortenson, and Bob Williams would go, and I would stay home.

I was heartbroken with Bill's decision. I didn't know Leo Harris, other than he was a former football coach, had negotiated the use of the Disney Duck as Oregon's mascot, and that Bowerman did not always get along with him. But I did feel I knew Bowerman. This was his decision. He knew my consistency in the five trials and he made the shoes I wore that day. In my mind, it just wasn't right.

The wrong I saw in Bowerman was echoed by my fraternity brothers—"How could he do it? Why don't you quit?"

Now what was I going to do? I did go to practice—didn't miss one. I coached the joggers and worked in the mill and attended reserve drills. But I stayed clear of Bowerman. If he was on the north side of the track, I was on the south. He'd move west, I'd go east. I stayed angry right through the holidays. Finally, one day I was the last athlete crossing the practice track heading up to Mac Court. A voice called out behind me, "Hollister!"

I kept walking.

"Hollister!"

A little louder and more pronounced. It was Bowerman, and I knew if he had to call my name a third time, I'd pay for it. So I stopped, not looking back. He came up to me, "Let's walk."

He put his long arm around me. "You're pretty pissed off at me, aren't you?"

At this point, every emotion was exploding at once. I loved this guy and would do anything to please him, yet I was furious with him at the same time. I was so choked inside, I couldn't answer.

"Well, looks like you have a decision to make. Either you can quit or stick around and be the best that you can be."

Years later, while being asked if there was ever a defining moment in my long career at Nike, I responded, "Yes, but it was much earlier."

It started with those two months, culminating that evening on the practice track. If I had quit then, it would have been much easier to quit later. I would have missed all of the life lessons. I had to see what I was made of and, to my surprise, Bill wanted to see that too. This was the defining moment. I just couldn't let him or myself down.

I had split my jogging class assignments with the women running at 6 a. m. at South Eugene and the men at Hayward Field in the evening. The women were surprising me. They were over a half-mile now with a continuous jog before walking. They were always cheerful, happy to see each other and came in all shapes and sizes, determined to improve both. My psychology professor handed out a challenging assignment to create our own test group on human subjects outside the classroom. The more I thought about it, I had a unique opportunity—a male and female jogging class, conducted separately. What long-term effect was jogging having on them psychologically? Were they happier? Was their self-esteem elevated? How was their energy level? Their libido?

My doctor, Larry Hilt, was one of those joggers. Larry seemed to start life all over at age 60. He started skiing, bought his first Porsche, and dreamed of qualifying for the Boston Marathon. If you asked him about sex, one eye would close behind his spectacles and he'd say "Off the charts."

I received an A+ in my psych class, and along with the same grade from Laverne Krause, I thought my GPA was looking good. I had one problem—physics, and had I not gone in to plead with my instructor, the D he assigned would have been an F. This did not go unnoticed by the watchful eye of Bowerman, and I was summoned to his office.

I had not been in Bill's office since I first met him my senior year in high school. He was reading *The Eugene Register-Guard* newspaper and told me, "Sit down."

So I sat, and I sat. Bill continued to read the paper for an hour without saying a word. The silence killed me. I didn't realize it at the time, but he was giving me a powerful demonstration of what it means to focus. It was as if there was nothing in that room with him but that newspaper. Finally, he put the paper down, exposing those crystal blue eyes that seem to poke through the front of my skull and read everything I was thinking written on the back. The stare was bad enough, and he hadn't said a word.

"Hollister, you don't know whether you want to be a great runner, a great lover, a great student, or a great politician. And you can only do two things well at the same time. If you want to be part of this team, academics comes first, running second, and that's all you'll have time for. You're excused."

How did he know I had a girlfriend? He never saw Lin Madden. By wanting to become a politician he must have been referring to the SAE house. Lin had just joined a sorority and had moved in, so I could see a conflict looming there. As for my own house, my brothers didn't seem to be changing their party-all-the-time ways. I found myself exhausted at times with the limited sleep I was getting, and the house had a real asshole for a president. Andy Jordan was a pre-law student from Portland filled with arrogance. He expected you to commit yourself to the house as though it was your duty.

Bowerman had other priorities when it came to duty. Everything came to a head in one meeting where Andy tried to reduce me to just another underclassman who really didn't need that extra sleep and certainly didn't require any special privileges. If I was going to follow Bowerman's directive about being good at only two things, I knew what I had to do. I picked up my belongings from the SAE house and walked down the alley to my parents' home. I had gotten Bowerman's message—I had to focus.

As for Lin Madden, the thought of backing off on our relationship seemed music to her ears, as she had wanted to date other guys anyway. Between her acceptance and my questioning how Bowerman knew, I walked away in a fog.

Bowerman reinforced his priorities in team meetings that often began with, "You are the men of Oregon," but quickly moved into how women can make you weak. "You lose all your energy in the chase. You need to be more like Jerry Tarr, if that's what interests you. Tarr would walk up to the bar at Foo's, meet a gal,"bam" get it over with, race the next day and win!"

How did Bowerman know anything about chasing women and the loss of energy that entailed? The Bowermans often invited us out to their home perched like a large nest high over the McKenzie River, above the large

Tarr held the American Record for the 120 yard high hurdles in 1962 at 13.3 seconds. He was paid to go to the Denver Broncos football camp. He got cut by the Broncos, but that payment robbed him of his eligibility to run in the 1964 Olympics, where he would have been the favorite to win a gold medal in his event.

expanse of farmland owned by attorney and close Bowerman friend John Jaqua. Barbara Bowerman was a second mother to all of us, getting us all to pitch in setting tables indoors and out on the patio. She made everything by scratch and put up with Bill's flatulence and belching, which he seemed to exhibit as something men should do, as with peeing. Seems a john was never close enough at the track. In the middle of a workout, Bill unzipped and just let fly against the southeast corner of the grandstand with his back to us, and under the watchful eye of Dave Wilborn, who seemed to admire Bowerman's animal behavior. Did Bowerman ever lose energy over a woman? Did he ever care?

Bowerman had his ways, and one was to band us all together as a unit off campus. It became another of his tests. Who followed his unwritten rules of common sense, and who broke them? Spring break was a bus trip to Hamilton Air Force Base, outside San Francisco. If you didn't make the departure time, you were left behind. And Bill always knew what time it was. "Don't waste my time, and that of your teammates." If you showed up late for a team meeting, he found a way to create regret. Once, as our bus approached the California border, Bill told the driver to pull over to the shoulder. As we looked out the window, he unzipped and peed over the guardrail. None of us got out, fearful he'd leave us behind.

The bus rolled into the town of Shasta and pulled up to the sorriest collection of rundown motel units you could imagine— they made the Nils Hult cabins look like castles. After a run and dinner, all we needed was a pillow to go to sleep on, hopefully devoid of the cockroaches that scampered in the corners to the playful delight of Wilborn, Williams, and Bowerman's middle son, Jay, a hurdler and self-proclaimed entomologist.

Frugal by nature, Bowerman seldom bought new clothes for himself, as though he were testing their durability. He spent the school's money as carefully as if it was his own. Bob Newland confided that Bill, on one occasion, was delighted with the savings following a phone call to California. When the bus pulled up to the establishment, Bill strode in, and just a few minutes later strode out red-faced without saying anything other than, "Drive on." The bus continued down the road. It turned out Bill had accidentally booked the team into a whorehouse. Imagine the disappointment of the ladies, as a bus full of college men pulled away.

I had to wonder if Bill ever slept—he seemed to be everywhere. Bob Newland had competed for Bowerman while he was at Medford High School. The football team was playing Bend High School in central Oregon. Newland was a good looking guy, and the Bend rally squad decided to give young Bob a tour of Bend, which back then should have taken all of 30 minutes. Returning much later, Bob snuck around in the dark back to his room, avoiding Bowerman, and quietly unlocked his door. He stepped in, removed his clothes, and slipped under the sheets in the dark. He suddenly bolted straight up—Bowerman was laying in his bed. Bill rose up, walked around the bed, opened the door, and, silhouetted in the moonlight, said "Newland, tomorrow I expect nothing but your best game!" Years later Bob told me, "I gave him one helluva game!"

Bill would later place Newland among the most talented he ever had the privilege to coach. Bob would win the state high jump, star on the basketball team, and quarterback Bowerman's State Champion Black Tornado football team.

Another reason I questioned if Bowerman ever slept was his unbending determination to create. Barbara would later say it was his ability to focus on what was before him. It was a laser focus that survived disappointment. On our return from California, he informed his distance runners that we'd be running our interval workout in the country at a place called Pleasant Hill, not far from the Kesey ranch where the Merry Pranksters bus, "Fuurther," (and yes, that's the way they spelled it,) lay at rest in a cow pasture. Bill had been experimenting with all-weather surfaces in the late '50s. One of his former throwers owned a tire company, and when Bowerman asked what would happen to a pile of discarded tires, George Lowe responded, "They go to the landfill, as always."

Way ahead of the recycling movement, Bowerman envisioned a way to solve an old northwestern track coach's problem. Had he coached in Los Angeles, the thought might not have occurred to him, with favorable spring weather for the track season, and enough sprinters, hurdlers, and jumpers in supply to field a powerhouse. But this was Eugene, and we got our share of rain. Bowerman never actively recruited, expecting the athlete to come to the Oregon track program for its own merits, and few sprinters did. So Bowerman concentrated on the distances, since sprinters, with good reason, preferred warmer climates.

On a blustery April Saturday, the track could be a lake out to lane 3, devastating our times. Bowerman went to work, mixing asphalt and shredded tire rubber in an old cement mixer. He determined the flashpoint of his concoction in the mixer by holding a blowtorch to the metal barrel. When it blew, he knew how long he could heat and mix the gooey black muck before pouring it over a sheet of precut plywood and raking it even to dry. He then took the sheets and butted them end to end on the jump runways for testing. Not convinced it would work, or how long it would last or even how to surface an area as large as the track at Hayward Field, he was reluctant to convert our cinder surface.

Pleasant Hill High School became the guinea pig. In 1966, two years prior to the first all-weather surface in Olympic history, Kenny Moore, Wade Bell, Mike Crunican, Bill Norris, Bob Williams, and I were all flashing smiles at each other as our feet felt an entirely new sensation. Not only was the surface new and capable of shedding water, it provided a cushion that could only be achieved by a shoe, a trail of pine needles, or grass. Whether it was exuberance or the surface itself, we were all one to two seconds ahead of pace. Bowerman looked at his watch, but contained any delight. He was not one to jump to conclusions.

Dave Wilborn had gotten quite ill, to the point that Bowerman pulled him completely off his training program. That left me and Wade Bell in the mile against UCLA's Bob Day at Hayward Field. Day had gone under four minutes, only the twelfth American to do so. We had an excellent new runner in Roscoe Divine, but being a freshman, he'd have to watch from the stands.

Back then, Oregon still played football at Hayward Field, and the south grandstands stood behind the south end zone. The mile started at the west end of the grandstands, so as the gun went off, the runners quickly disappeared from sight only to emerge 100 yards later on the east straightaway. Wade Bell, a hard charging 800 man, had made it his practice to enter the south bend behind on the last lap and either emerge in the lead or burst forward in an all out sprint with 300 yards to go. Knowledgeable fans, many with stopwatches in hand, would roar in appreciation. They knew exactly what was happening. I knew Wade loved to be tested by Day, and knowing my PR from my freshman year was only 4:18, I hoped only to improve and avoid total embarrassment. I had a good view of their behinds as I came into corner 4, well behind them, Wade urging Day to pace. After the half, I was losing them behind the stands. Bowerman always warned us about over striding when we tired, and he'd get vocal on the infield, trying to get you to recognize what you were actually doing and correct it. "Pitter patter. Pitter patter. Hot skillet, hot skillet," he'd yell as I went by, a slow and disappointing third, in what seemed like an eternity.

Sitting in the old east grandstands the next week, Bowerman approached, clipboard in hand. "Only one of you will win your event this week. What does that make the rest of you? Losers? Third place is one point, and that could make the difference between winning or losing as a team. I will tell you right now that you have a far better chance in life winning as part of a team than you ever will as an individual."

In fact, we were soon to find out that loss itself was relative. Upperclassman Bob Woodell from Beaverton had finished high in the Pac-8 long jump the year before. He was older, a field event guy and a Theta Chi, so I had limited contact with him. One sunny afternoon, he and his fraternity brothers were swimming a float down the Amazon Slough that had been designed by one of their architecture students. It was top heavy and tilted to one side. Some of the swimmers froze in place. Bob saw it coming and dove, exposing his back. The structure came tumbling down in one loud splash, a support timber hitting Bob just above the hips. At Sacred Heart Hospital, he had lost all feeling in his legs. Bowerman was a regular visitor, eyeing the prognosis and the mounting medical bills. He contacted the Eugene Register-Guard's Jerry Urhammer and told him to inform the public of a new meet. "We'll call it the Twilight Mile and put on the best race anybody could experience."

On a Thursday evening, the temperature was perfect, the flags were still, and the stage was set. If you didn't have goosebumps already, you did when the ambulance arrived from Sacred Heart and Bob Woodell was rolled out on a stretcher in front of all of us in the infield grandstands. Hayward Field was packed; the atmosphere electric, and I had tears coming down as the runners came to the mark with Ray Hendrickson's pistol held high. Half-miler Don Scott would take them out on perfect pace with veterans Dyrol Burleson and Jim Grelle in pursuit, with Bell and 19-year-old Divine following. Burleson, who could turn such a fast quarter that he anchored Oregon's 4x440 relay to a national championship and finished his collegiate career undefeated in the mile, would not let anyone touch him that day. He crossed comfortably into the lead as Scott dropped off, with Grelle 10 then 20 yards back. Bell tried his customary 300 meter burst, but precocious Divine had more than enough gear down the first straight. He held his lead on Grelle as both exhibited Bowerman's instruction to relax the chin and lips and fill the cheeks with each exhale to the finish. The crowd erupted as Burleson, Divine, Grelle, and Bell all finished in under four minutes—each member of this team feeling they were part of it all, and part of Bob Woodell.

I don't remember what provoked my anger, but one afternoon I approached Kenny Moore at his locker. I'm certain my words bounced off him, as Kenny used a vocabulary that sent the rest of us scrambling to our thesaurus to determine what he just said. What I do remember is that it was about the team. Kenny was setting himself apart, and I took offense. He displayed a certain selfishness that gave me my first understanding that this might be a way to get to the top. But there's a difference between selfishness, which is about ego, and Bowerman's idea of focus, which means you have to shut things out. For Kenny, it may have been the way he made the first of two Olympic teams, but it wasn't how I operated. For me, it wasn't about winning races—being on the team was everything.

CHAPTER 5: THERE'S SOMEONE I WANT YOU TO MEET

Early into the fall, Bowerman took me aside, "There's someone I want you to meet. He's from Portland, one of my former half-milers, Buck Knight. He'll come to your parents' house."

After knocking on the door, Phil "Buck" Knight and I walked down to the corner Dairy Queen for a cheeseburger and milkshake. He had a proposal for me. I would be allowed to travel the whole state of Oregon with a load of Onitsuka Tiger shoes and sell them directly out of the trunk of my car to coaches and athletes. He'd pay me $2 per pair and I'd have to pay my own expenses. We left the Dairy Queen and I distinctly remember paying for the hamburgers and milkshakes, as Buck forgot his wallet. Back home, Mom stood in the corner of the kitchen eying Buck, I suspect trying to determine a level of trust. After he left with instructions that I could pick up my first inventory at his parents' house in Portland, she unloaded her apprehension with, "You better get your teaching certificate, 'cause this shoe thing just isn't going to work."

Joyfully, I returned to Eugene with my little Sunbeam Talbot full of Onitsuka Tigers, and 1462 Hilyard became the unofficial Eugene Headquarters for what Knight called Blue Ribbon Sports. Buck needed a catalogue to display the Tiger selection, so Lin Madden and I drove the Talbot over to the coast as part of Professor Foster's photography class. I laid the shoes out on a coastal rock outcropping with the surf in the background, changed into a dark blue warm-up and Cortez's, and Lin shot one of the first BRS catalogue shots. Buck liked it. It was free.

Buck and Bowerman were both frugal. Bowerman started working hard on his uncle's ranch at an early age to help support his family. Knight was an accountant, and he knew how to count pennies. He'd learned in Business School at

Stanford that 25 out of 26 business failed. Counting pennies was his way of keeping BRS afloat in the early days, although his attitude about BRS was that if the business failed, he'd just start another one.

Driving home from the beach with the open sunroof exposing a sky full of stars, I was feeling good about life. Back at Hilyard Street, the doorbell was ringing, as word of the new shoe source spread among my teammates and in the jogging community. In my absence, my shoppers would dig through the inventory to locate the right size.

I was continuing to take a full academic load, train, and my women's jogging class had mastered the cinder track at South and was now completing a 6-mile run up through Hendricks Park and back. I was so proud they had broken free of the oval cinder track, and named them "Hollister's Cinderellas." That run through Hendricks Park had a steep up and down in the middle and these women were becoming athletes.

My doctor, Larry Hilt was complaining to Bowerman that the pavement was beating up his joints while he trained for the Boston marathon in Tiger Marathons. He handed a pair of shower thongs to Bill and said, "If you can place these between the outsole and the upper, I think I can make it." Bill did just that, and Larry ran the Boston marathon in that Bowerman prototype.

I would find myself in eastern Oregon or on the coast returning at night to Eugene. One or two late night cups of coffee got me back, just as they had got me up. I was drinking a lot of

Jeff Johnson met Phil Knight at an all-comers meet when they were both at Stanford, and he went on to become Knight's first employee, running the BRS store in Santa Monica. One of his customers, Gene Comroe, came to Jeff at about the same time with the same idea. Jeff sent the idea on to Bowerman, and Bowerman used the combined input to present what became the Tiger Boston to Knight.

coffee, cramming for finals and trying to keep up. Bowerman was back to giving us time trials and had a new experiment. Watching the success of his kiwi friend, New Zealand track coach Arthur Lydiard, and Arthur's high mileage approach applied to Peter Snell, Bill Baillie and Murray Hallberg, he divided all the distance runners into two groups. One would follow Bill's moderate 40-mile per week schedule. The other would graduate up to as high as 100 miles, and the time trials would measure any noticeable improvement. Wilborn and I were in the high mileage group. One run went 7 miles from campus, out Coburg Road, over and along the McKenzie River, winding through the idyllic countryside and up the steep Bowerman driveway. We'd fill up on Barbara's homemade raisin cookies and lemonade. The run back was always tougher.

Snell won Olympic gold medals in the 800 in 1960 and 1964, and in the 1500 in 1964. On August 24, 1963, Baillie set a world record for the 1 hour run: 12 miles, 960 yards. Hallberg won the gold medal in the 5000 in the 1960 Olympics.

Bill decided that we should practice this marathon distance in the Flat Mohawk Valley one Sunday morning. Williams and Wilborn seemed like naturals as they clocked mile after mile together. I started getting tighter and tighter beyond 16 miles—the farthest I had ever run around the Butte. At 20 miles my right hamstring cramped so tight I couldn't keep my leg straight, and in pain I hopped on my left leg across the right side of the road to a mailbox, sat down on my butt and leg and pushed in an attempt to straighten my leg out. I was in this compromising position when Bowerman returned in his van looking for me. After I got up and walked a bit, he said, "Here. You didn't get enough of this," and handed me another of his experiments. Bill was convinced, observing the salt that could cake on our sweaty bodies, that we were losing more than just water. We were losing minerals. So he mixed a concoction of lukewarm tea with sugar and salt and put it in a squeeze bottle. Bill called it Sheep's Piss. We hated it.

This was long before the first sports drink hit the market. But this was one more example of Bowerman's ceaseless creative urge—whenever he observed a problem, he had to come up with a way to address it.

I was making more and more trips to the Knights' house for shoes. Phil was kind of like me, in that he didn't have any money and had to rely on his parent's laundry room for space. But he did know how to work, and as with my parents, his choices also failed to resonate with his parents. Phil's father, William, was publisher of *The Oregon Journal*, competitor to *The Oregonian* and one of only two statewide newspapers. While Buck's school teachers were claiming that "A mile under four minutes was beyond the limits of human potential," William Knight drove his son up to Vancouver, B.C. to witness a match-up between Roger Bannister and John Landy in the mile at the Empire Games. As these two battled to both go under the barrier in the same race, the first such accomplishment in the history of running, William Knight, a most learned man, turned and said, "Son, we've just witnessed history. We will never see this again in our lifetime."

Young Buck would finish fourth in the state half-mile for Franklin High School, a race won by Jim Grelle of Lincoln High School. William Knight felt strongly that his son should attend Stanford for the best education. Both Grelle and Knight wanted to run for Oregon after Jim Bailey, Bill Dellinger, and Ken Reiser won their respective races in the Northern Divisions. This was all six years before Bowerman asked me "Why do you want to go to Oregon?" To that same question young Buck responded, "Sir, to be the best miler I can be!" I have no doubt that Bowerman made Buck see the error of his answer, just as he did with me.

William Knight lost out, and young Buck joined a loaded Oregon team of distance runners. Besides Grelle, all the other freshmen were either state champions or provincial champions from Canada. Then there were the supermen—first, Australian Jim Bailey who was the first man to run a sub-4 on U.S. soil, beating countryman and world record holder John Landy in the process. Both would go under four, rendering William Knight's prophecy hollow. Then there was Bill Dellinger, already an Olympian and world record holder for the two and three-mile. Ken Reiser had just graduated after winning the steeplechase at nationals. Talented, but a project for Bowerman, Bill could never figure out why young Ken could run only one race up to his ability. If he doubled, the first race was great, but the second was abysmal.

Despite his youth, Reiser had false teeth, and rather than race with them in, he'd hand them to a teammate to keep until the race was over. Bowerman started observing Reiser's every move. Reiser finished his first race, running brilliantly, recovered his teeth, got in the concession line and ordered a couple of hot dogs, wolfed them down, handed his teeth over to a teammate for safe keeping, and ran his second race as though he had a bellyache, which he did.

Oregon had a tight dual meet with Washington approaching, and a good double from Ken Reiser could determine the outcome. Reiser's first race gave Oregon 5 points as expected. Bowerman followed Reiser before his race, walked up to his teammate and said, "Hand over those teeth," and put them in his pocket. Reiser couldn't eat his hotdogs, but, just as Bowerman intended, he won his second race, and Oregon won the meet.

Knight would later confide that he learned more on the track at Oregon than he ever did in the classroom. As much as Bowerman stressed academics, his own "classroom" prepared you to get along in life.

But Bowerman could also inspire mischief among his troops. Following Oregon's team championship on a cold, blustery cross country day, Bowerman had the team line up for a newspaper photo. Knight was on the far right, Bowerman was dressed for the weather in his three-quarter length wool overcoat. Dellinger, Grelle, and Bailey were all freezing in shorts and singlets, with Dellinger holding the trophy. Unbeknownst to Bowerman, who was looking straight ahead at the camera, Bailey had removed his jockstrap and put it over his head to keep his ears warm when the picture was snapped.

For a young Buck Knight, that team photo said volumes about his future. Knight was not only affected by Bowerman, but by the team Bill surrounded Buck with. The team would become the conditioner of his own character, his love for sport, his own place in it, his understanding of team and his respect for those who were special—those who had the gift, that something extra on Saturday.

One of those who had the gift was Grelle. When Grelle finished, Knight was somewhere behind. Grelle would continue with an extended career on the track, while Knight pursued his MBA at Stanford. Grelle would finish with 2 Olympiads and 32 sub-4 miles, more than any man in history up to that point. He would go to Rome where a dynamic young American athlete would stop Grelle and his teammate Bob Schul to take their picture in the athlete's village. Returning to his seat on the flight home Grelle saw the same athlete, and stared at his gold medal, dangling by its ribbon from the overhead. After pointing it out to Schul, Bob looked up and said, "Oh yeah. That's Cassius Clay." They were among the champions of the world.

It was 1968, and that madman Dave Wilborn was having quite a year. Bowerman peaked him perfectly for nationals, where Wilborn clocked a most respectable 3:56.2, third only to Jim Ryun and Grelle, putting Dave on the U.S. team to compete in a dual meet against the Russians in Stanford Stadium. Against the Russians, Dave would have a disappointing experience on the track, and when he returned to Eugene, he shared a secondary disappointment. Following his mile at nationals, a representative from Adidas was all over him, and promised a bag full of their products—shoes, sweats, a rain suit. "The works!" said Dave. He didn't see the guy again until after his poor showing against the Russians. Dave walked up to him, and the Adidas rep passed him as though he were invisible. Dave never got the promised bag.

I couldn't believe what had happened, and the disappointment showed in Dave's face. Not even close to knowing what my future would hold, I told Dave, "If I ever have the same opportunity, I won't let this happen."

Bowerman wanted us all to compete at our best. He had convinced us that a one-ounce reduction in what we wore on the track translated to 55-pounds carried over the distance of one mile. Whether it was true or not, when you stepped to the line for the gun, you had a psychological edge. Grelle remembered when he put an Oregon singlet on for the first time in the '50s. Looking at himself in the mirror with a big "O" sewn on the chest, he felt like Superman with the "S."

By 1962, Bill felt the "O" weighed too much, so he removed it and had "Oregon" screened across with the lightest possible green ink. Even if it was a matter of mere grams of weight, no detail was too small to escape his attention. Then he made our green shorts out of a green, lightweight, parachute cloth. When you peeled off your sweats, you literally had to look down to ensure you had something on. They were that light.

Bowerman would occasionally weigh everything we wore on an old grocery vegetable scale in his trackside office under the wooden grandstands. I had been running without a jock and knew Bowerman would be impressed with how light my gear would be going into the mile. He had a slight grin, perhaps noting I was missing my jock strap.

As the stands were filling for the short relay, Bill called me over and, hardly looking at me, said, "Hollister, I'm running you in the steeple in 20 minutes. Get warmed up."

He'd switched my event from the mile, and my jockstrap was somewhere in a drawer at home. I had practiced hurdling the barriers during the winter with sweats or long johns over large cedar tree sections Bill had buried halfway in the ground on the practice track. A great training tool, it removed the fear of hitting the barrier, eliminated injuries in practice, and the circumference of the log required that we take off and land at a certain distance from the 34-inch elevation of a barrier. Your arms created the balance needed while airborne, but now here I was in the middle of the 7 and $^1/_2$ lap race, in front of a crowd, moving my left or right hand embarrassingly to my midsection to avoid experiencing a wrap around and scattering the family jewels into lanes 1, 2 and 3.

Promising newcomers to the 1967 squad were Tom Morrow, nicknamed "The Beak" for his prominent nose, Norway's Arne Kvalheim, and Norm Trerise, nicknamed "Tree" for his height. Trerise hailed from Vancouver, B.C., while Morrow was part of the continuing distance tradition at North Eugene. Dad was familiar with Tom, liked him and offered to drive us to the start of our planned Sunday long run one morning. It was so heavy with fog that Dad had to drive slowly out Coburg Road then east over the I-5 freeway with his headlights on. Although it was chilly when we stepped out onto the road, we discarded unnecessary clothes as we stood at the base of the Coburg Hills, barely making out the old logging road that wound up to the top in a series of

> Kvalheim was a Norwegian Olympian and held the Norwegian record for the 1500 and the 5000.

switchbacks. We started slowly and found our rhythm, working together as though pulling each other with each knee lift, arm drive and deep breath. The climb would continue for over 20 minutes in what appeared to be darkness at 8 a.m. Dew began to soak our cotton clothing. Then, gradually, an even light began to appear as the road reduced its pitch. The fog was becoming patchy and fluffy like cotton candy, and then we punched through the top into pure blue sky. The scene stopped us in our tracks as we rotated 360° with wide smiles, "Look at this!"

We were on top of the fog bank that stretched across the Willamette Valley to the west and to the Cascade Range in the east. Snow-capped mountains punctuated where the ranges were and reflected the bright sun in the distance. Speechless, we started moving again, winding south through conifer forests and open clear cuts all the way south, entering the Bowerman property on a gravel road.

You have thousands and thousands of runs over the years, but a run like that, you never forget.

My training continued to go well, always having partners who pushed me and made the effort seem easy. But you had to gauge yourself and not leave your best effort for Saturday somewhere in a Wednesday workout. If you ran with Arne Kvalheim, you might as well hold back, as he would not let anyone put their chest in front of his. If you did, the pace picked up. Another competitive guy in workouts was steeplechaser John Woodward, the Oregon high school record holder from Marshfield High School. Forman's Hill was a tough elevation climb south of campus, then a series of downhills back to Hayward Field. Bowerman had taught us to always finish our tempo runs as if we were approaching the end of a race. Stay under control, but pick it up.

As we got more fit, the first runner to break had added a block or two from the prior week. Woodward was leading a large pack of us down a long paved straight that veered right to access 30th Avenue below on the left. A metal guardrail kept cars from going off a steep embankment. All of a sudden, Woodward hurdled the guardrail, shot down the embankment, and the race was on. "Woody" was the first across the four lanes of 30th with the rest of us in pursuit, looking both directions for traffic, then onto the upper green slope of Laurelwood Golf Course and down a hill Bowerman had us run hundreds of times to practice balance with our arm carriage while accelerating. Now we were taking the lesson to the extreme as we were still blocks away from the track, all locating the final gear that brought us all back together, some laughing, some cussing.

My workouts had been sharpened, and I was in the best shape of my life. A sophomore half-miler from Pendleton, Jim Gorman, proved to be a perfect training partner because we matched up closely in both speed and endurance. We often trained using a Scandinavian technique called "fartlek," meaning "speed play." We'd pick a landmark along our running route—a tree, or a telephone pole— sprint to it, slow down until we'd recovered, and then repeat the process.

Bowerman had asked us to finish an hour tempo run through South Eugene and finish at Hayward Field. Jim and I hit a respectable pace, then on our return to campus straight down 11th Street I started picking up the pace farther out than I had ever tested myself on Jim. Gorman protested with a slight grunt, and then matched my stride. I picked it up a notch. Now we flew by Maxie's, then the Dairy Queen and into the campus village area. By the time we reached the president's office in Johnson Hall, I shifted to an all out sprint, across the quad and down to Hayward Field. "You son of a bitch!" Gorman wailed as we came to a stop, hands on our knees as Bowerman walked up.

"Okay, I've marked out the end zone with cones. I want a dozen repeats race pace and slightly faster." Bowerman had the

A basic Bowerman formula was to move his athletes from "date pace," at the beginning of the season, to "goal pace" late in the season. An early season "date pace" for Jim and me in the steeplechase might be 9:30. By the end of the season our goal pace would be 9:00.

green infield manicured, and it provided relief to the pounding we had just subjected ourselves to on the pavement and concrete. We handled the repeats with ease and knew we were ready. Bowerman added Canadian steepler Cedric Wedemeier to the line up, knowing that if his top sprinter Mike Deible got blanked in the 100, Cedric could add points in our event.

At the end of the workout, Bowerman handed me something special, a pair of blue Tiger spikes. I don't know if this was Bill's way of saying, "Sorry," but he had convinced Tiger to start trying nylon uppers in their training flats, and technology now made a sandwich of a smooth nylon woven against the skin, a layer of foam, then a coarser, more durable nylon exterior. The Bowerman prototypes were glued together, but these were sewn. Bowerman didn't know how to sew, and he wasn't about to start. The new shoes came in a yellow canvas bag with a draw string and were a far cry from Bill's effort my sophomore year. With the shoes, my expectation for Saturday hit a new level. I was ready.

Ray Hendrickson brought us to the line for the start. USC's best entrant was Chuck Schultz who sometimes ran the 3-mile. He approached the line tan and blond, a stark contrast to us Ducks, who hadn't seen much sun since October. Ray Hendrickson pressed the trigger on his starting pistol on the far side of the track for the 7 $^1/_2$ lap 3000 meter race, and we quickly sprinted past the smell of gun smoke into the first turn.

I'd learned to love the steeple. At the end of the first 220, there was an imposing 6x6 inch black and white striped barrier set at 34 inches, another at the end of the turn, then a water jump that Bowerman had placed on the north infield. The jump required the runners to exit the track left at almost a 90° angle around a steel pole hammered into the grass. You approached the barrier across the grass infield instead of cinders. I was pretty limited in coordinating a left foot take-off, springing off the barrier with my right foot to land as close to the end of the water jump as possible, knowing that each successive lap would increase the difficulty. My dad was the hurdle chief, which included having his crew move the other four barriers into position, which we were to clear without touching and then regain our stride for the next 100 yards.

I found the steeplechase's jumps kept me aware and alert to the pace, unlike the 3-mile, where I'd drift off, and so would my time. Gorman and I went stride for stride through two laps. I was on the rail, Jim on my shoulder at a pace we had not yet attempted. We were fast, with Shultz and Cedric a stride behind. As I approached the barriers, I had to ensure that I timed my stride for a right foot take-off, so at the same time you had to block out banter coming from your teammates on the infield and the roar of the crowd from the old green wooden grandstands.

Gorman and I were approaching the barrier where the timers were waiting to record our finish. We were down to three laps to go. Gauging my approach, I took off, airborne, my lead foot extended. I had taken off too soon and in a split second, hit the front end of the barrier with my heel. My momentum carried my compressing body over the barrier, and I was heading for a nosedive to the cinders as I did years before in Canby. But this time, several thousand knowledgeable Oregon track fans were watching.

My hands extended forward to brace my fall and just as fast, four fingers and a thumb lifted me up under my armpit. It was Gorman. Talk about having your teammate back you up, this was it. He had a powerful upper build, unlike most distance runners, and his quick gesture kept me on my feet. Shultz and Wedemeier avoided me, and chased Jim, who hardly broke stride.

I was running with a strange hobble, as my left knee complained from the impact of the immovable barrier. I struggled to maintain contact. Gorman maintained pace, Wedemeier was secure in second and Shultz was coming back to me. On the other side of the field Dad was yelling at me and couldn't see why I had let Cedric and Shultz in front of me. My broken stride only increased the effort, as Gorman finished, Cedric got 2nd, and I passed Shultz to claim the final point. It was a sweep. Jim was elated with the win, but more so with his time. His 8:53 was the fastest time in the U.S. that season and would stand for six more weeks.

As for me, I could only think of what might have been, considering all those days I had run as well or better than Gorman in practice. It was a glum two weeks while my knee recovered before Bowerman would let me run again.

It seemed like an eternity, but by Northern Divisions, I was ready to race again. Running at Oregon State, they had a water jump barrier that wobbled when you stepped on it, but I had a smooth run, finishing third to Washington's John Celms, and setting myself up for a successful run in the Pac-8s.

The following week, Tom Morrow and I drove up to Corvallis for the state high school track championship. Tom had a former teammate, Doug Crooks, running well in the mile, and we sat on the opposite side of the noisy grandstands on the backstretch with a stopwatch, waiting for the 2-mile. The puff of smoke preceded the sound of the gun on the far side, and one figure in purple separated himself immediately. I was hopeful it was someone from South, but when he flashed by with a 10-yard lead, it was a blond-haired Marshfield Pirate. This guy settled down to a consistent 68 second pace. We were impressed, and then on the next lap it happened. I called out "68" and his eyes rolled up into his head to somewhere we had never been. You could only see the whites of his eyes and he still had half the race to run.

This was Steve Prefontaine, and he was putting on a show. Afterwards, we admitted, "He could be good," and wondered if Dellinger, who had joined Bowerman as an assistant, was having any success recruiting him.

I had started expressing concern to Buck and Bowerman about what to do with the shoe business when I left for the Navy following graduation. We all knew it couldn't remain at my parent's house. I had located an empty, narrow brick store downtown at 885 Olive Street. You'd think I was bleeding Buck dry to get the $50 a month rent. I told him we could open it cheap, and he agreed. The paint for the exterior was free not only because it was in my parents' basement, the paint was in the basement when my parents bought the house. It was chartreuse green. On our occasional date, Lin and I picked up sand and fishing net from the beach and barn wood from the countryside. I bought two pine boards to carve a sign that would bear the store's name. We called it "BRS West."

The second question was who should run it? I'd be gone for three years. Bowerman had a suggestion—Woodell. I was incredulous. Woodell had never given up trying to walk again, and after a year of therapy without progress, had returned to his parents' home in Beaverton. When I asked how he could possibly get to the schools throughout the state, Bowerman responded that with special controls, Bob was driving.

Buck said, "You'll find out, cause he's driving down to take you on a trip."

Bob drove up in his shiny 1968 Mercury Cougar and off we went to the Oregon coast with his wheelchair in the backseat. I was impressed with the hand controls. Bob could accelerate and stop with the touch of a finger. I pulled out my appointment book and we made it on time. On returning to the car, Bob slid off his wheelchair and onto his driver's seat, and I started to fold his chair to slip it into the back. "Hollister, you're going to fuck it all up!"

Woodell would be the next BRS West store manager.

Bowerman had never spoken to me before a race, except when he changed my event from the mile to the steeplechase. What needed to be said had been covered days before. It was 1968, and here I was in my first and only NCAA championship. Bowerman walked up to me just before I went onto the track for strides, and even though he pulled me in close so I could hear above the noise of the crowd, I couldn't get the message. But it was the gesture that made me feel special and sent my adrenaline out of control. It was a warm day, the gun went off and I tore around the turn into the straight and hurdled the first barrier with the pack a stride or two back. As I approached the second barrier, the crushing sound of spikes into cinder behind me had disappeared. Not looking back, I came through the first lap, "61!" What had I done? I just ran a lap over barriers faster than I had ever run a lap for the mile, and I have 6 and a half to go.

Track and Field News would later quote Kerry Pearce saying, "That Oregon guy really had me worried for a while." It took him 3 and a half laps to catch me, but once he did, it was like a freight train, with one after another passing as I tried to keep my composure. I couldn't count anymore as the tenth runner passed me somewhere before I got to the finish line. Not able to distinguish a horizon, I swung onto the grass infield and did a face plant, waking up horizontal somewhere with my teammates in the stands. Those who saw it said I didn't even put my arms out to break my fall. I simply hit the grass flat and sure as a Douglas fir on its last day in a clear cut.

Knight had opened an L.A. store, and he made the decision that Woodell and I should join L.A.'s BRS employee John Bork at the South Lake Tahoe Olympic trials. Bowerman would be there as part of the coaching staff, as would many of my teammates who qualified. The idea was that by holding trials on a new synthetic track built at 7000-foot high Echo Summit, you could simulate conditions anticipated at Mexico City. Great for the sprinters and jumpers, but tough for most of my teammates.

Bork was a former half-miler, older and more informed. Woodell and I would stay at his cousin's house on the other side where *Bonanza* was filmed. As I entered the unique competition site with huge conifer trees left standing in the middle of the track and portable grandstands sitting in the high desert dust, kids started running up to me with their programs. Wearing my blue BRS track suit, Cortez's on my feet, my Tiger bags over my shoulder and looking like a runner, they shouted, "sign, sign, sign!" Surprised, I obliged, and then it happened at another corner. After seeing one of the boy's expression of disappointment when he turned the program upside down to read my name, I asked, "So who do you think I am?"

"We thought you were Gerry Lindgren." And I laughed.

The next time I saw Gerry, I shared what had happened. He squeaked with his high-pitched voice, "Gee Geoff, that's great, 'cause you're a lot better looking than I am."

If only I had Gerry's wheels.

CHAPTER 6: SHOOTING STARS

I spent the next three years in the Navy assigned to the USS *Guadalupe*, the second oldest ship in the Navy. "The Guad," as she was known, was a converted ESSO tanker when the U.S. entered WWII. She fought with distinction and survived what was truly a naval war. Our Chief Quartermaster Lance had survived all of that and could point to any sunken ship marked on a chart and tell you its name. He could also name the stars in the sky without referring to a book. That skill, of knowing the stars, would be a skill that I had to acquire in order to fulfill my duties as a naval officer.

I was sent to San Diego for a few days in advance to study the demands expected of the navigator, but this training did not fully prepare me for what was to come. We set sail for the Philippines, and from there, we would support the U.S. war effort by refueling Navy ships off the coast of Vietnam. At twilight each evening and morning, Chief Lance would quietly pull down a handful of stars to a clear horizon and plot them along our Dead Reckoning course. Every time we changed course or speed, a new D.R. had to be laid. I would occasionally pull out a sextant to test my skill, and as my plot lines scattered over the chart, I saw myself waiting for the next horizon to update my inadequate positioning of the ship. Without Chief Lance's experience and skill, the Guad might have ended up in North Korea instead of the Philippines.

Sometime after we arrived in the Philippines we were informed that a major typhoon was approaching the Luzon coast. The fleet would sortie out of Subic Bay to reduce the risk of damage dockside and would rendezvous at a designated latitude and longitude that would place us out of harm's way. The skies had thoroughly darkened when we exited Subic Bay, and we stole through the night to a coordinate that placed the fleet at a position where the typhoon would least likely turn. Still, the wallop packed from over 100 nautical miles away brought the seas to 40 feet. Work ceased on the lower decks. With only 10 feet of freeboard on the tank deck, the 553-foot long *Guadalupe* rode like a Cadillac even when she was empty. Fully loaded with bunker fuel, she rode even lower, her bow knifing through the oncoming swell, sending spray clear over the bridge that stood one third of the way back. Once through the swell, you could only imagine the exposure of the keel as the ship's steel quivered and groaned before settling back down. I never actually got seasick, but felt listless and without energy the entire day. The whole experience would provide a never-forgotten memory, one that would save my life and that of others when I was older.

After the storm passed and a stop in Singapore, we crossed north between the coastlines of Luzon Island and Taiwan, headed for Hong Kong. I was learning that the navigator found sleep when he could. Every cruise or speed change required my return to the bridge to re-plot the D.R. The *Guadalupe* started picking up mountain peaks on the rugged coast of China at 50 miles in the dark, muggy night air. Twenty miles off the island of Victoria, a flashing light began to signal us. A signalman wrote down, "Turn back, turn back. You are in Chinese territorial waters." I informed Captain Brown, who left his stateroom to check our position on the chart and our D.R. We concluded it was typical harassment for any ship entering Hong Kong in international waters, and we maintained course and speed. Twilight exposed the rocky coastal island, topped with an occasional house on the exposed southeast side amid gnarled trees older than the Guad herself.

We reduced speed, and as we swept around the bare island, junks began to "chunk-a-chunk" by with their one-lung diesels and fanlike lug-rigged sails that had more patches than a quilt. Atop all wood hulls, live-aboard family perched from stern to bow. As soon as our anchor dropped, small punts with work crews were attached to our hull. Chief Lance rode ashore with me in the motor launch to the Navy pier. I was all eyes at the vast array of concrete buildings that climbed the interior hillsides bordering the British Commonwealth city on the water. There was energy in the air, and an audible ambition, the chatter and banter of commerce, Asian style.

The chief pointed over to an older lady overseeing a soup kitchen. "See her? Mary Sue. What a beauty in her day—she was a prostitute up in China. When the communists took over, she was smuggled down the river and ended up here. She started the soup kitchen and all those workers in the punts at the Guad are her crew. She's already struck a deal with the Chief to paint the ship in exchange for brass shell casings and anything else she can salvage. Can't tell it, but she's rich." Looking back on it now, Mary Sue was, in her own way, showing me what it was possible for a determined entrepreneur to accomplish.

As the *Guadalupe* crew prepared to steam back to Long Beach, a concern of the Executive Officer and the navigation team was Chief Lance's impending transfer to another duty upon arrival. The XO fully expected that my celestial navigation skills would have to improve. I prepared myself for numerous sun lines, azimuths and star fixes, and we once again set out into the vast Pacific Ocean. I laid a D.R. that would swing us down from the north and home. We sailed under cloudy skies, and the sun would not appear the whole transit. The blanket of clouds deprived us of any loran signals to the east. For thousands of miles, we relied only upon my D.R. until we picked up faint loran lines off the west coast of the U.S. Radar contact with the Channel Islands confirmed our position. Without a single celestial sighting, our position was right where I had plotted us on our 4500 mile Dead Reckoning. Finally I had a reason for some confidence in my own navigation skills.

Tying up at the Long Beach Naval pier, the crew, in dress whites, faced a line-up of wives, girlfriends, and family, but I had to drive to Eugene to see my nearest and dearest. I drove north for a Christmas celebration on Saratoga Street with my parents and sisters. Before I returned to Long Beach, my dad, perhaps mindful of the lonely life of a sailor at sea, gave me the name of a former girl's gymnastics coach and teacher who had gone through a divorce and moved to Long Beach. On my return to the ship, I gave Carol Kienlen a call from the phone booth on the pier and met her at her apartment. I learned that she grew up in Champaign, Illinois, graduated from the University of Illinois, was nationally ranked in gymnastics and was one of the oldest gymnasts on the competitive circuit. Her coach, Dick Mulvihill had moved his club to Long Beach, and the big new name with promise was Cathy Rigby from a competing club. I found myself attending gymnastic meets, where the talent and courage to perform seemingly impossible moves left someone like me asking, "Why?" Running was so simple by comparison.

Carol's apartment was right on the beach, and we had fun beachcombing together. We found a large hatch cover and a round wooden wire spool that we hauled back to the sparsely appointed apartment. I pulled old unused charts and resined them to the tops for a nautical theme. One evening after dinner, a thick dark fog rolled in, and you could barely see a foot beyond the windows of the high rise building. I made the excuse that it might be dangerous to drive back to the base, and we turned the lights out. Not returning to the ship became a habit.

Before I shipped out again for the far east, Carol and I decided to get engaged, but we wouldn't get married until I got out of the Navy. I agreed with that, as I saw the stress life overseas put on both husband and wife among my shipmates. Carol sewed a new flag for the Guad to fly when we did our at-sea refueling stops, or "unreps" as we called them. The flag featured an old lady sitting in a rocking chair with knitting needles in hand, and surrounding her were the words "She may be old, but she still puts out." Despite Captain Barnes' lack of any sense of humor, he agreed to let us fly the flag.

I had quite a changeover of personnel in navigation, headed by my new Chief Quartermaster, Hall. Where Chief Lance would stand like an immovable rock, say little and do his job, Chief Hall was jumpy, running from one side of the bridge to another. The chemistry on the bridge was already speaking to a different kind of cruise for 1970.

As we left the California coastline behind and started our celestial navigation, I realized that all my quartermasters needed to shoot sun-lines and celestial fixes. We had perfect conditions to obtain a horizon as we made for Hawaii, and I needed to know what I had to work with. To my surprise, Chief Hall's fixes were not matching the plots of some of my younger quartermasters. I mentioned this to the XO, and he asked me to verify if there was a problem and match my own plots. I was questioning my own confidence at this point when my own plots were off from the chief's. I waited for another horizon, and tried again, then confirmed with the XO that my plots matched with Jim Taylor's, a 19-year-old quartermaster out of Glen Bernie, Maryland. Taylor was obtaining the largest cluster of stars of any of us. It was becoming a contest to obtain a seven point star fix, and Taylor was up to five, his celestial fixes meeting pinpoint on the chart. I had to ask Chief Hall to re-compute his sightings, and he was still off. The questions lingered as we reached Pearl Harbor.

There was a certain level of anticipation as we threaded the narrow entry into the harbor, all of us realizing the significance of this place in naval history, the great ships that had preceded us, and the reverence for those lost in a national tragedy. Our stay in Pearl Harbor was brief. We refueled, and then we were off for Subic Bay again. I kept working with Chief Hall, but I relied on Taylor. By the time we reached port, Chief Hall was so stressed by his failure he was reporting chest pains.

The chief went to the base hospital and was med-evaced to Japan. Commander Bailey had his lips tight as he handed me a copy of Dutton's Navigation.

"Better learn that from cover to cover. We are totally counting on you now for the safe navigation of this ship."

I walked around the corner to my room in shock. What if I screwed up? I had 200 plus men relying on me.

At quarters, I relayed the medical condition of the chief and called Jim Taylor to the wing of the bridge. He was only 19 but was the brightest I had.

"It's you and me. You're the man, and I've got to get better myself." The challenge left a smile on his face, and we set about reading every spare moment we had.

From the highest level of the bridge Taylor and I would take turns—one would shoot the stars on a clear horizon with the sextant while the other recorded the sighting. If you identified the stars correctly ahead of time as they showed their brilliance, you could move in one succeeding 360° turn and get as many as seven. Then we worked together on the computations. When it all went as good as it can get, you were rewarded with a seven point star fix. The celestial fix and sun lines with a noon azimuth were like a roadmap on the water. You not only knew where you were at that exact moment, but from that point, you knew where you were going.

I thought to myself, as crazy as it was losing the Chief, I had far more confidence in this 19-year-old kid, and I had more confidence in myself. I couldn't lean on many people, I had to do it, and I might not ever have such a level of responsibility again in my life.

By now, no one present in the wardroom had spent more hours on the bridge than I had. Along with the hours came responsibility. I became the senior deck officer, and would be on the bridge supervising other officers, especially during unreps, when the safe handling of the ship was most critical.

This meant tedious, minute adjustments and orders to the helmsman and engine room, every change being entered in the ship's log. On our first unrep, Commander Bailey beamed as we hoisted "The Old Lady," sitting there in her rocking chair with knitting needles in hand. A cheer went up from the crew on deck awaiting our first customer, and it was obvious that Carol's flag was a big hit.

I went ashore in Hong Kong to locate a trading company Phil Knight had asked me to contact. Once again, I was a cheap way for Knight to get something done. He had a laundry list of things he was interested in—including ping-pong paddles, "wet look" nylon jackets, blue baseball mitts, and a price for 1000 dozen T-shirts for May delivery. Not the list of a company that knew exactly what it was doing.

I introduced myself, and was invited to visit a bag factory the next morning in Kowloon. I will never forget turning a corner to see an old, wrinkled lady curled up and sleeping on a pile of stamped pieces, waiting to be sewn. I didn't ask questions and no one supplied an explanation, but I thought back to children I'd seen in Kaohshiung, and looked down at this woman who must be reaping the reward of laboring all her life in this factory.

By December 1970, I was back in Long Beach, and I was off looking for a new escape— my own sailboat. I looked at all sizes and fell in love with an older wood New Zealand ketch, but probably wisely decided against what looked like a project, despite its perfect lines. In Marina Del Ray, I found a bulletproof looking Meridian Seaquest, basically a Coronado 25'. The Meridian had a slightly modified bow shape that gave you a little more room to handle the headsail and anchor. I paid $5,000 cash to the broker, signed all the papers and set off with our supply officer Ron McVickar and his wife south to an awaiting slip in Wilmington.

Fourty-four years after my hero Glenn Davis autographed my scrapbook at Hayward Field, I meet him again at the 2004 Olympic Trials with scrapbook in hand.

1964 S.E. Axeman Year Book

That's me, fourth from right, surrounded by South Eugene teammates as I hold the Willamette Invitational Team Championship trophy with my co-captain Paul Weiseth. The trophy was presented by 100-meter world record holder Harry Jerome (center, behind microphone).

Lin Madden

I'm sitting on a rock cropping on the Oregon Coast with Tiger model shoes, available at the 855 Olive store in Eugene. Knight loved it for a catalog image—no model or photo rights. It was free.

Bill Bowerman as I met him in 1964.

Geoff Hollister

Arne Kvalheim, Wade Bell, and Dave Wilborn in a track workout in California. Along with Roscoe Divine, they were all teammates and sub-4 minute milers—the reason I became a steeplechaser.

Buck Knight (second from right) stands with Bowerman and his teammates after they captured the Northern Division team championships. It was cold out, and Bowerman doesn't know that Jim Bailey (third from left) has his jockstrap over his head to keep his ears warm.

Buck Knight in his customary position behind teammate Jim Grelle. This says volumes about what Phil Knight became—competitive.

Bill Bowerman would weigh everything we wore in a race. He was obsessive about weight.

Jim Gorman leads me, Cedric Wedemeier and Chuck Shultz in an Oregon steeplechase dual with USC.

1964 USS Guadalupe Cruise Book

The "Guad" "unrepping" with a carrier to port and a destroyer to starboard.

Hong Kong as I found her in 1969.

My navigation team on the bridge of the U.S.S. Guadalupe. Young Jim Taylor is sitting at the bottom, far left. That's me with the mustache, standing on the left.

John Fassero (right), my roommate on the USS Guadalupe.

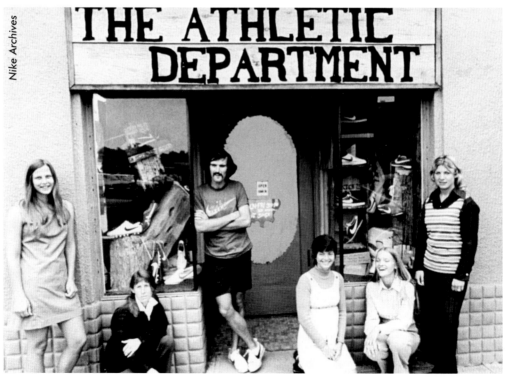

My staff in front of the original 855 Olive Athletic Department in 1972. I have an all-female staff, they are all athletes and it's the first year of Title IX.

Don Dickover

Bowerman with his sub-4 minute milers at the grand opening of the second Eugene retail location in 1973.

Nike Archives

Nelson Farris at work.

Phil Knight in his kimono before we sit down for breakfast in the Ishibashi mansion.

Phil and I in Kurume Japan at the Bridgestone Rubber Company.

Blue Ribbon Sports had sent an Oregonian down to manage the California business, and I started visiting Dave Kottkamp to get in a run, have dinner and catch up on the business. Dave was a friend of Bob Woodell's, and they had met during the successful campaign for Neil Goldschmidt's bid for mayor of Portland. It didn't take long, and Bob was down for a visit. Typical of Bob's confidence, he felt confident and comfortable going for a sail with me, wheelchair and all. He wheeled down the dock and quite easily slid over the cockpit boat cushions and we were off, taking in the somewhat narrow channels with huge ship piers and warehouses surrounding us. Not the most scenic sail, and the wind would gust and bounce from different directions. Suddenly, I realized my tiller was overpowered by a back-winded headsail, and our bow was headed for a tall creosoted piling. Bob was now less confident and yelled, "Do something!" I said, "Take the tiller," and sprinted forward to fend us off. Over time, I learned that you could stay in the cockpit and control everything with jib sheets and earlier anticipation. It would come with experience.

As the end of my Navy hitch approached, Carol and I made wedding plans. The Captain's wedding present was to deck haul my car and sailboat aboard the *Guadalupe* to Seattle where I would be out on arrival. By then my closest friends were John Fassero, the deck officer who was also my roommate, and Emanuel Witherspoon, who was our XO. John and Spoon rode with me from Seattle to Eugene for the wedding party dinner. My Uncle Elzie and Aunt Jane drove down from Port Angeles, Carol's parents, sister, and brother were out from Illinois, my sister Laura and her husband Fred arrived from Hawaii, and Jeff Galloway was clicking away with his camera.

The next day, I stood at attention on the grass in the middle of the rhododendron gardens in a corner of Hendricks Park with Spoon, Fred, and John as my best man. We were awaiting the bride, escorted by her father, Fred Olson. Steve Stageberg and Jim Thomas were in attendance from my high school days, the Bowermans were there and Galloway quietly clicked his shutter to capture the moment from the cover of various large pink blooms as we all stood there in line in our matching tan bellbottoms and the pink paisley shirts I had purchased for my wedding party.

My last glimpse of the USS *Guadalupe* was in the north end of Elliot Bay. John, as the Deck Officer, already had the sailboat in the water and rigged. Carol and I boarded the Meridian Seaquest, which we had christened the *Mugwump*, and Captain Barnes ordered two blasts from the *Guadalupe*'s bellowing steam whistle. I responded with two from my hand held air horn.

CHAPTER 7: HOT OFF BOWERMAN'S WAFFLE IRON

After a honeymoon week in the San Juan islands, I was in Beaverton at Blue Ribbon Sport's little office, which amounted to a hallway outside an insurance office. Bob Woodell was now my boss and doing impressive work. Bob could share a laugh with straight talk as he informed me, "Hollister, the future doesn't look good for selling Tiger. Hell, I don't know, maybe we'll be selling umbrellas!"

I responded, "I could do that. Oregon would be the perfect state if you had to sell umbrellas."

Down in Eugene, Bowerman was dealing with his own version of that problem—running fast in a rainy climate. Bowerman had always been a product of his own environment, and when that environment created problems, he set out on an endless quest to solve them. Times had changed, and with those changes, new challenges arose. The University of Oregon had installed Astroturf at Autzen Stadium. Neither the manufacturer, nor the school had thought of contacting the shoe companies, which only produced football shoes with molded cleats for grass. The fact was, there was not a shoe in existence for this new surface, and it was not only the Oregon coach who was concerned with the problem. An old Bowerman friend, USC's John McKay, had played for Oregon and was an assistant under Oregon's Len Casanova prior to developing the highly respected Trojan program. McKay was concerned about his quick tailbacks' ability to stand up on a wet Astroturf surface. The Oregon players had resigned themselves to wearing basketball shoes, as they provided lateral support and the herringbone tread pattern gripped better than cleats.

Bowerman was working away in at his hillside home over the McKenzie River in response to McKay's need. He started with a modification of the standard cleat, adding bars of surface area where he felt the pressure from a foot-plant would require it, but it was still too high off the surface for stability. Bill was looking at anything that would provide a clue. One morning he stumbled on it, staring at the pyramid shapes on Barbara's waffle iron. It has always sounded like a good story that Barbara, a devoted Christian Scientist, was at church when Bill, started his experiment. But it didn't happen that way— Barbara was there and saw the whole thing. The first time Bill tried it, he poured the urethane on the wrong side of the griddle, so he got innies instead of outies. Of course, that didn't stop Bill. He just poured another batch on the other side of the griddle.

I received a call from Bowerman one morning. Kenny Moore and I were to report to his home by 9 a.m. When we arrived, he pulled out some old Tiger flats and turned them bottom side up. Stuck to the outsole were strange looking tan nubs of urethane. He instructed us to put them on and run up the gravel road that passed an old pioneer cemetery in the trees to the left. The sensation under foot was remarkable. This little change felt like pillows. We were only gone for five minutes, but when we returned, the nubs were gone. Bill looked at them curiously and said, "Well, it looks like I have more work to do." I left, not expecting to see this idea again.

A debenture is an unsecured loan to a business or a corporation. Nobody had heard of this animal called a "venture capitalist" back then.

Carol and I had been living in an apartment on Coburg Road, not far from the Bowermans'. On one of my training runs through South Eugene, I spotted a shingled two-story home that I found out had been designed by an architect. Phil Knight had been seeking debenture holders for his Blue Ribbon Sports Company, and Bowerman discouraged many of us from investing, suggesting we could lose it all. I had a choice. The house was up for $25,000. I put $5,000 down and bought it. My first house—I'd spent two years at the U of O studying architecture, and I never really have gotten the architect out of me.

Not having much left for furniture, I made a table out of a barrel and hatch cover. We patched and sewed pieces of carpet together, and I built bookshelves with ladders and wood planks. The look went with my longer mustache, hair and sideburns, to which Bowerman responded, "What's that turd on your lip?"

It was around this time that I heard about an incident involving Bowerman and Mac Wilkins. Mac Wilkins was a real character who mixed discipline with fun. In Bowerman's P.E. class, Bill taught the elements of every event, including the difficult approach for the javelin throw. He would measure out the stride with, "One, two, three, bam! Just like stepping on a cow-pie." While demonstrating the technique with discus thrower Wilkins in the front row, he slammed his plant foot down, completing his imaginary release with his head close to Wilkins, and farted with the effort! "Don't you say a thing, Wilkins."

"Bill, was that the cow-pie?" That was Mac Wilkins— irreverent, quick-witted, and earthy. His comment left the class in stitches and Bowerman red-faced and, for once in his life, retreating.

My primary job was to manage the BRS store at 855 Olive. I changed the exterior color and the staff, hiring all women, and every one of them an athlete. Bowerman encouraged me to join the Oregon Track Club and attend their monthly meetings. I was comfortable with old family friend Bob Newland as a major player in the club, and soon found myself in charge of putting on their monthly road race. All the races had been conducted at the same location in Alton Baker Park, and they would simply change the distance. I moved the early sign-up to the store and started looking for new sites and more creative formats.

Bowerman had been appointed head Olympic coach for the 1972 Munich-bound track and field team. Eugene won a successful bid to hold trials at Hayward Field on Bowerman's lightening fast urethane track, and Pre was everywhere on back roads, running up hills and turning in blistering laps at Hayward Field. He usually trained under Dellinger's watchful eye, often warming down with "the young Bill." I had been training with steeplers Mike Manley, who had moved into town, and Steve Savage, who had won an NCAA title. They were above me, and although I could match them in workouts, I had little left to compete on Saturdays. But between their help and my many runs around the state with high school teams and coaches, I was getting in the best shape of my life. The workouts ranged from runs at altitude with former Oregon state half-miler Jan Underwood, now living in Gilchrist, to sprints in the surf and up Oregon's coastal dunes.

Manley and Savage were ranked 1-2 in the US rankings for the 3000 steeplechase in 1972. Both made the Olympic team.

Bowerman started phoning nearly every morning around 7 a.m. with the marching orders for the day. Carol was pregnant, hadn't been sleeping well, and failed to appreciate the urgency of a new shoe idea or a problem to solve. This was the beginning of a long running conflict for me. Finding a balance between my family life and the demands of working for Bowerman and Knight's shoe enterprise was not going to be easy.

CHAPTER 8: WE CALLED HIM "PRE"

I had not had much contact with Prefontaine, but I had marveled watching him at Hayward Field. I had always thought my teams in the '60s lived up to the great fanfare, but Pre took athletic showmanship to an extraordinary level. It was like a three-act play—first the warm-up, then the race itself, and finally the victory lap.

We didn't do victory laps, and, like most distance runners, I preferred my warm up before a race in solitude. I usually chose the cemetery across the street from Mac Court. Pre started right in front of the crowd, usually jogging and chatting with a teammate on the warm-up lane Bowerman had installed of tire shavings. Pre would then remove a jacket or sweat top and run a stride, remove his pants and break into a sprint on the turn, under the watchful eyes of the Eugene faithful. He followed his American 5000 record of 13:29.6 with what I considered one of his most memorable efforts in the upcoming Twilight Meet.

When the time for the traditional Twilight Meet arrived, I felt in decent enough shape to PR in the mile. Earlier in the week Bowerman had given Kenny and me new outsoles on our old Tiger spikes. He had stripped off the spike plate and heel and replaced it with a black rubber material with the same nubs as before. "I went back to the drawing board," Bowerman said, "and thought back to the old Pleasant Hill track built with truck tire rubber. This is what Wyatt calls logger 5, used for log trucks. Myrmo's machine shop machined the plate to withstand the heat and pressure to press the sole." Kenny and I danced down the street impressed and decided we'd race the Twilight Mile in them. Bowerman's idea would go on to be patented and would become known as "The Waffle." We've made millions of them, and virtually every shoe company has some variation on it.

I was lacing my shoes up in the bullpen sitting in the middle of Hayward Field. Pre was next to me lacing up his Adidas. Dad was still the hurdle chief and walked up, "Hey, you ought to try these new waffles Geoff's wearing."

Pre looked up, glowering at my dad, "When you're going to run 57 seconds for your last lap, you have to have spikes on your feet."

I froze. He just told me what he was going to do. He's going to run 57. He's that confident. I'm nowhere near that. I just wanted to crawl under the dark bowels of the west grandstand and hide. Pre ran 3:56.7, I PR'd at 4:09 and Kenny ran 4:03 in waffles, one of the fastest ever without spikes. I decided I would devote my energy to doing whatever I could to help this guy called Pre.

Little did I know what I was getting in to.

On a sunny day in May, Pre had his hands full with a talented Ethiopian pre-med student, Hailu Ebba. Pre was challenging Ebba in this specialty, the 1500 meter run. A customary strategy of Pre's was to take the lead, which he did as Ebba was content to hold and kick off a pace that would take them both under two minutes at the half. Pre held the lead into the final turn and you could see Ebba coming, impatient to get to the final straight. He was on Pre's shoulder, and head down, Pre wouldn't let him by, holding him in lane two and insisting on maintaining a slight lead in the straight, where Pre started running a diagonal down the track, holding Ebba to his right, forcing him to run wide.

Pre 3:39.8. Ebba 3:40.4. The two jogged together to thunderous cheers from the stands, smiling as they both circled the track to satisfy all who had just witnessed a great contest.

In the store, we were awaiting a shipment of a new brand, and a phone call from Knight and Woodell had prompted us to think of a new name. I stayed in the zone of Puma with my suggestion of Peregrine. Knight went for Dimension 6; we thought perhaps for his love of the pop group The 5th Dimension. Jeff Johnson was three hours ahead of us in Massachussetts, and awoke with "Nike." He calmly emphasized 2 syllables and the importance of a "K" or a "Z" sound and, "Oh, by the way, Nike was the Greek goddess of victory." Typical of many early decisions, he didn't hear back from Knight, as though the process took place in a vacuum.

Knight had already bumped into Carolyn Davidson in a hallway at Portland State where he was teaching accounting, flashed her 30 bucks and she came up with the swoosh. We all had a hard time seeing it as a success, but Knight said, "It will grow on you," and we had a brand.

It would be called Nike. And, it had wings.

With the good fortune of the Olympic Trials coming to Eugene, I started thinking of any strategy that would allow us to have a Nike presence. We had no money, but there was the store, and I knew some of the athletes who would compete. My old South Eugene High School teammate Steve Stageberg had come as close as any to beating Pre, running just 1 $1/2$ seconds behind him in the previous year's AAU championships. My old ROC buddy, Jeff Galloway, had improved dramatically, teaming up with Frank Shorter and Jack Bacheler in Florida, and then going to altitude in Boulder. They formed the nucleus of the Florida Track Club. Back from Cornell, Jon Anderson

Shorter won four straight U.S. cross country championships from 1970-1973, and took the gold medal in the marathon in the Munich Olympics with a time of 2:12:19. He won the silver medal in the same event in Montreal. Bacheler ran ninth in the marathon at Munich.

Anderson, a member of the 1972 U.S. Olympic team, won the 1973 Boston Marathon in 2:16:03. He was the son of Eugene mayor Les Anderson.

had matured and gotten faster. I was hoping I could get these guys to wear our shoes.

Our problem was we had training shoes, but to get runners in racing shoes, we had to build them ourselves. Bowerman was focused on coaching his Olympic prospects, and he didn't have time to build shoes. I couldn't do all the pattern work that Bill could do, but Knight ordered a batch of nylon uppers from Japan. Once I had those I would be able to put the rest of the pieces together, but I was struggling with Bowerman's mold for the waffle, a 6" square that required two pieces butted together at the mid-foot to make one shoe. Sarge milled the molds at Myrmo's Machine Shop. Sarge was their master machinist, and he admired what Bowerman was doing, so he took on the task himself. I had gone to South Eugene High School with George Myrmo, and they did good work, but Bill would not spend another penny for a new mold.

A guy named Smitty pressed the logger 5 into the mold one at a time in a little shop across the street from Wyatt's tire, and you couldn't get any waffle from him unless Bowerman signed a purchase order I couldn't do anything about the mold, I was running out of waffles, and the uppers had arrived in Eugene. I was getting desperate.

Bowerman was standing on the grass, stopwatch in hand in the middle of Hayward Field. I walked out behind him as he shouted a split to Kenny "62," and with one look, I could sense I was an aggravation.

"Bill, I need some more waffle."

A machine gun line of expletives was followed with, "Damn it, can't you see I'm coaching."

Well, if I had learned anything from Bill, it was focus. I was going to get those shoes made, and I drove off to Smitty's shop and said, "Make 'em. I'll beg for forgiveness later."

The next day, Smitty had a stack of 40 waffle sheets in a box, and I took them across the alley to a shop called Jim the

Shoe Doctor. Jim the Shoe Doctor was owned by Ed Thompson, a former state policeman who became a cobbler. We laid out a production line in his shop to produce what would be Nike's first competition shoes. Each waffle stud had a thin, round, rubber piece extending from the top. Sarge thought it might be necessary for the material to flow to the edges. Bowerman called them "tits," and I was the guy who got a pair of shears and did what Bill called "The tit trimming."

Knowing that all my contacts were distance runners, I glued a white crepe mid-sole to the bottom of the upper and added a little more to the heel before applying the waffle outsole. I started thinking back to some of Bill's shoes not going the distance and watched Ed's staff operating a McKay stitcher that could stitch an outsole to the upper. We tried it and then covered the stitches inside with a Spenco sock liner. The final touch was taking a star punch and perforating the upper for ventilation. Janet Newman was watching with interest as the shoes came off the line and wrote about them in an article for *Runner's World*, "Hot off Bowerman's waffle iron." The shoes were ready two weeks before the trials.

Bill was so focused on the Olympics that I never had to beg his forgiveness. None of our guys made his team, so that was a non-issue, and his runners all wore Tigers or Adidas.

Meanwhile, we were getting more Nike models in the shop. We switched customers to the new brand as often as possible—it might just be our future. Initially, my print ads in the *Register-Guard* had both Tiger and Nike, but by spring of '72, Nike was dominating. We printed a T-shirt that combined the winged mark of the shoe with a scripted font that said "Nike."

I started taping the *Guard's* articles on the trials to the long south wall of the store. Jim Gorman was our newest employee, even though he had qualified to run in the trials in the 1500. Jere Van Dyk had also qualified. But as enthused as

I was, it was difficult to get anyone to try the waffle for the track, even my good friend Jeff Galloway, who was entered in both the 10k and the marathon. It looked like my best bet would be the marathon, and with my best selling point being "Bowerman's waffle sole, sewn on so it won't fall off," I managed to give the 10 pair away, and 5 would be brave enough to wear them.

Adidas was everywhere when Eugene and Springfield swelled with athletes and spectators. By now, the little store had half the wall covered with pictures and stories. I could identify athletes' faces, and each was offered a Nike T-shirt. We hot pressed their names on the back. A green T with gold ink said simply "Pre" on the back. Long jumper Arne Robinson asked for a black T, and another athlete had us print "Dump Nixon."

Robinson made the Olympic team, and a picture of him wearing this shirt appeared in Track & Field News. *He took the bronze medal in the long jump in Munich. Four years later he took the gold medal in Montreal with a long jump of 8.35 meters.*

Cassell was on the 4 x 400 relay team that won Olympic gold in Tokyo in 1964.

The AAU, run by a somewhat arrogant former 400 runner named Olan Cassell, was also everywhere. Under the amateur rules, branding was not allowed on the field of competition. The stripes on the shoes were ruled functional and not touched, but backtabs, the tiny labels on the backs of shoes, were taped over, as were logos and brand names on athletic bags. Even branded T-shirts were not allowed. But something curious was happening. The scripted Nike on our new brand looked like "Mike" and to our delight in the stands, a lot of Mikes were running around on the infield at Hayward Field. As inauspicious as it seemed, a new brand had emerged out of nowhere in the Pacific Northwest, where there was no footwear industry.

I built on this success by inviting athletes out to the house for a barbeque and beers. The fun would often continue well into the night. In contrast to our competitors, who relied on the old standby of cash under the table, I made it my business to give these athletes whatever I could in the way of support and the comforts of home. What I did was done out of necessity—BRS didn't have any money to give away. But BRS was a company made up of athletes and former collegiate runners, and we knew what it was like to be far from home.

I was making a cup of coffee one morning when I heard behind me, "That looks good," and I turned to see Nike debenture holder Chuck Cale standing there in his bathrobe. Cale was a friend of Knight's, and he'd arrived the day before and come out to the house for a party. Carol and I had gone to bed, and unbeknownst to us he'd slept somewhere in our house that night.

Galloway, Bacheler, and Shorter had taken up temporary refuge at my parents' home, where I found Jeff thinly slicing raw liver and downing it. As I watched with disgust, I didn't know if he saw any nutritional value, or whether he simply wanted me to spread the word to scare off his competitors.

The American team was showing its potential at Hayward Field. Jim Ryun would make the Olympic team for a second time, Bob Seagren was calm, cool, and confident on the vault runway, and Dave Wottle's white hat headed down the back stretch of the second lap of the 800, only to have it snatched by an over-exuberant junior high boy while doing his cool downs. Dave had enough left to chase it down and wear it to a world record and gold medal in Munich.

Seagren won the gold medal in the pole vault in the 1968 Mexico City Olympics, and the silver in the 1972 Munich Olympics. He held the world record 4 times from 1966 (5.32 meters) to 1972 (5.63 meters).

Jim Gorman advanced through the quarter finals, but missed by one place to race Ryun in the final. Disappointed, he went out drinking only to awake the next morning to hear that one of the athletes that advanced was injured and could not run. At this point, neither could Jim.

The store now had people in line clear out to the parking meters. They read the articles on the wall, picked up their T-shirts and bought shoes. I noticed one guy in line pretending to be an athlete. He was a fat kid from Philadelphia, and I knew that he worked for one of our competitors, Puma. I challenged him in front of the athletes, "You're no athlete—now get the hell out of here," and escorted him out. I don't think I understood it at the time, but I was making a statement: BRS was a company run by athletes, for athletes. Those courtesies were not going to be extended to a pretender like the guy who worked for Puma.

It was a business approach that caught on. Watching were Villanova's Marty Liquori and Florida coach Jimmy Carnes. They observed what was going on, the "buzz" in this tiny little shop, and started to plan. This was the beginning of what would become the Athletic Attic.

In high school, I thought Stageberg looked so good in the 440 that I told him he should run another lap. He resisted, saying "Run another lap? That's too far." But he went on to become America's #2 runner in the 5000.

Steve Stageberg was injured, could not compete, and didn't even return home to Eugene to watch Pre systematically dismantle veteran George Young and Leonard Hilton with excruciating laps in the 5000 that ended up in an American record 13:22.8. Pre also had a new look. Four short weeks after his NCAA win, a tanned Prefontaine sported a mustache, long sideburns, and flowing sun-bleached hair. Pre got away with some things that the rest of us couldn't because Bowerman recognized that Pre did everything he needed to stay focused, and he gave absolutely everything he had to give on the track. With the new look, and the third best performance in the world, Pre had added confidence. He told everybody "Nobody will beat me in Munich."

Frank Shorter, Kenny Moore, Bacheler and Galloway all toed the line at Hayward Field for the marathon trial. Somewhere hidden in the crowd of runners were five pairs of the waffle-soled running shoes on the feet of runners who were brave enough to wear them. Knight and I were sitting high up in the east grandstands. A few seats over was Portland Mayor Neil Goldschmidt, a big track fan in a white T-shirt, chewing on a cigar. The gun went off, and after a circle of the track, the runners were on to Agate Street, the footbridge over the Willamette and then a long loop through Springfield. Updates were covered on the radio.

"We are at the 20-mile mark. It's Frank Shorter and Kenny Moore side-by-side and, oh my God, a freak is going to make the Olympic team!" Not far behind in third was Mark Covert from California sporting a long beard and curls over his shoulders. On his feet were Nike waffles.

Sitting in front of Phil and me was Puma's promotion guy, Art Simburg. The fat boy worked for him, along with a guy named Cubi. Simburg had married top sprinter Wyomia Tyus and catered primarily to sprinters, jumpers, and hurdlers. He wore Tom Jones styled pants, but didn't have Tom Jones' ass. A bit of a gut sat below his open shirt and frizzled hair. Rumor was that at the '68 Olympics in Mexico City, Adidas had arranged to have Simburg thrown in jail, thus eliminating one competitor. Those were cut-throat business tactics, and they couldn't have contrasted more with how I preferred to operate.

The runners started streaming onto the track with Shorter and Moore leading, matched stride for stride. Then it was Bacheler, and the team was made. Galloway, having already qualified in the

10,000, had backed off, pacing his club mate onto the team and crossing the finish line 4th in Nike Bostons. Jeff Galloway was the first athlete to cross a finish line in Nikes during a major event, and he was followed by Greg Brock in 5th and Don Kardong in 6th, both in Nike Bostons. Covert had faded to seventh.

In amazement, Simburg stood up and started clapping, "I'm surprised. We're doing well." He had misinterpreted our mark that curled up. His curled down. Knight tapped him on the shoulder, "That's not a Puma, that's a Nike."

"What's a Nike?"

"A new brand."

"That's okay. There's enough room for both of us."

Little did Simburg know how much room we would require.

Bowerman was off with the U.S. distance runners to a training camp at Bowdoin College in Brunswick, Maine prior to departing for a second camp in Oslo, Norway. Pre, Galloway, Moore, Shorter, Bacheler, Anderson, Ryun, and Wottle would fine-tune their preparation for Munich and present themselves as the last competitive distance group to represent their country in the 20th century. No American Olympic distance runners have performed this well since.

Back in Eugene, my mom still had her eye on Phil Knight and his plans for Blue Ribbon Sports. She didn't trust him, and she insisted I get my teaching certificate as a fallback. That fall I student-taught at South Eugene under my old art instructor Maurice Van and student-coached cross country and track under Harry Johnson. My former head coach, Don "Barney" Barnhart had passed away while I was in the Navy, and Harry immediately took South to the top in both sports. I ran with his team in workouts, and after seeing Tom McChesney win the state cross country and 2-mile titles, and   Mark Feig run 4:05 for the mile, I thought "This is easy." Little did I know that Harry had a work ethic few would match.

As much as I enjoyed the teaching and coaching, I did trust Knight and Bowerman. I loved the work and remembered Bowerman always saying to the team, "Find something you love and work hard at it. You'll have a much better chance of success." I hand-built cross country waffle shoes for Harry's state championship team, and then came the big challenge— USC's order of football shoes. We were using white basketball shoes for uppers. McKay would not allow white shoes on the field, unlike crosstown rival, UCLA, so we had to spray paint the uppers black and then strip off the black wings that later became known as the swoosh, creating a white contrast. Add the waffle sole, and 60 pair later, we were done.

I watched the Munich games on television from Eugene. In disbelief, we sat there as Jim McKay and Chris Shankel tried to maintain calm while communicating the confusion of what appeared to be a terrorist attack on the Israeli dormitory in the athletes' village. The problem was, they didn't have any details to tell us.

Most of what I know about this I learned later. Bill Dellinger, who was not an Olympic coach, was staying in an apartment nearby. The Olympic Village security force, dressed in lederhosen, were still not keeping people out, even after the attack began. Dellenger went in to the Village, got Pre, and drove him across the border to Austria. Pre was so upset he wanted to go home. Dellinger wanted to get inside his head and get him focused. He told Pre that his competition in the 5000, "Viren, Bedford, Stewart, those guys are going to be ready for you. You need to get ready for them."

Another factor was all Olympic competition was postponed one day because of the attack. Pre knew this meant Viren had another day to recover from his win in the 10,000 final, which took place before the attack.

Dellinger predicted that David Bedford would set a fast pace because he lacked a finishing kick. Pre's strategy was to tuck behind Bedford and save energy. The pace dawdled, the runners bunched up in a pack, with the lead held not by Bedford but by runners who had no chance to win. Pre was getting elbowed and bumped, and even for a runner with his incredible gifts, this was hard, especially since he preferred to run in front. But this race was tactical, a battle of competing strategies, rather than a race he could win from the front.

At the Olympic Trials in Eugene, Pre had boasted not only that he would win in Munich, but that he would run the last mile in 4 minutes. With a little over a mile to go, Viren had moved through the pack to a striking position. This was the moment for Pre to make good on his boast, to get into that grinding 60-second pace. He had a little over 4 laps to go. He took the lead, and Viren and Tunisia's Gamoudi went with him. The three of them ran at 60-second pace, but Pre ran wide and Viren owned the inside lane, a tactical error on Pre's part. Worse, Pre kept surging, grabbing the lead and then letting off, using a lot of energy in the process. You surge because you want to break somebody, but Pre's surges were ineffective. He was 21, and he was running against experience.

Viren had been here before, and he knew exactly what he was doing. He had those long legs and that quick turnover in his hips, as well as a beautiful flowing stride, very deceptive. Gamoudi was right there, but he was tiring. You knew, because when he tires, his head starts bobbing from side to side, and it was bobbing now. Coming off the last turn, Pre still looked good, running third behind Viren and Gamoudi. But Ian Stewart was coming hard, and Pre's tactical errors were about to catch up with him.

Viren breezed to the tape untouched. Gamoudi took the silver. Pre was so exhausted at ten yards out that he was practically staggering. Stewart passed him, reaching his body forward for the bronze. Pre finished fourth.

Years later Phil Knight said, "Pre certainly didn't lack courage. He'd rather go for the gold than take the bronze."

Pre was disillusioned with himself when he came back to Eugene. "They'll name a street after me in Coos Bay," he said. "Fourth Street."

On the Oregon coast, BRS was hosting a sales meeting at Otter Crest where Woodell had purchased a condominium. Buck and I were running along the sandy beach near the surf as pale misty air blocked our full vision. I saw something bubbling in the water. It was a green glass Japanese float about a foot in diameter. I plucked it out, ran up, and placed it behind a log. Further down, we found another, then another. On the return, we put the floats in our hands and returned to the lodge. As we arrived, Knight said, "Here, you take two, I'll just keep one."

Impressed with Buck's generosity, I returned to my room, rinsing the sand off, toweling them dry and just staring at the two floats. They had crossed the great expanse of the northern Pacific, taking years, eventually traveling south in the one knot Japanese current down the Washington and Oregon coasts. No doubt occasional storms reversed their course, but they finally arrived unbroken at the moment of our run. And now I was working with Buck Knight selling a product that originated in Japan, crossed the same waters by ship and were on the feet of thousands of runners across our continent.

CHAPTER 9:   AFTER MUNICH

Bowerman returned to Eugene just as disillusioned as Pre. Going into the Olympics, he had been concerned about the lack of security. He wanted simply to protect his athletes in preparation for their events. He believed that fans, autograph seekers and journalists were too much of a distraction for the athletes at the time it was most important for them to focus. Once he arrived at the Olympic Village, Bowerman, unimpressed by the lederhosen-wearing guards, asked the USOC officers for more security. They wanted him to justify this.

"I'll give you two good reasons," he said. "World War I and World War II." They turned him down.

After the attack started, he was on the phone calling his half-sister, Jane Bowerman Hall. Her husband was Bill Hall, Undersecretary of State. Bill Hall sent in the U.S. Marines, and the U.S. compound in the Village was secured. But what should have been the pinnacle of his career—head Olympic Track coach—had become, in his words, "the worst coaching experience of my life." He retired as track coach at the University of Oregon within weeks, much to everyone's surprise. But he had options after all—his partnership with Phil Knight would give him an outlet for his inventive side, something for his restless nature to focus on.

Dave Taylor later became VP for worldwide production at Nike. Knight wanted him to be president, succeeding Tom Clarke, but Taylor had to decline for health reasons.

When Pre returned to Eugene, he had a full year of eligibility left. Dellinger was running the show now, and together with Pre, they decided to red-shirt Pre for cross country so he could have more time to recover from the Olympics. Dellinger already had a competitive team that included Dave Taylor, Randy James, Gary

Barger, and Terry Williams. Red-shirting Pre meant he worked out with the cross country team but did not compete, which preserved his last year of cross country eligibility until the fall of 1973.

We had been evicted at the 885 Olive store as part of the downtown urban renewal. Woodell negotiated a lease for a new construction at a small mall two blocks to the south. The contracting was my first experience with unions. I had hired a non-union carpenter, and the other trades threatened to walk. A union plumber couldn't finish a simple job because he was not allowed to use a hammer, so I did the job myself. Hayward Field's old west grandstands had been torn down, and I bought hundreds of board feet of the old 1918 seats, pitted with marks from track spikes and each seat with an embossed scrolled number. I thought, "Ah, if these seats could only speak of the events witnessed."

I hot pressed "Nike" in block letters on the left chest of a warm-up suit to give to Pre to try on. It was getting quite noisy as the city was demolishing the building behind us, and we were next. Pre went to the tiny restroom in the rear of the store to change. The suit fit, and he left. Twenty minutes later, the wrecking ball slammed through our wall, while taking out the last of the adjacent wall. Bricks fell everywhere. We looked wide-eyed as workers peered in from the other side. By the end of the day, they had bolted thick plywood slabs to both sides to patch the hole. Pre had dodged a bullet.

There was a lady who kept bringing Cortez's back to the store, demanding a replacement for her son. I asked her what he used them for, and she said "running," although I could tell they had been used for tennis or another sport. Our policy was to back our product, so I gave her a replacement rather than lose a customer. When it happened again, I leaned towards losing the customer. Sure, BRS was all about taking care of our customers, but there were limits.

Our monthly road race was a potluck run at Skinner's Butte Park bordering the Willamette River. Two laps with a good hill in the middle created a nice 5k challenge for the runners before we settled down at picnic tables for a shaded meal. As I came off the finish line, Mike Manley informed me that some guy was walking toward the river with a case of our beer. I caught up to him as he walked straight-armed, his hands wrapped under the case. I told him to "Stop and drop the beer." He continued. I repeated my demand as he failed to turn around. He kept going. The third time, he dropped the case and you could hear bottles breaking. He kept walking and I tapped him on the shoulder. As he turned, my fist was at his nose. He fell backwards clutching his nose and ran off. I put the glass shards in the box and returned what was left to the party.

The following day, the lady I had problems with regarding her sons' shoes walked into the store with her son. He had a white bandage over his nose. It was the boy in the park and I thought, "Oh no, she's going to sue me." She didn't take long and informed me that her son told her what happened, and that she came in simply to tell me I did the right thing.

For me, this was a lesson in customer relations. We'd come to a mutual respect, and a mutual understanding. She left, but returned as a customer, and never brought in another "defective" shoe.

Bowerman was struggling with Prefontaine's racing spikes, trying to fashion a snug-fitting pattern with a one-piece toe. Pre had a broad foot, and the nylon seam down the top of the shoe's toe was abrasive. Bowerman made a special last for Pre. When he laid the thin, dark green leather flat, it looked like a butterfly before he glued it together on Pre's special last. Bill had carefully modified this last, adding material to broaden the toe box. Always absorbed with reducing weight, he cut out swooshes from gold tape and pressed them on the side of the upper. He cannibalized a plate from another shoe and handed me the finished pair to give to Pre. "He'll run some strides at the track this afternoon," Bowerman said.

I met Pre on the west straightaway; he laced the shoes and pranced in a circle, his T-shirt already wet from his warm-up run through Hendricks Park. On his first burst down the straightaway, the swooshes floated off both shoes and fell to the track.

I could see in Pre's eyes a certain discomfort, wondering what would come off next. He knew Bowerman's shoes were glued together, not stitched. I took the shoes back to Bowerman, and unaffected, he had heavier swooshes stitched on. Now that he was Knight's business partner, Bowerman had to compromise just a little on the weight issue. Compromise was a rare thing for him, but the swoosh had become our signature, and we couldn't allow our shoes to be worn without it.

The one-piece toe seemed successful, but Pre only wore it in practice. Bowerman warned Pre, "I build these shoes to last one race. They don't always make it."

Not long after, it was race day, a quad meet against WSU, where Pre would open with a 3:56.8 mile, then come back two hours later with a 13:05.4 3-mile. Oregon needed his points in both events to win, and Pre did more than rise to the occasion. Pre's April 14, 1973 performance was considered the best distance double in history. The thrill wasn't diminished for me even though he didn't run in our shoes that day.

The following Monday Jon Anderson won the Boston Marathon in a pair of Nike Bostons that I had modified for his outside foot strike. Anderson, at 6'2", was broad shouldered and had a long powerful stride, so the outside ball of his foot really took a beating. I replaced the gum rubber outsole with a wedge of Bowerman's waffle sole. We had our first win in a pair of Nike shoes, and it was the Boston Marathon—could it have been more auspicious?

But the biggest thrill for me was still to come. Nearly two weeks later, Pre pulled Bowerman's spikes out of his bag and laced them up in the bullpen. He led a good field in the Twilight Mile that included teammates Knut Kvalheim, Scott Daggett, Mark Feig and Todd Lathers. Pre finished in 3:55, recording the third fastest mile ever by an American.

Jim Gorman was in his warm-ups trackside and must have had a 30" vertical leap when Pre crossed the line. My heart felt the same. The air was filled with the rhythmic stomp and clap of the Hayward faithful. They kept it up, matching the cadence of his stride as he took his victory lap.

I ordered new vanity plates for my van, "Nike 1." No, I wasn't Nike 1, but Nike had just won something. Twice. Nike was now a changed company.

In Eugene, final preparations were being made for the new store opening. My contractor, Lorie Cross, and I conferred on how the lock would work on a large sliding front door made from the Hayward Field seats, set on a diagonal. We used more of the seats—long, 2x12 planks of old growth Douglas fir—for paneling on the inside. Not only was all of this wood from Hayward Field historical, but it was cheap because it was salvage. We used some of the big timbers that supported the stands as shoe displays.

We had changed the name of the retail outlets to The Athletic Department. I had taken the old 855 Olive sign down, and to avoid increasing the overhead, simply turned the pine planks over and carved the new name on the back side. The only remaining fixture I would keep from the first store would be the old 4-bladed G.E. ceiling fan.

Mile PR's for these runners are: Pre, 3:54.6; Feig, 3:58.5; Daggett, 3:58.6; and Divine, 3:56.3.

I invited all of Bowerman's sub-4 minute milers to the grand opening, and I made a special exception for impressive 1500 performances. We were approaching 1974, and it had been 20 years since Roger Bannister had dipped under the once-unattainable barrier. We had several of the milers locally now who also claimed the distinction, so it seemed the natural thing to do. Pre, Mark Feig, Scott Daggett, Bill Dellinger, Roscoe Divine, and Jim Gorman were among those who joined us. Also there was a new "mouth from the south," a transfer from Rice by the name of Paul Geis. We all said, "If this kid can run as fast as he can talk, he'll be good."

Dellenger PR'd in the 1500 at 3:41.6, and Gorman at 3:41.8, for mile equivalent performances strong enough to get them into this elite group.

Geis made the 1976 Olympic team in the 5000. He finished twelfth.

My fellow steepler Jim Gorman was a geography major and presented Knight with a retail strategy he called "the cluster theory." The idea was to open multiple outlets in strategic areas in higher population communities. We moved Gorman to Portland, Oregon to test the idea, where he managed three locations.

BRS then experimented with the same concept in L.A. with five locations. One of the guys we brought on board to manage one of the stores was a wide-eyed Long Beach State graduate with a brush moustache to go along with his L.A. street smarts. He could dance, sing and speak with foreign accents when I first met him at lunch in the BRS head office behind the Grandma's Cookie factory. I laughed at his natural ability to entertain and said to myself, "Good fit." His name was Nelson Farris, and he'd teethed himself on the business, partnering with Long Beach State track and cross country coach Ted Banks. Banks accepted the same position at Texas El Paso and Nelson started looking for work. Bob Woodell's mother, Meryle, was running the Nike warehouse in the old White Stag building on Burnside in Portland. Nelson would call and ask her. "Why don't you hire me? I've been selling your shoes anyway." Meryle called her son and said, "Why don't we hire him—he's a nice boy." We did.

At Knight's house, Nissho's Tom Sumeragi, who managed Nissho's Portland office, joined a small group of us to celebrate the million-dollar mark of Nike sales. The mai tais were poured regularly and then Woodell made a toast and shared, "You know, if we really do it right and don't screw up too bad, some day, just some day, we might just be a $14 million dollar company. Now wouldn't that be something."

Years later, Knight said, "We were pretty schizophrenic. We were going to take on the world, but we couldn't make payroll."

After a tough ending to his '72 season, Pre was bouncing back and willing to take on all comers. The fast-talking Geis was the first on his list. Pre shook his head at the talent he saw in Paul, and now he had to test him head-to-head. The plan was to share the lead and alternate laps, but Geis didn't do that. Instead, he sat on Pre's rear and let Pre carry the pace, lap after lap in a grueling 2-mile that left Pre sprinting in an all-out fit of rage, stomping and cursing off onto the infield, barely the victor 8:24.6 to 8:24.8. The minute he stepped off the track, he said, loud enough for anyone near him to hear, "Enough of this bullshit!"

Pre then collected his fourth NCAA 3-mile title in Baton Rouge, the first runner to ever win four straight titles in the same event, with a time of 13:05.4. Next he took the AAU 3-mile title in Bakersfield, running the race in 12:53.4, sixth best in the world at that time.

Back in Eugene, Bowerman, a wily promoter and fundraiser, had his finger on the pulse of Eugene. He wasn't afraid to drag his athletes along on meetings to acquire concrete from John Alltucker, architectural plans from John Stafford or glue lam beams from a timber baron. Pre was a natural choice for extra leverage, which left him wanting to return the favor. He'd do so with a unique contest. At Bakersfield, he invited Dave Wottle to come up for an attempt at Jim Ryun's mile world record. Pre promised to set a hot pace and he'd get the word out to pack the stands. Bob Newland scrambled to set a schedule of events and mobilize the Oregon Track Club officers in what would be called the Hayward Field Restoration Meet. Wendy Ray announced the mile field, and Wottle, who had won a gold medal in the 800 the year before in Munich, trotted onto the field to slowly building applause.

Then Ray started to announce, "And now American record holder at 2 miles, 3000 meters, 6 miles—" and the crowd noise drowned him out, as Pre exited the bullpen, arms swinging freely and feet pumping. A puff of smoke blew from the barrel of Ray Hendrickson's starting pistol, and the race was off. Pre didn't have to take the lead at the start, as the pacer kept the field honest for the first lap. Then Pre took over and with head down and arms pumping, you could see the effort on his sweaty face. Wottle's long stride seemed to float effortlessly behind Pre's struggle. On the last backstretch, Wottle's trademark white cap rode above a blur of leg speed. With great knee lift and what seemed like reserve energy, Wottle hit the tape one and a half seconds short of the world record in 3:53.3. Pre followed in a PR of 3:54.6. He was running out of his class, and the crowd knew it, but he didn't disappoint.

Pre and Dave Wottle were off to Europe with a series of meets primarily in Finland. Intermediate hurdler Ralph Mann would join them as they traveled by car, train, and plane to meets setup by a former Finnish hurdler and Olympic team captain, Jaakko Tuominen, throughout his homeland. At one small stopover, Pre was making eye contact with a young waitress. Despite the fact that she could not speak English, and

Mann was an NCAA Champion hurdler. He won a silver medal in the 400 hurdles at the 1972 Olympics. Mann has a PhD in biomechanics and is an expert in the biomechanics of sports performance.

that Pre knew only one Finnish phrase from Jaakko (paska husen—"shit pants"—of little use in this situation) it didn't stop his advance. Wottle and Mann were fading and turned in, leaving Pre in the hunt.

The next morning, a car was waiting to take them to the airport with Wottle and Mann in the back seat. Prefontaine was not to be seen, and they couldn't afford to miss their flight. Just as they instructed the driver to leave, Pre broke out the front door on the run, bags slung over his back, sporting a wide smile, "Ha ha! It was great! She made me eggs for breakfast and everything!" It was no surprise that Pre's running was less than stellar. He set an American Record in the 5000 in Helsinki, but he lost that race to Puttemans, and he lost to Wottle and Norpoth in two other races.

Pre returned to Eugene for a training break. He poured beer at the Paddock Tavern not far from my house for rent money. One afternoon he drove up in a butterscotch MG roadster and parked across the street next to our mailbox. He dragged me down to look at it, a newer model than the one he owned. "Whadaya think?"

"Don't buy it—I've had my share of British cars."

"I already have." And he jumped in over the door, settled in, started it up, and took off for "The Pad."

I stood there shaking my head, asking, "Why'd' you ask?" I wrote it off as asking for "big brother" approval.

Buck invited me to go to Asia with him. It would be my first return since 1970. The primary business was to place footwear orders with the mammoth Bridgestone Rubber Company. We were driven by private car to the owner's home, the Ishibashi Mansion. Ishibashi in Japanese means "stone bridge" hence the name of his company. I used Bridgestone radial tires on my Avanti and was impressed with that segment of his sprawling business.

We never saw Ishibashi at his home, but were given free reign, including two rooms and kimonos that we had to pose with in the gardens the next morning. We rode to the Bridgestone grounds, which were surrounded with concrete buildings constructed with thick walls that could withstand an armed attack. During the war, they manufactured army boots. Now, we were negotiating for a new Nike model. It would be called the Waffle Trainer, and would combine all of Bowerman's advances— a nylon upper, a cushioned midsole, elevated heel, and waffle sole, along with recommendations from Dr. Stan James for a bevel at the toe and heel and a slight flare outward of the midsole for added stability. These features had never been combined in one shoe.

> Dr. James was a doctor at the already-famous Orthopedic and Fracture Clinic of Eugene, headed up by Dr. Donald Slocum.

We toured the noisy factory first, amid the clanging of hydraulics and metal die stamp presses and hisses from high-test hoses. One room would be filled with rubber dust, another's concrete floor covered with drips of dry cement adhesive. The workers were quick in all their movements, and they paused to look and smile at us as we walked by. I asked for the men's room and was escorted out to what amounted to a covered trench with tiles overlaid to step on. Water ran on a slope beneath. It smelled, but when you've got to go, you've got to go. I was more than shocked when a little old lady walked by, slowly cleaning the floor tiles behind me. But she totally respected I had something I needed to do, and so did she.

Buck and I were escorted up to the conference room, where nearly two dozen managers sat with notebooks, all in matching short-waisted cotton jackets with nametags. Knight entered in his Ray Bans, something he customarily wore to protect his sensitive eyes. I was having the same problem after three years of reading tiny fathom markings on charts under red lights. Buck's was from reading millions of numbers. It was what he was good at, and here he stood amid all his short, dark-haired Japanese counterparts, a tall, blond, curly haired man.

The negotiations went on for almost two hours. I was standing on Knight's right as he departed, proudly displaying his knowledge of Japanese customs by bowing as he shook hands. "Domo. Domo arigato," he said. The metal door out of the room was right behind Buck's head, and as is typical of pre- WWII structure, it was lower than his 6-foot height. In addition, it was the style at that time that many of us Americans wore a boot with added heel height. Buck no sooner finished his last "Domo," turned to walk out, and banged his forehead into the metal door frame. I was on his left side now as he winced and not wanting to display any loss of face, spoke to me through his teeth, "Grab my arm. God, that hurt!" He must have been seeing stars as I clutched his arm with both hands and we slowly walked out.

The next stop would be Taiwan, and after landing in Taipei, it was a long train ride down to Taichung, home of a small footwear factory, overseen by Japanese managers. The Chinese and Japanese were happy to have us there and threw a lavish dinner party in a private upstairs restaurant. I told our hosts that I didn't drink mixed drinks when they introduced me to Mao Thai's. Buck leaned over and said, "You have to. It's tradition." Reluctantly, as a host toasted me, I downed the drink, to a round table of "Kompai!" Not bad, and I couldn't really feel it, as plates of delicacies were delivered. "Kompai!" "Kompai!" What you didn't feel immediately from the drink was latent, and it had a kick. Buck was getting wild, almost combative, and we were both carried down the stairs to our awaiting cab. I couldn't remember what I had eaten, but would soon find out as my head spun like a top, surrounded with speeding bright neon Chinese characters on buildings. "Bluaghh!!" I had just redecorated the inside of the taxi cab with the evening's dinner, and with my boss sitting next to me. How impressive.

The next afternoon, I awoke to realize I had missed the factory tour. No matter. At the train station to witness my departure, the factory managers were laughing and clapping as I waved out of my car window. I was a hero.

Buck Knight had married a cute young lady by the name of Penny. At a dinner party, he once introduced her as "Kitten," the go-go girl. Someone expressed their surprise later, and he said, "Well, I couldn't tell them she was one of my students." (Knight was a full time accountant at Price-Waterhouse at this time, and he was moonlighting at Portland State University, teaching accounting.) They purchased a modest ranch-style home in Beaverton, where they lived with their first-born, Matthew, a toddler at the time. Both Penny and my wife Carol were pregnant. When Carol and Penny slid into their backyard pool Buck referred to them as "the whale sisters." No one in the company had any money, and BRS was losing $50k in 1973. When we traveled to Beaverton for meetings, we'd stay at the Knights' house.

Looking back, I can't help but think how ironic that a couple named Buck and Penny would become billionaires. What were the odds?

In the fall of 1973, Pre ran with Dellinger's cross country team in his last season as a collegiate athlete. Whenever they ran, I was there. I ran workouts with them, bought a movie camera, and started filming them. To my surprise, that footage would remain the only known footage of Prefontaine on a cross country course.

The first meet was at Tokatee golf course. Just call it a little all-comer's meet. Pre's competitors for the day included Norwegian Olympian Knut Kvalheim, U.S. Olympians Jon Anderson and Mike Manley, sub-4 milers Mark Feig and

Scott Daggett, All-Americans Randy James and Dave Taylor, and Paul Geis. Bowerman was there and Pre's latest girlfriend, the tall legged, crystal-eyed Nancy Alleman stood among the scattered gear bags. It was a foggy morning as the gun went off and the pack disappeared into the mist. As they wound back through the first loop, Pre was leading Knut and the pack was now a single line. Pre had taken time off following the Munich experience and had gained weight, but it was now obvious—he was back. He put his head down, and he charged to the finish line.

Knut Kvalheim is Arne Kvalheim's younger brother, and he also held the Norwegian records in the 1500 and 5000.

I was spending more time with Pre, and I started to realize that no one seemed to pack more into one day as he did. Author Ken Kesey would later tell how in one day, you'd see Pre running in Springfield, and then later at Hayward Field, and then later still on a road in south Eugene. "He was," Kesey said, "a moving monument." He ran fast, talked fast, and met all the girls fast. But he didn't waste his time in pursuits he didn't feel deeply about. As I got to know Pre, I learned that he only got involved if he really cared about something.

At the Northern Division Championships, Pre would match up on a Corvallis golf course with Kenyan John Ngeno of WSU. Pre and Ngeno were locked in a battle of wills up and down the hilly course that was only decided at the end with Pre's driving arm carriage and knee lift, the final uphill finish on a punishing course.

I drove down to Stanford for the Pac-8 Championships. Pre would contest Ngeno again. In addition, Stanford coach Marshall Clark had recruited a talented state champion from New Mexico named Anthony Sandoval, but Pre had improved and simply distanced himself after one lap of the Stanford golf course. This was the same course where high school runner Dana Carvey watched wide-eyed as Pre and Gerry Lindgren came to the tape almost as if they were holding hands. They were that evenly matched.

Pre's final collegiate competition would take place at Hangman Valley golf course outside Spokane, Washington. I checked out the best camera positions to cover the race and positioned myself on a rise over the starting line so I could pan across the uphill first half mile. You could see the starter's pistol smoke rise and the mass was off like scampering ants in formation. The sun was reflected brightly off a mane of gold hair in the lead. It was not Pre. With a powerful long stride, an English runner from Western Kentucky was setting the pace—something Pre would normally do. Nick Rose was exacting a punishing pace, intent on running anyone off their legs. Pre was next in the chase, but remained back the first three miles. But as the runners came off the hills and circled into a series of switchbacks in the valley, Pre had cut the gap down to 30 yards and was coming. The spectators now lined every bend in the course, and Pre's record was on the line—he'd been undefeated since his freshman year. He finally pulled even with the prancing mane of Rose, who looked straight ahead. He knew who it was. With 800 to go, Pre fought forward. His stride was not as smooth as Rose, but his wild, driving arm swing matched cadence with those magnificent legs, and he found the precious yards it took. Pre won and so did his team. Backslaps from his teammates under a bright sun punctuated the end of possibly the most dominant running career in collegiate history.

I looked down at Pre's red Nike America's spikes, shoes I had modified with a flat heel wedge and a piece of waffle for downhill traction. He wanted these shoes because he was worried that Bowerman's custom shoes wouldn't hold up over the length of a cross country course. He confided that the waffle was working but that the Americas would not be good enough for the track. He showed me his bloody second metatarsal, and said "I'm tired of this shit."

We were going to have to get rid of that toe seam.

Streaking was a fad, a dare, a risk. You could go to jail for doing it. Simply put, a streaker ran naked in public, and the more people who saw you, the better.

Paul Geis was watching all of this, not able to compete for a year with his transfer from Rice. Perhaps it was pent-up energy, or desire to out-perform Pre at any level, but he and a friend decided to streak the campus village record shop. Runners were used to running with just shorts all over campus, so it was only a one-square-foot piece of nylon to leave behind. The plan was to go through the front door, out the back door and retrieve their shorts for their return to their dorm. They bolted around the corner and through the front door to the surprise of those in attendance. As planned, they ran to the back door only to find it locked. Shocked to see everyone looking at them, they each pulled an album cover from the table, and placing it strategically, ran back out on the street. What would they have done if the CD had been invented?

I never knew if part of this was due to the stories handed down of our "totem scrotums" at Odell Lake, but Pre had earlier led a band of teammates on a nude trail workout in Hendricks Park. They went unnoticed until they boldly came down a path and turned at the bottom on pavement just as a lady bus driver was dropping off elementary kids at their homes. Before Pre and his followers could get their shorts on and get back to Hayward Field, Dellinger was awaiting their arrival. He had already spoken to the bus driver.

Word of Geis' dash had spread around campus. As a counter, Pre made his move at the Valley River Mall, the huge retail complex on the Willamette River. He cut out holes for his eyes in a brown paper bag and placed it over his head after stripping down to his shoes, and ran his bold dash past the shoppers, like Zorro riding his steed. Again, Dellinger got the call. "Pre, you honestly thought no one would recognize you with a bag over your head? Everyone has watched you run. You have the most recognized stride in the world!"

Knight and Bowerman had begun talking about Steve Prefontaine. When Pre finished the season, they wanted to give him $5,000 so he wouldn't have to take a job and compromise his career. Because I knew Pre so well, I had begun to question the decision when Bill called me. "Well Bill, I think Steve needs to feel more involved than that. He should work in the store some and learn to deal with the customers, learn to build shoes next door at Jim the Shoe Doctor and go out on the road with me and talk to the kids and the coaches." You could almost see the smoke coming out of the phone—Bill was pissed and yelling so loud at me, I had to hold the phone away from my ear. Then he hung up.

After Pre graduated, Bowerman's neighbor and close friend called one morning with a voice that slurred as though having consumed a little Jack Daniels. John Jaqua said, "I was just talking with Bowerman, and he thinks it would be a good idea if young Steve would work at the store some and get to know the customers, go next door to Jim the Shoe ..." It was verbatim what I suggested to Bill, but he couldn't tell me. He sent Jaqua. Knowing that I had persuaded Bowerman to change his mind was a rare pleasure, one that few people on earth can claim to have experienced. I laughed at the circumstance but couldn't wait to get started.

Pre was enjoying the trips visiting the teams in Oregon. I was driving an Avanti at the time, but I found it impractical and sold it. To replace it, I bought the ultimate vehicle for driving around with lots of shoeboxes. It was a box itself. The vehicle of choice was a VW bus. We traveled to Bend, Madras and Prineville in eastern Oregon, Siuslaw, Newport and Reedsport on the coast, as far north as Portland, and south to Medford.

There was a dealer in Medford who didn't want to carry Nike. "I'll stick with Tiger," he told us. With Galloway in town on a visit, I called the schools in the area and Jeff, Pre and I held a clinic at one of Medford's parks. We sold Nikes right out of my VW bus, and the dealer called Knight the next day to complain. I responded with, "I'll make you a deal. You carry Nike, and I'll never come back." I never had to go back to Medford.

The phone rang in the store when the word got out that I was bringing Pre to speak to the high school track team in Reedsport, close to Coos Bay, his hometown. It was the Reedsport principal asking, "Would you mind if we let the whole student body attend and hold it in the gym?"

That's how powerful Pre's charisma was and a perfect example of how effective our marketing strategy was. You put our shoes on an athlete like Pre, and they pretty much sold themselves.

Former Oregon sub-4 miler Scott Daggett had a new job, working with touring music groups. He called me and asked if we'd make a special shoe for Elton John. At Jim the Shoe Doctor's shop we built a shoe with a rainbow-striped, stacked midsole three inches high. We cannibalized the upper from a Nike Cortez—white with a red swoosh, glued the midsole to the upper, and sent them off. A couple of months later, I got a letter from Elton John, thanking me "ever so much."

Nelson Farris was already selling shoes to Alice Cooper and Farrah Fawcett. While Fawcett was skateboarding on *Charlie's Angels*, she wore a pair of Nike Lady Cortez and sales took off immediately. It was huge. The Lady Cortez was one of the first athletic shoes made on a women's last, and its success showed just how big that market was. Being the dumb bunch of guys we were, we didn't get the message right away.

Up in the BRS office in Beaverton, we had hired an employee who was not an athlete. Sporting a goatee and an attitude, I could see I was going to struggle to get along with him. Jim Moodhe would become my opposite within the company. When he set up the powerful chain of Meier & Frank with Nike, I exploded and called Buck and Woodell. My message was laced with expletives. "Hell, they just hired one of the best running coaches in the area to manage their sporting goods department and their ad budget is huge. They'll kill me!" I should have been fired.

Soon after, Pre and I drove up to Beaverton for a meeting. Buck wanted to have lunch at his favorite Chinese restaurant, and as we sat around the table, Moodhe prodded me about the Meier & Frank deal and I lost it. I stood up and left, preferring to stay in the parking lot as Pre ate his lunch. Pre looked at my full plate, then at Buck, asking, "Do you think he'll come back?"

"Don't think so."

"Then he won't need this," and Pre grabbed my plate and consumed it.

Back at the office, the discussion was a letter that had been written by the AAU's Dan Ferris, saying that Pre had been running on the streets of Eugene with Nike on his chest. If he continued, his summer travel visa to compete overseas would be in jeopardy. I had a solution. We would print up a new suit, leave off Nike and just hot press the swoosh on the left chest. Pre was the first person to ever wear the swoosh on something other than a pair of shoes.

But there was a problem. On a pair of shoes, you had a left facing swoosh and a right facing swoosh. No one had ever done this before, so which one were we supposed to use? We had to pick one, but as it turned out, Nike later picked the other. Pre's was backwards.

I had visited Pre and his roommate and teammate Pat Tyson in their aluminum-sided trailer in Greenwood, and Pre was ready to put his newfound money to work and buy a small home of his own. Usually, there was a weekly party in town, either at our house, Jon Anderson's, Kenny Moore's, or Mike Manley's, All of us took care of each other. Pre had to be carried out of our house one night. No one would allow him to drive, and Mark Feig drove his MG Roadster to his trailer.

In Portland, Blue Ribbon Sports and Onitsuka Tiger were engaged in a federal lawsuit. Tiger had asked for controlling interest in the growing BRS, but no one had controlling interest in Bill Bowerman. By the time Knight, Bowerman and Jaqua had set our course of action, Tiger had already sent distribution proposals out to prospective sales agencies who would collectively replace BRS under Tiger's management. BRS employee John Bork had jumped ship and joined Tiger. Shoji Kitami had been sent to the U.S. to manage Tiger's interests. When Kitami and his Japanese team arrived at Eugene's Mahlon Sweet Airport for a final meeting, a briefcase was lost. Gorman and I were sent to the airport to drive them into town, and with the briefcase and valuable papers missing, Jim and I were accused of taking it. We were deposed prior to sitting in Federal Court. A big, bearded attorney prepared me for the deposition in the offices of Bullivant, Wright, and informed me that Kitami would claim that through the papers in the briefcase, BRS learned of Tiger's strategy. In fact, BRS found out when a loyal distributor forwarded a copy of the proposed distribution network to Phil Knight as a warning. A big smile came across the face of the big attorney, and he laughed. "In addition, you will see Kitami testify in Japanese and pretend to the judge that he doesn't understand English."

"But he does!" I was incredulous.

Rob Strasser now stood up, stretching his white shirt underneath his loosened tie. "You'll do fine. The judge will find you believable. It's all part of Katami's defense. I think it's wearing thin on the judge."

By March of 1974, the judge had a ruling. BRS would retain the copyrights to the names of the footwear products that Knight had registered, forcing Tiger to change their product names and compensate BRS for sales. Tiger retained all of Bowerman's innovations, which Nike could also use, with one exception.

If Tiger had waited two months to sue us, we might have already given them the waffle. The waffle was highly patentable. It would be hard to imagine the future of Nike without it.

CHAPTER 10: A DREAM COME TRUE

Pre and I continued to hit the road in the van that spring. The store was booming, and I hired U.S. AAU decathlon champion Jeff Bannister and his friend, a basketball player from New Hampshire nicknamed "Spider" to help manage the store. We were seeing so many injured athletes that Bowerman, Stan James, and Dennis Vixie, a talented local orthodist, started what we called the Footcare Clinic. We would screen patients at the store, first looking at their footwear. If they were training in a pair of basketball or tennis shoes and suffering shin splints, we simply moved them into a Cortez. If they were already wearing a decent training shoe and suffering, they went on to Stan and he gave them a free analysis and catalogued the visit, building a thick file of cause, effect, and hopefully, solution.

Jeff Johnson provided guidance to our Japanese factory for a new seamless toed spike. This shoe would go the distance, solving a problem that Bowerman had struggled with. We named it the Pre-Montreal in anticipation of Pre's upcoming 1976 Olympic effort. Pre wore the new shoes at the 1974 Twilight Meet, and Jeff was on the Hayward infield with camera and lens focused on Pre's red, white, and blue Olympic jersey and matching spikes. Jon Anderson was equally matched just behind, as Pre charged out one brutal lap after another, finally coming home in a new American record for the 10,000. His 27:43.6 would be the sixth fastest in history.

Pre had been talking to me about an idea he had. He delighted in the wonderful woodchip trails that adorned almost every city in Europe. "Here we have to run miles of pavement to get to trails, and it's killing my Achilles. In Stockholm, I can run right out of the stadium, and miles of trails await me. We can do that here in Eugene."

We went for runs, looking for the perfect location and settled on Alton Baker Park, a county park named after the founder of the *Register-Guard*. It was bordered by the Willamette River that already had a paved ribbon of asphalt for a bike trail alongside. The county had built a waterway down the middle that meandered along and spilled back into the river below the Ferry Street Bridge. Pre got excited. "We could put one mile of woodchips right here. That would be a start, and we could lease a building over there. Hold meetings and have speakers when our friends come through town. Lockers, healthy food, a place to stretch." Jeff Bannister overheard the conversation.

"Not only could people run, they could bike the path and canoe right from the front door."

We were ahead of what later would be called "cross training," but Pre's raw energy and enthusiasm along with our collective ideas led us to incorporating. We called it "The Decathlon Club."

Pre would join me at the Sheldon High School track to work with the joggers we had signed up for the club. My sister worked during the day in an office in the mall to place calls and hand out membership forms. Pre would stop by to check the progress, then come into the store, briefcase in hand which made him look organized until he accidentally dropped it, spilling everything from his airline bookings, passport and checkbook to his little black book. He came in one day with his dog Lobo, swearing a blue streak, "You can't believe what just happened! This fucking policeman told me to stop in the mall because Lobo was not on a leash. Hell, I have total voice command over Lobo. I gave him the magic finger wave and kept running."

All the while working himself into prime condition to handle the best in the world, he was suddenly off to Europe and beat

Olympic 1500 champion Pekka Vasala at the 3000, then steeplechase world record holder Anders Garderud at the same distance. He hated losing to our old Oregon teammate Knut Kvalheim at 5000, but they both set national records in a duel that would leave Pre a second and a half behind at the tape. He would follow with American records at 3000 and two miles before deciding to return to Eugene for a needed break.

I questioned Pre's return both from an energy standpoint and the expense of returning, but usually he arranged a ticket with the European promoters. This time he did not, and we started scrambling. The idea was to announce to the Eugene public that Pre would run a sub-4 mile in a workout. Guaranteed. If we passed the hat, we might collect a few hundred dollars to help buy a ticket to Europe.

It was a perfect day on September 3, and the time was set for the workout. The word had spread, but so did a field burn warning. The Willamette Valley grass seed farmers were allowed to burn their fields after harvest. When the wind blew from the southwest it pushed the smoke north, away from Eugene. But on this day the wind reversed. By the time I drove to Hayward Field, I had to turn my headlights on to see, and it was supposed to be broad daylight. Pre had concluded his warm-up as spectators were taking their seats. They could barely see the other side of the track. It was like a coastal fog. I told Pre he didn't have to do this, that under the circumstances people would understand. "No, I said I'd do it. Now I have to."

He got up, took a couple of quick steps, checked the bottom of his spikes and treated the crowd of several hundred to a 3:58 mile. Oh how Pre loved to deliver the goods in front of a crowd. A few of us wound through the crowd with our baseball caps held upside down, collecting one and five dollar bills. $500 went a long way to return Pre to Europe.

Pre and I sat before the Lane County commissioners and pitched The Decathlon Club's request to place the woodchip jogging trail at Alton Baker Park. Professor Fredrick Cuthbert, the former U of O Dean of Architecture, was violently opposed, citing that the park should be left in a natural state. A former landfill, we wondered just how natural it could ever be. Our request was tabled for a future meeting.

Pre bitched loudly as we traveled out to visit cross country teams, "Jesus, we're talking about improving the health of their citizens—don't they get it?" I told him the professor was an old man, set in his ways, and I doubted we'd ever change his mind. We'd have to convince the others.

By the time we arrived at the first school, the excited welcome transformed Pre, as the kids jogged behind and alongside him as if he were the pied piper. I'd unpack the shoe boxes, set up the price list and ready the cash box. Pre was now stretched out on the West Albany grass in front of students from Albany and surrounding farm communities like Turner. Stripped down to just his shorts, he'd answer any and all questions. I pulled out my Nikormat and started capturing the moment. Overhearing him, I was shocked to see him going off on a tangent on safe sex. "Safe sex?" I thought to myself. "Pre, you don't have a clue as to what that is!" Before I knew it, he was back to safe training and racing.

"You've got to have goals, and I suggest you write them down. If you write them down, you own them. Don't waste your time."

This was when he pulled out the jewel, "To give anything less than your best is to sacrifice the gift."

Both in terms of understanding how running could improve public health, and that an athlete's gifts should never be squandered, Pre was giving voice to two of the core principles that helped shape Nike.

Pre was back over to Europe and lost a close 5000 to Viren at his home Helsinki track. He matched up against a tough Englishman named Brendan Foster in a 2-mile in London.

Kip Keino lowered the world record in the 3000 by 6 seconds in 1965, won Olympic gold in the 1500 (1968) and the 3000 steeplechase (1972), and silver in the 5000 (1968) and the 1500 (1972). Puttemans set world records in the 2 mile (8:17.8, 1971) the 3000 (7:37.6, 1972) and the 5000 (13:13, 1972). He took the silver in the 10,000 at the 1972 Olympics.

Brendan was a "Geordie" from the northern town of Newcastle, an area that made you tough as nails just to live there, let alone train. Foster was one of those few, like Keino and Puttemans, who could race anyone from 1500 to 10,000. He was full of grit and determination. Pre was up for the challenge, then inexplicably stepped off the track mid-race, grabbing his chest. It was the only race Pre failed to finish. Tests would show torn tissue in the diaphragm, most likely from the torturous run in the smoke in Eugene. Pre's season was over.

Pre and I were back out on the road for another cross country season that would take us on a run in the Oregon Dunes and on a group run through the high desert pines. The conversations were wide ranging, but Pre was a man with dreams. He wanted to own a European style pub, where you could order a good beer to go with a big salad. We were still working on the trail and the Decathlon Club, he was involved in his latest scrape with Olan Cassell and the AAU, and he was in contact with Jaakko to bring a group of Finnish athletes to Oregon to compete. On the list was Lasse Viren.

Pre spent part of the winter cross country skiing with his close friends the Gauthiers in Madras, and with Frank Shorter in Boulder. Bannister, Pre and I attended yet another county commissioners' meeting on the trail project. Over dinner, our proposal was debated then again tabled for further and later discussion. Pre left in a huff, his patience lost, "Damn it! They buy us dinner, then postpone. What the hell's wrong with them?"

The winter of 1974 kept us busy. Nike was beginning to grow as a brand. We were up to about $3 million in total sales. Pre's letters in the shoeboxes continued to go out from the store in Eugene. This personal touch was typical of how Nike grew its business in the early days. The following went to Bill Rodgers in Jamaica Plain, Massachusetts:

Dear Bill,

First of all congratulations on a fine race in Rabat. You have really improved this past year and hopefully will continue until the Olympic games.

The reason I'm writing is because Jeff Galloway told me you were interested in training in our shoes. I'm sending you a pair of Boston '73s and a training shoe. Just feel free to drop me a line and let me know what you think.

Wishing you continued success for '75.

Sincerely,
Steve Prefontaine

Rodgers let Pre know what he thought when, that April, wearing a GBTC singlet, painter's gloves and the '73 Bostons, he won his first Boston Marathon. It was one of several successful conversions by Pre while he was battling with Olan Cassell, Executive Director of the AAU.

Pre had been corresponding and phoning his Finnish promotions friend Jaakko Tuominen for months. Jaakko was Pre's favorite European race promoter, but their friendship ran a lot deeper than that. Jaakko introduced Pre to the sauna, and Pre ended up building a sauna at his own home. Jaakko got Pre into the European circuit, made sure he got money for his appearances, and Pre reciprocated by twice setting American records while running in Helsinki.

Pre wanted Jaakko to send a Finnish contingent of athletes to compete in the Northwest with Eugene as a base. Cassell's belief was that this was the federation's work, not that of an actively competing athlete. Pre didn't get it. "Why can't I organize it?" Pre's promise to Jaakko was that he would raise money for the athletes from each meet performance with a guarantee of five meets. He could count on Eugene and looked to his hometown of Coos Bay, Vancouver B.C. and the Gauthier's in Madras for additional venues. Cassell toyed with Pre, but Pre said, "I'm doing it."

As the arrival date got closer, I pressed Pre to show me his plan somewhere between his daily doubles and his flurry of other activities and time with Nancy. He pulled "The Plan" out of his briefcase, a series of notes, letters, and phone numbers. He stacked them neatly. "What if we got this all on one piece of paper?" I suggested.

I typed everything up. "Now, how are you picking them up?"

"I'm driving out to meet them at the airport."

"How many athletes?"

"Seven and Jaakko."

"And you are going to pick them up in your MG? Where is Antti going to put his pole vault poles?"

Pre looked at me as though my questions were an annoyance and unnecessary.

"Look," I said, "Let me help you organize this. Where are you going to put them up?"

"They'll be here a month."

"A hotel would be expensive. We'll go to the next Oregon track club meeting and ask the board for volunteers for home-stays."

As it turned out, we could have hosted twice as many athletes. Carol and I would host the only woman in the group, world-class jumper Pirrko Helenius. Board members snapped up the rest and an old teammate of Jaakko's, now an assistant professor at Oregon, Reiner Stinius, one of the few men to ever long jump over 27', took Jaakko.

On April 29th, we drove out to Mahlon Sweet airport, and I met Jaakko for the first time. Pre had told me so much about him, and I commented how good his English was. "I graduated at BYU in 1968."

"You ran NCAA's that year?"

"Yes, intermediates."

"I'll be damned. We competed in the same meet."
Jaakko gave Pre a big bear hug and Pre was excited to show off his state. He had been busy completing a sauna in his house, a real test of hospitality for his friends, even though it was already warm as a summer day in Finland.

There was one notable exception in the arrivals. No Lasse Viren. Pre was devastated when Viren pulled out—racing Viren was his main reason for bringing the Finns over. Now he was committed to all these meets, but he lacked the big draw that his competition with Viren would have been.

Lasse had complained of a sore Achilles, and Jaakko brought trainer Ilpo Nikila instead, a barrel-gutted man standing under a ball cap with arms and hands that could easily tear phone books in half. In response to whatever you said, he nodded, smiled, and said, "Yah, very, very good."

I found out what that meant and why Ilpo was nicknamed "Mr. Tickle" when he offered to give me a massage at my home. On my stomach, he ran his thumbs down my hamstrings, separating the muscle groups and going to what felt like the bone. I jumped, "Aahh!"

"Yah, very, very good." Ilpo muttered away in Finnish as he laughed and kept the pressure on. Pirkko interpreted that as, "You are very fit, but a little tense."

"I'm tense because I'm in severe pain!"

"Yah, very, very good!"

We allowed our new Finnish friends to adjust to the time difference and then transported them in our vans to Eastern Oregon's high desert country, sightseeing along the way until we reached the hospitality of the Gauthiers' in Madras. As an investment, Bud

Gauthier, a big man of 250 pounds, had opened a pub on the outskirts of town, which was popular with the athletes. Bud's day job was dentistry, and he picked up the tab.

On the day of his Madras meet, a strong desert wind blew across the track east to west. Despite the hindrance, Pre ran 8:26 for 3000 and Antti Kalliomaki showed why he had the skill to be an Olympic medalist in the pole vault, adjusting and playing with a shifting wind to achieve a world-class height.

Pre was proud to take the Finns to his hometown of Coos Bay. He arranged a charter fishing trip out of Winchester Bay, had the group over to his house, and just two blocks away, organized an evening meet on his old track. Despite all this, Pre came ready, and raced an American Record 2000 meters, a seldom run distance, but one that demanded 60-second laps to finish in 5:01.4.

Six days later, Pre and the Finns would compete at the beautiful Swangard Stadium in Burnaby, a suburb of Vancouver, B.C. All this led to a final competition at Hayward Field, before the Finns departed home. By this time, strong friendships had developed between athletes and hosts, and behind the scenes, a final farewell was being planned. Ray Atkeson Oregon picture books were purchased for each member of the Finnish team and food was ordered for a large gathering at our Dillard Road home, along with a cake with white frosting and adorned with the Finnish flag.

Pre was nervous about ticket sales without Lasse. He had a decent match-up in the discus where old teammate Mac Wilkins would go up against world leader Pentti Kahma. I thought Mac was big, but Pentti was huge and gentle. He hoisted my son Tracy up, and the smile of a two-year-old beamed below Pentti's blond hair and massive shoulders.

With the need for another draw, Pre called Frank Shorter and got him to commit to come in from Boulder for a 5000. "I really need your help Frank." Pre was actually behind in gate receipts and knew that the Hayward faithful would have to make it up. Frank agreed to come, and Pre relaxed for at least a second.

Sports Editor Blaine Newnham and the *Register-Guard* staff did their job and packed the stands. Mac had a tremendous come-from-behind win over Pentti to get the fans on their feet. The night of May 29 would conclude with Frank doing his part to set a decent pace, leading Pre through a 8:40 two-mile split and staying in the hunt for a few more laps. Then Pre, wearing a black Nord Italia singlet he had traded for in Milan, exploded into the lead, finishing with a 60-second final lap and just missing his P.R. by less than two seconds. It's the only time I saw him wear black on the track, and he pulled the singlet up after finishing, exposing his 6-pack abdomen covered in sweat from the effort. In appreciation for those in attendance, he moved into a jog and waved goodbye to the crowd.

I was off to the house getting food prepared, beer on ice in a cooler on the back deck and opening windows to cool things down. Ray and Elfriede Prefontaine arrived early with Pre's sister, Linda. The Gauthiers and Pre's high school coach Walt McClure walked in. All had long drives home. Bowerman was early, smiling with a pat on my back, "Hey, not a bad all-comers meet."

Eventually, the athletes appeared with their families, Frank and Kenny, Mac and lastly Pre with Nancy Alleman at his side. Pre was a vision of relief, the pressure of producing this track and field tour for his Finnish friends now behind him. There were a lot of hugs, backslaps, and thank you's. Reiner Stinius and I immediately had Pre cornered next to my wood burning stove. We told him that his effort tonight was great, but if he truly wanted to be the best in the world, it would have to be in the steeple, 10,000, or marathon. Pre rebelled at the suggestion that he follow the typical runner's progression of taking on longer distances as he grew older.

I said "Steve, these are events that require the most guts, and that's your strength." The debate went into the details for nearly an hour with interruptions and then we realized Pre had not eaten. We wandered back to the kitchen, and Carol brought out the cake, which looked perfect with the sky blue Finnish cross until Frank Shorter swept through it with his finger, plunging the frosting into his mouth.

With the cake in the center of the room, I brought out the Oregon books, and Pre addressed the collective group, thanking them for all taking part and making a dream come true. No sooner had he finished than Ray and Elfriede gave Steve a hug and were off to Coos Bay. The Gauthiers were off on a 5-hour drive to Madras despite our concern and offering to put them up for the night. In exchange for the books, the Finns broke out a bottle of vodka for their hosts. Kenny Moore had already left to write his story for *Sports Illustrated* on the meet, and Pre was heading off with Frank and Nancy. Pre and I agreed to meet at the store in the morning to wrap up details of the tour and coordinate transportation for the Finns to the airport. Jaakko had set up a world record 10,000 attempt at Helsinki for Pre. He'd be departing soon after an obligatory race for Olan Cassell and the AAU.

After several departures, some of the Finns and hosts opened the vodka and started toasting each other. But I too was tiring and called it a night, informing the remaining revelers that I would see them in the morning.

CHAPTER 11: OUR BELOVED SON AND BROTHER

The phone rang early, just before six. I was wondering why Bowerman would call so early with his "marching orders." But it wasn't Bill. It was Buck. "A friend just called me who heard a radio report that Pre died last night in an automobile accident."

"It can't be true. He was just here last night. I'll call Bowerman and check."

Bowerman answered the phone. "It's true, Geoff. I don't know the details. I haven't picked up my newspaper yet."

I called Buck back to confirm from the kitchen, ran back to the bedroom and hit the bed in uncontrollable tears, waking Carol. "Pre's dead," I yelled loudly. It all seemed so impossible. He of all of us seemed so invincible.

I called Jaakko in tears—he immediately thought it was one of his athletes.

I waited for the *Register-Guard*, and Pre's photo by Brian Lanker dominated the front page. The big, dark brown eyes fixed somewhere beyond the camera. The accident had taken place on Skyline Boulevard, a favorite running route for all of us who trained in Eugene. It seemed as though he was by himself. I read all I could through a blur of tears and called Bowerman again. I had to come out.

I pulled into the Bowermans' drive a little after 9 a.m. Bill met me at the door. He was solid as a rock—what I needed. I couldn't put the loss in perspective. I didn't believe it. Bill had experienced the loss of life many times on Riva Ridge in Italy, during World War II. Some he did not know. Pre we knew, and it hurt. As I poured my heart out, Bill remained strong and mostly silent. As always, his words were few.

"You were there. Pre didn't have that much to drink. The police said his blood alcohol was 0.16. He had a hard time finishing one beer with Reiner and I."

Although Bill said little, just going to the hill and sitting down with him helped, and I returned home. Kenny called. He was changing his story for *Sports Illustrated* and invited me up to his house. Ray Prefontaine called. They were on their way back to Eugene. "Geoff, can I ask you a favor? Can you pick the pallbearers? We have a lot to do, and I'd appreciate that."

Phone calls started pouring in. Galloway was on the line. I was doing okay, then I just lost it. The store staff called, then the host families. It all seemed a blur until the hosts and the Finns were all assembling in the home of Norm Thompson on University Street, close to Hayward Field. It was silent; no celebration at the end of a successful tour as we waited to head to the airport to see our friends off. Jaakko and I looked at each other in a different light. It was no longer two people with Pre in between. It was now just the two of us, a strengthened bond, but Pre was always there in our thoughts.

The Finns were off, and a group of us were sitting in Kenny's living room as he scribbled on a note pad as we collectively responded to the loss. I had already asked Frank and Jon Anderson if they would be pallbearers. I asked Pre's childhood friend, Jim Seiler, and Pre's roommates in the house, Bob and Brett Williams, sons of my old wrestling coach, Bob Williams.

It became obvious that as much as we all thought we knew Pre, we didn't know him. One of my surprises was the jogging club he'd established at the Oregon State Penitentiary. "Why'd he do it? Why didn't he tell me? He kept it a secret, like so many girlfriends."

As for the girlfriends, that became an issue. They seemed to be everywhere. Ray also asked me to invite certain people to a private dinner. I found out after inviting Nancy Alleman that I left out one Mary Marckx, a girlfriend from Pre's freshman and sophomore years and one I had never met. There was his older cousin. There was his high school girlfriend who got married. And whatever happened to the mystery girlfriend he brought to my house?

I sat down at the dinner table across from Ray's shiny eyes with Elfriede to his left. They had been to the funeral home. I didn't go. I didn't feel it was my place. Instead, I visited the site of the accident, where fluids were still on the road from the overturned MG. There were no skid marks on the pavement. I drove to the wrecking yard and looked at the car. It's left front fender was crushed back to the wheel. Elfriede was talking about her Steve running the 5000 this weekend. I looked at Ray's eyes, and he gently shook his head. As much as I had a hard time believing Steve was gone, Elfriede was not letting him go.

Lane County's Mike Dooley called, informing me that the county had just approved a 10,000 meter wood chip trail in Alton Baker Park. We would name it Prefontaine Trail. It still amazes me, as it did then, that it took such a tragedy to move a government to the right decision.

In Coos Bay, Walt McClure and Bowerman eulogized Steve Prefontaine in front of family and a full stadium. I had instructed the pallbearers to all wear track suits and running shoes. Ray and Elfriede had Steve dressed in his Olympic Team warm-up, his Waffle Trainers and that black Nord Italia singlet that he only wore once. I positioned Frank and Jon in the lead. It was fitting, as they wore their '72 Olympic warm-ups. Then we lifted the coffin and carried it to the back of the hearse, sitting on the track in front of the grandstand.

The door closed and the hearse slowly drove around the two turns of the track in tribute to the many run at a furious pace by a younger Pre. We arrived at the cemetery overlooking a backwater that dumped into Coos Bay. Dirt was piled in front of a granite marker with the Olympic rings and the inscription *Our beloved son and brother who raced through life now rests in peace.*

I concentrated on the task at hand as we lowered the coffin to its final resting place. I looked out to the water and stared at nothing. The job Ray had given me was completed. I promised him that I would be back. As pallbearers, we had only been in the car a few minutes to return to Coos Bay, and I totally and uncontrollably broke down again. He was gone. There was no doubt. He was gone.

Pre came to us in dreams. Usually, he would be on a run with you. In my case, he was coming the opposite direction down Dillard Road, around a bend as I was going up. We waved, and he was gone.

My dreams were always in color and seemed so real. Only days after Pre's death, I was dreaming that he walked into the office in the back of the store, briefcase in hand as he always did. It was as though nothing had happened. Spider and Bannister were with me and we all stared at him. "What?" he said.

"So this was another of your damn practical jokes, Pre? This one isn't funny! Hell, we all thought you were dead."

Then there was the truth of going into the store, knowing that he would not come in, that the seat that he'd occupied alongside me at my desk would be empty. The office staff realized that I was staring at my work but not getting anything done.

I was not the only one. Nancy Alleman was also struggling. A group of French athletes that included Guy Drut and Jean Claude Nallet had arrived in Eugene and it was suggested I drive them over to Black Butte Ranch to see the country. I took Nancy along to get her out of town. Her crystal eyes were glossier than normal as we talked while the French dropped their jeans at poolside, exposing skimpy bikini briefs, and dove in. I learned that my friend Whitty Bass, who we called 'the running rev,' was going to marry Steve and Nancy when Steve returned from Europe in September. Now Nancy reflected on a broken dream of a husband and a family and a house, all those things in life that I had and Steve had wanted.

I thought back to his quote, "To give anything less than your best is to sacrifice the gift." Pre had no idea he would only live to age 24, but he did know how to live life fully and without compromise. Only years later would I realize how special those two and a half years with Pre at Nike would be. It set the tone and created the formula for something much bigger. As our first employee Jeff Johnson remembered, "You know when Pre was down on the track and we were up in the stands, he represented what we could be if we were only willing to work that hard."

As a navigator, in charting the stars, three perfect sightings gave you a celestial fix, a roadmap on the water. For this infant company, Bowerman was the first star. Buck was the second, representative of all of us who worked there. Pre completed the Nike corporate celestial fix. He was so demanding, yet so inspiring. We knew that if we could satisfy him, we could satisfy anyone.

CHAPTER 12: MONTREAL—
AN EXPERIENCE,
NOT A VICTORY

The loss of Steve Roland Prefontaine came at many levels. Don Kardong and Dick Buerkle were among a U.S. team just returning from competition in China when they heard the news on arrival. Stunned, Dick returned home to Atlanta and wrote the following tribute on the plane.

Ode to S. Roland

You came out hot and flashing
Like a Spanish fighting bull,
Your chest went stretching forward
Straight hair flying from your skull.
Your knees came high, the arms they swung,
You sneered around the bend.
Leaping, diving, baring all
Exhausted in the end.
You called the fouls and formed the words
That told it as it was.
A warrior running rampant, wild.
In pain you never paused.
For six short years we followed you;
You always grabbed the lead.
And now it's over, just like that.
The hearts begin to bleed.
No more will dirt in London, Oslo,
Crush beneath your feet.
It's up to other artists now
To make the tempo sweet.

No more to pound the dusty roads
Or touch the emerald green;
No man again to taste
Your thrilling madness in Eugene.

Bowerman and Knight discussed what Pre had been contributing to the company. How that work must continue. Over a month had passed, and I was continuing to work in a fog, unable to deal with the loss. My friend Dr. Stan James called me in early July. He said he and his wife Branwyn would take Carol and me hiking for a few days in the Three Sisters Wilderness, part of the Cascade Range. "Just bring boots and clothes. We'll take care of the rest." On the fourth of July weekend, we were climbing up snow-packed trails past rushing creeks swollen with snowmelt, arriving hours later in a world of white. Stan pitched our tents and set up camp and together we prepared dinner. To the west, the sun set, illuminating an orange haze of contrails. Our time in the mountains gave Stan and me time to talk about life, the meaning of it, and the opportunity that drives us. We discussed Pre's ego and Stan admitted, "I have an ego. Without it, I would not have accomplished what I have." I looked at Stan, a man I highly respected—not only a skilled surgeon, but a multi-engine pilot, a fit athlete 15 years older than me. "How do you do it?" I asked.

"If I don't put that workout in first, nothing else falls in place. If I take care of myself first, then I have the ability to take care of others." I had never heard that truth spoken so plainly and honestly.

We alternated the talk with play. Close to our camp was a plunging bank of snow that descended several feet to what was probably a frozen creek bed. From the top, you couldn't see the bottom. Stan mounted an air mattress, grabbing the front with his hands and jamming the heels of his boots on each side into the snow. Up went his boots and off he went, yelling "Ohwhowhowho!" as he disappeared.

"Oh great, there goes our orthopedic surgeon," I said. "What happens if he breaks a leg?"

I came off the mountain with renewed energy and a sense of purpose. It was good timing as Bowerman and Knight called with the news of a job change. I would no longer manage the store. Instead I would spend full time working with the athletes as Pre did. How I did it was up to me. I'd have to come up with a plan and strategy. I had few shoes, no apparel, and no budget. In the back of my mind, I thought Bowerman would be happy to see less of me meddling in the shoe lab. To him, I think I had become a pest, and he preferred his freedom.

Through my business friends in Eugene I found a basement location on Pearl Street. I could keep a small inventory of shoes there and not look like a retailer. With an address and a phone I was in business, and I began where it had all started, writing personal notes to Pre's old friends, who happened to be some of the best runners in the world. The letter went in with a box of shoes with no obligation to me or Nike. "Just try them."

Knight drove down to approve the location in his old white Plymouth. He agreed to the lease and left. Then he returned and I thought, "Oh, no. He's changed his mind."

"Hey Geoff, do you have a set of jumper cables? My battery's dead."

The 1975 Nike Oregon Track Club (OTC) Marathon was starting to draw attention. When we first ran it, we repeated four loops, but it was flat. I started driving in search of an alternate course and found that going over the I-5 freeway was only a 16-foot rise in elevation, and we could still run a flat course and finish along the Willamette River. Bannister and Spider pitched in and set up the finish line and we divided the duty of covering each 5k mark. To broaden the appeal, we added a half-marathon distance.

Race day: I clicked off my last split time and hurried back to the finish, elated with how the runners were performing. I returned amid a certain chaos as the first official who saw me put his arm around me, ushered me to the parking lot, and in a low tone informed me:

"We had a fatality."

"What! Who?"

"Larry Vollmer."

"Larry Vollmer? Couldn't have been. He's run almost every run!"

We were now in front of my own doctor, Larry Hilt. "Geoff, I was right here. Larry finished the half marathon, walked a few steps, and collapsed. I think he was dead before he hit the pavement. We couldn't get him back."

I found it impossible to believe. Bowerman was there and told me that the two of us should pay a visit to Larry's parents, who lived up the McKenzie River. So we drove up. They explained that he worked in a fiberboard plant in eastern Oregon, and that running was his passion. He died doing what he loved.

Rob Strasser had now joined the company. Knight needed an attorney and perhaps more than his law skill, Knight saw something in Strasser's personality. A student of military history and strategy, combined with a rough and tumble demeanor and a touch of theatrics, Strasser, a large, even rotund man, would earn the nickname "Rolling Thunder."

I would devise my own strategy to try to compete against Adidas, our powerful German rival. Montreal was right around the corner with no time to spare. I took the schedule and worked backwards. In our favor, the track and field trials were again awarded to Eugene. Putting athletes on the U.S. team in Nike shoes would become a focus. I then looked at competitions prior to the trials where I could observe and meet people.

Strasser and I discussed what went well in the '72 trials. Offering my home as a base to the few athletes we knew was a no cost way to show them how special we thought they were, and we'd try it again. So what about Montreal? I would meet Strasser in Montreal on my way out to the Millrose Games in New York City.

Montreal in the dead of winter is not an enjoyable experience. I went for an early morning run in the dark and came back with a frozen moustache to the surprise of Strasser, well insulated with his double wide body, who stood outside wearing only a Hawaiian shirt. He wouldn't walk even a single extra step. We couldn't have been more different.

Armed with a map, we drove each direction out of Montreal, looking at resorts or inns that could accommodate up to 12 Nike staff, feed larger groups, and provide our athletes a place to run or shower. After several dead ends, we came upon a cozy establishment outside St. Marc on the Richelou River called The Hanfield Inn. Operated by Pierre Hanfield, The Hanfield Inn was established by his parents. Pierre toured us around the frozen grounds, complete with a French restaurant, bungalows, and even a ferryboat, used for theater shows. We agreed on dates and a price and looked forward to August. Now we just needed some athletes.

I traveled into New York City for the first time for the Millrose Games. I was used to Eugene and its remarkable cleanliness, but as my cab whisked by garbage-strewn streets, I saw homeless shopping carts and graffiti-painted walls. My hotel was close to Madison Square Garden, and I looked out my window straight across at a brick wall, black with soot. I walked down the street hungry, and to avoid some of the questionable people I saw on the street, ducked into an old diner and took a place on a stool. I ordered what was advertised as cordon bleu, and it arrived on my plate, looking like it had come out of a can. I picked at it and left still hungry. I returned to my room and, feeling very alone, I dropped backwards onto my bed, looking up at the ceiling just in time to see a piece of plaster rocketing down to hit me in the forehead. I looked in the mirror, and wiping the blood off my head with a wet towel, I said, "I'm never coming back here!"

At the meet, it was easy to stay anonymous. We didn't have any athletes, and I didn't have Nike apparel to wear. So I sat in the stands and took notes on who looked good, what they were wearing, who they competed for. I couldn't wait to get home.

I attended the Portland Indoor, which I had once competed in. Pre had been a star there, and I knew my way around. I could wander the back halls where athletes warmed up and if I wanted, I could be more aggressive. One athlete who had impressed me was USC sprinter Donald Quarrie, from Jamaica. I had to listen closely to understand his clipped English, but I liked his attitude and invited him to lunch before he flew out to L.A. I learned that Donald was under contract with Adidas through Montreal, but that he was very interested in Nike when his contract ended. He felt that Adidas had so much dominance that they treated athletes with indifference. He felt he could help in our selection of athletes, "Don't just look at their performances. Look at what's under them. Some, you do not want to touch. But first, your shoes have to improve. The shoe is key."

One of those athletes would be Harvey Glance. He was charismatic, a sharp dresser, and the kind of guy who laughed his way through life—a good fit for Nike. He was no more than 5' 8", but I watched him in the parking lot of the Dogwood Relays as he showed off his vertical leap, which put him on top of a Volkswagen Bug.

Because of the Waffle Trainer for which Buck had successfully negotiated production, distance runners were writing back and returning my phone calls. I already knew from Harry Johnson's repeat state cross country trials that the Waffle Trainer was a hit. Jeff Johnson had communicated all of Bowerman's developments, plus the flare contributions of James and Vixie to our Japanese factory. Communication was

Nike would head into Montreal with annual sales at $7.5 million.

by telex. Once the Waffle Trainer reached retail, they flew off the shelves.

We were attracting distance runners and saw that as a direct avenue into the real market. Knight felt that we didn't have a true headliner, a standard bearer. We saw Bill Rodgers and Frank Shorter as a possible solution. I invited Rodgers to come to Eugene, and he and his wife stayed with us. I thought our talks went well, only to learn later that Bill's next stop was Japan, where he visited Onitsuka and a deal was made.

I traveled to Boulder and met with Frank and Louise Shorter. Frank and I went for runs in the Flatiron Mountains and spoke of Pre. Frank was an educated attorney and I found him somewhat guarded. But he seemed willing to work with us. Again, the issue was the shoe. Frank had a slightly banana shaped, narrow size 10 $1/2$ foot. When you ran just off his shoulder and tried to emulate his flowing stride, you seemed to follow effortlessly with him. It was like magic. But he did toe in and landed on the outside of the ball of the foot.

Onitsuka had a master custom cobbler who made one-offs for world-class athletes. Frank showed me the yellow masterpieces. The detailing was perfect and they fit. That was going to be tough to compete with, but Frank did agree to fly to Eugene and have Vixie cast his feet. Looking ahead to a predictably hot and humid Montreal, we were experimenting in the lab with a new mesh upper material that would breath. Vixie was working with an extremely light foam midsole material. We would attach a new version of Bowerman's outsole we called the "mini waffle." In talks with Strasser and Knight, we decided that we should secure Frank for three years at $15,000 per year. Frank negotiated his own contract.

Leading up to the trials, I traveled the country, remaining as inconspicuous as possible. Once, at the Drake relays, I mistakenly opened my sample bag in a hotel lobby to show a shoe to one athlete. Immediately I found myself surrounded by inquisitive athletes. At the Dogwood relays in Knoxville, I was walking amid a crowd of sprinters and jumpers out of the stadium, and a guy with a severe limp and a coordinated but errant hand and arm swing said, "Hey, the 'Nyk' dude's here! Need to find him and get some shit."

With little time and limited budget, our approach was a single assassin's bullet versus a shotgun at a turkey shoot. I saw what I wanted, what was do-able, and what was a waste. I went from Knoxville to Nashville and met the wise old Ed Temple, coach of Wilma Rudolph, Wyomia Tyus and Madeline Manning. He was as solid and no nonsense as they came, and a good friend of Bowerman's. As he toured me around the Tennessee State Tigerbelles' austere facilities, he pointed off the track to rough trails through fields. "I don't let them run in their trainers there. They have to wear heavy boots." I looked surprised. "It works. They put those spikes on after this and they scoot!"

And scoot they did. Brenda Moore-head, Kathy McMillan and Chandra Cheeseborough led the top short relay in the country. Ed was direct and to the point. "You give me the equipment, they'll stick with you."

Kathy McMillan competed in the long jump in the Montreal Olympics, winning the silver medal the summer after she graduated from high school.

When you had a measuring stick like Ed Temple, you shouldn't make a mistake, but I did. At an indoor meet, I met Alex Woodley of the Philadelphia Pioneers. One of my top 800 runners, Thomas McLean, would compete for Alex during the summer. Alex was a hustler and Philadelphia street smart, but as I'd learn, not to be trusted. You'd give him "the swoosh" and wonder later why the guy he promised you was wearing Puma spikes and an Adidas warm-up.

Across the country in Los Angeles, Fred Jones ran the all-girls L.A. Mercurettes. Fred would charm you with his smile, but rumor was that between that leather jacket and barrel chest he packed some heat. Fred reached way down into the L.A. age group program and developed talent like Ros Bryant and Jeanette Bolden.

In New York City, an educated, sophisticated attorney named Fred Thompson also developed national and world-class talent, and created new competitive opportunities like the Colgate Games. He developed Olympians Grace Jackson, Lorna Forde, and Diane Dixon.

All the time, Adidas was watching mildly, almost taunting us, and certainly not taking us seriously. We marveled at their product engineering and production skill. They also had bags and apparel. Their promo reps tended to look the same, sporting three stripes everywhere. What were we going to do?

Jeff Johnson was sitting on a multicolored inventory of nylon-covered upper material in Exeter. Stan James and I had taken an average composite of metatarsal head locations from all the foot care patients. We determined that the spike placements should be positioned just behind the metatarsals for maximum thrust. Thus the Vainqueur spike plate was born, and although Nike had established a production color for retail for both the Vainqueur and the two-piece toe version called the Triumph, Johnson would exhaust his fabric excess for our Olympic trials order because of all the custom shoes we built for the different teams.

Early on, Nike purchased the old Wise Shoe factory, located in Exeter, New Hampshire. Exeter was Nike's east coast research and design lab for shoes, as well as its U.S. production facility. Its location placed it in the heart of what was then America's shoe industry, with a wealth of expert shoemakers available for hire.

At the same time, I was struggling with our brand image. The scripted Nike over the swoosh seemed confusing. From the stands, it was hard to read. I began to sketch some options. The swoosh by itself was asymmetrical and did not stand alone well, in my opinion.

Geoff Hollister

My VW van with Nike 1 license plates.

Nike Archives

The first car I sold the Nike brand out of was my 1963 Studebaker Avanti.

Pre and I have a discussion in the new retail store—I call it the eyeball-to-eyeball shot.

Steve Prefontaine sits on the grass in front of Oregon high school runners and coaches. He told them "To give anything less than your best is to sacrifice the gift."

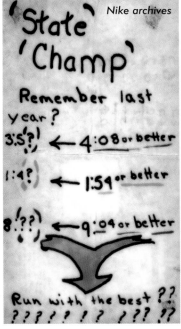

'State'
'Champ'
Remember last
year?
3:5 ?) ← 4:08 or better
1:4 ? ← 1:59 or better
8:!?? ← 9:04 or better

Run with the best ??
?? ?? !? ??? ??

The goal sheet Pre had taped at his bedroom desk in Coos Bay.

Geoff Hollister

Pentti Kahma holds Tracy.

Geoff Hollister

Prefontaine sits in front of his Finnish guests in Madras, Oregon. Everyone except Pre signed an enlargement of the photo I passed around at the party the final night. He said, "I'll be in the office in the morning to sign it."

Nike Archives

I often preferred to remain incognito—although these were for Nike International Halloween parties (the left, sans wig and mask).

I sit with sprinter Harvey Glance at the Pepsi Invitational. He still has his Pumas on but not for long.

Nelson and I scout the L.A. Times Indoor Meet.

THE LESS WE SEE OF THEM, THE BETTER.

These are not the kind of people you want hanging around the office.

And we've done our best to keep them brushing their teeth in airport washrooms. For one simple reason. In their own bizarre way, they have the ability to work with athletes.

Take Nelson Farris, on the right. One minute, he's leading three world class runners through the Ramada Inn in Fresno, singing breakfast cereal commercials at the top of their lungs. The next, he's getting their feedback on a prototype racing flat. So it can be right when it hits the market.

From day one, he's been on the road. Holding clinics anywhere there was a high school. Attending meets so small even the parents wouldn't show.

And if there's a race for women in this country, odds are Pam Magee will be there. From the outset, she wanted women to have more races, longer races, the same chance to travel and compete as men. So she set up the first promotional program in the business to see that they did.

Geoff Hollister is the same kind of raving idealist. He not only works with athletes, he helped give them the first corporate-sponsored marathon — the Nike/OTC. Now he's working with the Long Distance Race Directors Association to see that prize money is sensibly introduced into the sport.

Farris, Magee and Hollister are loose cannons. Keep them behind a desk too long and they'll short circuit.

As our representatives to the running community, they never once pretended to care about the athlete.

They never had to.

Beaverton, Oregon

Nike Archives

Early Wieden & Kennedy print advertisement.

Nelson and me—would you trust your Olympic effort to these two guys?

Nike Archives

Geoff Hollister

In the heat and humidity of Mombasa, Henry "Superman" Rono springs from the high water jump barrier to a world-class time.

Geoff Hollister

Rono fires back at me with Klutmeier's bazooka lens.

Pam Magee and me.

Orthopedist and good friend Kent Davenport tells me, "Not only did they run tough, they're great people."

I started playing with what would be called the Sunburst; a symmetrical joining of eight swooshes in the middle, which allowed for the printing of a school or club above and below. This would be the case for the Tigerbelles, the Colorado Track Club, the Jamul Toads, Texas El Paso, and more.

Dellinger asked me to have a couple of his new recruits out to my home for dinner. Rudy Chapa from Hammond, Indiana had just set the new American high school record for the 10,000. Cuban-born Alberto Salazar had already run for the Greater Boston Track Club with Billy Rodgers. A big part of Dellinger's success in recruiting these talented young athletes was that they would get to train with Pre. They were like two sponges, soaking up every story I could tell them about Prefontaine. They knew the records he'd set, but they wanted to know the man. More than anything they wanted to be like Pre, but I told them, "No, be yourself. Be the best person you can be."

As we moved closer to the trials, I started sketching a bolder Nike block that couldn't be mistaken from the stands at Hayward Field. It would be bright, tie-dyed, and would repeat down the chest and back. I called it "the Nike Billboard," and I selected a tight stretch T-shirt fabric so every ripple of a fit athlete would show.

Any promising athlete needed to travel to events for competition. In the world of amateurism, an athlete was on his own to qualify for the very competition the AAU controlled. The AAU pocketed all of the ticket money, advertising money, and television money without giving any back to the athletes who brought all that money in. In an attempt to remedy this situation, Oregon Senator Mark Hatfield and Washington Senator Henry "Scoop" Jackson were concerned over the unwieldy AAU governing structure and their continuing battles with the NCAA. In response, they introduced the Amateur Sports Act, which in effect broke up the AAU. They cited the life of Steve Prefontaine as an example of how wrong things were. However, track and field remained officially under Olan Cassell and the AAU. Little effectively changed the lot of those who showed promise but lacked the resources to train and get to the meets. Beaverton gave me approval for a budget item called the Athletes' Assistance Program, whereby an athlete who competed at a certain standard, who had shown loyalty, and had a need, would qualify. Marathoner Don Kardong would be among the first, along with Jon Anderson. They would get four domestic trips or could combine for an equivalent international trip.

For the '76 trials in Eugene, we moved the promotions base and inventory to my house so Bannister could control the retail environment. We made a decision for no new athletes. Here's what was happening—the athletes figured out pretty quickly that they could play one shoe company off against another. You'd give a runner shoes, and he'd wear them through the preliminaries, but then at the final they'd be in a competing brand. We didn't want to play that game, and couldn't afford to anyway. Instead, we relied on having good relationships with our athletes, and for the most part, they stayed loyal to us, whether we had them under contract or not.

Bob Newland again organized a spectacular Olympic trials. Frank Shorter would again win the marathon, and as we agreed beforehand, he would wear his Tigers, while Vixie built the final version of his Nike racing flat. We concentrated on the middle and long distances with a goal of placing Nike athletes on the Olympic team, a giant step for a fledging company in an arena dominated by Adidas.

The athletes strode out onto the track in their Nike gear, and none looked better than the Tigerbelles. Their slow walk from the bullpen to the start of the 200 was catlike in front of the east grandstand. We had printed the "Nike Billboard" on the back of their pink and blue rain suits, and each had his own colored Vainqueur spikes produced by Jeff Johnson in Exeter. Adidas was a little confused, as colors ranged from 800 runner Mark Enyeart's silver and black to Easter egg combinations of three colors, but we stood out.

One event after another, Nike athletes came through and made the team, from the 800 to Kardong's third place qualifying run in the marathon. Beyond that we had built goodwill with the potential to expand our athletic base the next year. We did this by treating athletes as special. I had been an athlete myself and I understood what they were up against, and what they needed. The athlete had a choice between a fat guy with Pumas, a former world class athlete carrying a briefcase full of Adidas' cash, or me, and I could run with our athletes in their workouts. Don Kardong said, "We and the guys at Nike were one and the same."

As we marched through the 10-day competition placing one athlete after another on the team, it was time to celebrate out at the house. Knight appeared and was jubilant. He was staying at the same motel as the Adidas contingent. His door was open as they walked by, not knowing who Knight even was. "And they yelled 'Fuck Nike!' I just smiled. I knew we had 'em right where we want 'em."

I selected my team for Montreal. It would include Nelson Farris, who could get into anything and talk his way back out if he needed to, and Pam Magee, who was unusual for a Nike employee because she wasn't an athlete, but who had a gift for developing a good rapport with the women. John Philips was the cousin of NBA star Paul Silas and showed great skill with the few sprinters, jumpers, and hurdlers we had. Our Canadian distributors volunteered a former English marathoner, Dave Ellis, who was based in Toronto.

Farris, Magee, and I decided we would go to the U.S. training camp in Plattsburg, New York first. We would then rent a car and carry replacement Vainqueurs and Elites in our bags in the trunk. On our way out of Plattsburg, we saw a guy hitchhiking on the side of the road. As we got closer, we realized it was Puma's promotion guy, Simburg. "Should we stop?" As we got closer, we smiled and waved. "Nah!"

Simburg had a tough Trials. His key sprinter Steve Williams didn't make the team. His coach, Brooks Johnson, tried to circumvent the rules to get Steve to Montreal, but he was turned down. When I caught Brooks snooping around Vixie's lab asking questions about what we were doing, I told Dennis not to let him in again. "There are guys you trust, and guys you don't."

We were off and across the border with our prize cargo, arriving at the Hanfield Inn on a hot muggy afternoon, a stark contrast to the chill of winter. Pierre Hanfield hustled us around the compound and showed us our bungalows and rooms, reserved for our guest athletes whom we would rotate in and out as they prepared for their particular events.

Frank and Louise Shorter arrived early as did Carol with 2-year-old Tracy, now happily sprinting across the lawn. With a pool and a river within sight, he would have to be watched carefully. Frank and Louise gladly accepted sharing that responsibility, and Frank was in the best mood. He was cracking jokes, affable, and it was his kind of weather, hot and humid—just what he preferred. He had won the 10,000 trials in the new racing flats and expressed confidence they would work.

Dave Ellis arrived from Toronto, then the Phillips, and we drove the 20 miles into the center of Montreal to scout the Olympic complex. Following the Munich tragedy, the Canadians took precautions and encircled the Athlete's Village with a chain link fence and plenty of barbed wire. This did not deter Nelson from figuring out a way to get in. Our Canadian distributor, Paul Nemeth, was a former Canadian wrestler and head Olympic coach. Nelson used Nemeth's connections to the local organizing committee to acquire a visitor's badge. The badge gave Farris open access to the Olympic Village. Once inside the village, it was amazing what Farris could get for a pair of shoes.

Adidas had taken over a corner motel across from the village. They had a giant staff to cover all their sports, they carried briefcases, and they dominated the uniforming of teams. In the world of "shamateurism" we knew what was in those briefcases—cash for payoffs to athletes. We couldn't compete against this. We wouldn't try. We had our own methods, and they were working.

Nelson and I saw the Olympics as a bridge to the future. We might not beat Adidas here, but there would be another day. This was but one step. Adidas distance runner Brendan Foster, from England, met with us and expressed his desire to run for Nike after the Games. He liked the shoes we sent from Eugene and knew other athletes who would join. A former Norwegian 800 record holder and good friend of the Kvalheim's introduced himself. Konrad Ystborg had a great sense of humor and explained, "I and my partner Yohan Kaggestad are very keen on importing Nike into Norway."

Back at the Hanfield Inn, we started our days with a morning run. It was the best time to beat the heat. Dave Ellis would be gone for an hour or more, return dripping wet, didn't shower, and changed right into his street clothes. This didn't go unnoticed by John Phillips and his wife, who took more than one shower a day, did their laundry daily, and neatly pressed their clothes.

We watched the competition mostly on the television in our bungalow as we had few tickets. Much of our time was spent driving athletes to and from the Village. "Dirty Dave" would drive some of the trips, still having not showered. He'd turn the air conditioning on. That simply recycled the air around him. Some athletes lowered their windows anyway to breathe.

Lasse Viren ran and won a tactical 10,000 against a field that was absent of Africans due to their boycott. Lasse, running in front, would surge, then slow the pace while runners behind him stepped on their competitors, chopped their strides and lost their rhythm. He sprinted to the tape unchallenged. Lasse ran in the 5000 next and it was rumored he would also run the marathon.

Frank's disposition was beginning to change. He brought me his shoes and asked if I could make some changes. I found a little cobbler shop run by a French Canadian behind his home only a few kilometers away. I could not speak French. His English was minimal, but he was impressed that I knew how to run his equipment. I paid him hourly for the time in the shop. His buddies would assemble and talk away in French. I sewed and reshaped Frank's shoes, returning them for him to test.

Our athletes were getting eliminated one at a time, few reaching a final—Matt Centrowitz, Craig Virgin, Dick Buerkle, and Gary Bjorklund all fell away. They were America's best, but it was like sending kids in against gladiators. Viren was impressive enough, but when you saw the kiwis in all black with just the silver fern on their chest, it had to strike fear. They were tall and mature. Dick Quax and Rod Dixon were well over 6 feet, but none were more impressive than John Walker. A running machine, Walker was the first man to run under 3:50 for the mile.

At the 1976 Montreal Olympics, Walker won the gold in the 1500, and Quax the silver in the 5000. Dixon won the bronze medal in the 1500 in the 1972 Munich Olympics.

Back at the Hanfield Inn, current and future Nike athletes like Donald Quarrie appreciated the hospitality. In the bungalow, the Phillips eyes were riveted on "Dirty Dave" who was sitting in his running shorts and T-shirt picking his toes, then his nose, and then moved his hand down towards Tracy who was at the foot of the couch. "No, don't!" they warned, but Dave was oblivious to the issue and concern. John followed with, "Going to do a load of laundry—got anything I can add, Dave?" John went to the store and bought extra bars of soap, "Here Dave—these are for you!"

My routine revolved around meeting Frank for breakfast with the latest change on the shoes. Each day he had a new request as he got more intense and nervous. It was a complete metamorphosis from the jovial, confident Frank of a week ago, and the weather was beginning to change, too. Predictions of rain loomed on the day of the marathon.

Frank couldn't control the weather, but he could have his shoes altered. I was going back and forth—adding one day, taking off the next. I called Dr. Stan James. "Stan, I'm going nuts. I need help." Stan flew out and joined us in the discussion. We went to the track and watched Frank do repeat 200s. He was fit, very fit. The muscles rippled down his thighs like a washboard. All Stan could do was reassure him, "Frank, you really look ready to go."

Viren won the 5000 much like the 10,000, with everyone obediently lining up behind, as Lasse altered the pace from the front. An easy win, he was heading to the marathon, and Frank was losing control. Carol and I drove Frank and Louise into the Village. Defizzed Coke sat in marked bottles in the back seat, Frank's preferred liquid replenishment on the course. Louise accidentally tipped a bottle over with her foot and Frank blew up, swearing at her. He was on edge. This was his day to repeat as Olympic gold medalist in the marathon and nothing was going to get in his way.

We dropped Frank and Louise off under threatening skies and grabbed some lunch. We then headed for a spot two miles from the start where we could view the pack from under an umbrella. The wait seemed to take forever and finally a helicopter appeared over the leaders in the distance. Numerous motorcycle policemen in two rows kept spectators on the curb as you could see the wet reflection of multicolored uniforms appearing. One of our best hopes, Dave Ellis' Toronto friend Jerome Drayton, was in the lead. You never saw Drayton's eyes. Even today in the rain, he was wearing his signature sunglasses. The leaders were all in a pack, and I picked out Bill Rodgers' bouncy stride easily, and then I saw Frank, and I'm thinking 'here comes Frank, here comes Frank. There. There goes Frank. Oh shit, he's wearing his Tigers!'

My spirits were as gray as the weather. We found the car and abandoned the plan to follow the course at various checkpoints. I drove to a liquor store, bought a bottle of wine and returned to the Hanfield to watch the race on television. I called Beaverton, "Buck, Frank switched shoes. He's wearing his Tigers."

Penny Knight would tell me later that Buck turned off the last light in the room and sat alone in the dark. Coach Sam Bell told me that Frank called him over at the practice track during his warm-up and asked him to run over to his room in the Village and pick up his Tiger racing flats.

Drayton dropped back and an East German named Waldemar Cierpinski dominated the later stages of the race. When Frank finished second and saw it was an East German who won, he said, "Blood doping." Amazingly, Don Kardong was in this race, battling for third, with Belgium's Karel Lismont. Lismont headed into the last lap around the stadium track with Kardong in pursuit. Unfortunately for us, Kardong just didn't have enough left to catch Lismont, and he crossed the line just two seconds shy of the bronze.

We didn't see or hear from Frank and Louise again in Montreal. Carol and I took Kardong and his fiancée Bridgette out for a dinner to discuss what might have been.

Carol, Tracy and I left Montreal for her parents' farm outside Champaign, Illinois. So much had gone into the effort with Shorter, extending all the way back to the loss of Pre. The contract, the trust, the shoe development, the daily shoe modifications in Montreal--you pour your heart out not only for the company, but for the athlete. You were there together for the prize. I spent the majority of eight days on the farm in bed. It might have been the only time in my life where I was seriously depressed.

CHAPTER 13: AFTER MONTREAL

Upon returning to Oregon, I drove up to Beaverton and sat down with Knight in our little BRS office. "Was it as bad as it seemed?" he asked.

"Worse," I said.

"If I didn't spend $50,000 on an ad in *Sports Illustrated*," Knight said, "what could you do with it?"

"Our guys were like kids going in for a slaughter," I said. "There's such a gap between our college program and the age where they'll run their best. There are clubs, but not with a fulltime coach and a competitive environment."

"If you had a club, who would run it?"

"I know just the guy," I said. "Harry Johnson. Nobody works harder and his track record is the best in the country for high schools."

It was agreed that I should approach Harry and see if he would be interested; what would be his input? The idea fascinated Harry and we discussed initial needs—who would we recruit, what was needed for a facility, what would we call the club?

Harry's South Eugene Axemen would win another state cross- country title that fall and by winter the collective ideas for a club were beginning to take shape. I found a larger basement location across the street on Pearl and moved over in advance. We were narrowing the options down for a club name, and Harry's wife Jody was sewing a uniform design. I was making phone calls to prospective members.

In the meantime, Carol was pregnant. On one of my runs, I noticed a unique home under construction a few blocks away. It was a fifth year project for a group of U of O architecture students. I was impressed with its openness and reversal of space, putting the bedrooms on the ground floor and one large living area, kitchen and dining room upstairs with large picture windows looking up a grassy hill. We put the Dillard home up for sale, doubled our investment and moved into East 43rd. That home would later be nicknamed "The Hollister Hilton," a home away from home for Nike athletes visiting Eugene.

In the meantime, I was still trying to grow our running program. Chapa and Salazar were beginning to show promise, although Alberto dropped out of the NCAA cross country meet on a cold, windswept day in Denton, Texas. We were walking down the street outside of our hotel, and Rudy and Al told me that they were thinking of leaving Oregon and running somewhere else.

My advice to them was simple. "If you quit now, it'll be much easier for you to quit something else later."

They stayed. If I ever felt like a mentor, it was that day.

That winter, Carol and I accepted an invitation to stay with Dr. Kent Davenport, a Honolulu-based orthopedist I had met, who ran in our Nike-OTC Marathon. He was impressed with our race in the fall where Kim Merritt set an American women's record and a Rice graduate sprinted past a strong men's field for the win—Jeff Wells had a future. I was asked to speak at the Honolulu Marathon Symposium and share how Eugene's event developed into such a competitive marathon.

The Marathon Symposium was headed by the dynamic Dr. Jack Scaff, an island fitness guru of sorts, who loved beer and ran to shed the obvious pounds. With the symposium it was a unique opportunity to get race directors to share their experiences. Race safety was the primary concern. I explained that we put ice cubes in our water containers, we kept the course as flat as possible, had an early morning start time, and ran in September with a predictable temperature in the 50s with clear skies. In addition, I insisted on a ratio of one volunteer to every four competitors. The top 5 men and women from the Nike-OTC Marathon were rewarded with a trip to compete in Honolulu, followed by a fun-filled two days in Maui to bodysurf, golf, and party.

On this particular trip, Kent had arranged for a friend to take a group of us out on his 32-foot French-built sloop on the windward side. Among other athletes, Don Kardong and Gayle Barron agreed to go, and we left the harbor to sail out to a small rock outcropping and back. I loved the feel of the wheel for steering and the power of a bigger boat as we plowed through the windswept sea of green and blue. But Gayle's perfectly manicured complexion had faded to green, and Kardong's long body was stretched out on deck face down on the port side. The boat's owner found himself coping with the sick and left me on the helm, which I thoroughly enjoyed.

Back in Oregon, we were into basketball season and I was asked to go meet with Dick Harter's "Kamikaze Kids," the most popular Oregon team perhaps since Oregon's 1939 NCAA champion "Tall Firs." The Kamikaze Kids had worn Converse up to that point. With the starting line-up of Ronnie Lee, Greg Ballard, Stu Jackson, Ernie Kent, and Mark Barwig in the room, Harter's east coast bluntness rang out. "From now on, we're wearing Nike only—got it?" With no dissent, the first Nike collegiate team would take the floor.

Up in Portland at the Memorial Coliseum, our basketball guy, John Phillips, had given me an assignment. The New York Knicks were in town to play the Trailblazers and Spencer Haywood needed a pair of Nike Bruins personally delivered to play in. I drove up to Portland and checked with security at the back of Memorial Coliseum. "Ah, these are for Spencer Haywood." I was escorted down a long underground hallway to a locker room. Here I was, all 145 pounds of me waiting for this unhappy big guy who had the ability to flatten me with a forearm. "What's this runt doing to upset my game?"

I just stood there and lifted up the box. He opened the lid, looked at the shoes and a smile spread across his face. "Thanks man, thanks."

It was like Christmas, and I was Santa Claus. You wouldn't get that kind of reaction today from an NBA star, but back then, those shoes meant a lot to him, and his reaction made me feel great, too.

CHAPTER 14: THE ARRIVAL OF RONO AND ATHLETICS WEST

At about the same time as the Portland Trailblazers, led by Bill Walton, were winning the 1977 NBA championships, our daughter Kaili entered the world. Surrounded by sports people, activity, and travel, plus a 4-year-old brother, hers was a fast-paced life from day one.

With Nike sales now approaching $20 million, I was traveling more and the company was on a roll. We held our sales meeting at Black Butte, a resort in Oregon's Cascade Mountains, and between rounds of golf, runs on the trails, and mixed doubles on the court, we actually managed to get some business accomplished before heading to the bar. With the success of the Trail Blazers and Nike players Sidney Wicks, Geoff Petrie and Dave Twardzik, basketball became the hot topic. Nike decided to select key players across the country, which put a regional strategy in play.

John Phillips knew the kind of players we wanted, guys with personality, guys who understood what loyalty meant, and guys who weren't just about the money. The deal was structured so that the whole group got a shared royalty based on Nike's basketball profits. That meant they had to be willing to hang in there with us for the long haul. We ended up with at least a dozen players, guys like Moses Malone, George "The Iceman" Gervin, and Paul Westphal. The strategy would be called "The Supreme Court." Roundball would become a major thrust for Nike. Strasser and Knight loved it.

I drove up to Seattle in the fall of '77 to see Alberto Salazar and Rudy Chapa perform at Green Lake Park in the Pac-8 Cross Country Championships. I was excited, jogged the course for the best vantage points, and adjusted my Nikormat for the Seattle haze. To my surprise, it was another runner from Washington State that caught my attention. He had a fluid stride but a more muscular build than a distance runner, and he would glide up and down a hill seemingly not touching the ground with his feet. When he set the pace for his fellow Kenyans Kimeto and Kimombwa, his surges left Salazar and Chapa hanging back. I had just witnessed Henry Rono for the first time.

John Chaplin, track coach at Washington State University, was impossible to contain—"Motor Mouth" had his usual machine gun banter in high gear. He was proud of his new find, acquired through a pipeline back to Kenya courtesy of Pre's old nemesis, John Ngeno. It was enough to drive me back to the serenity of Eugene, even though John had many of his runners in our shoes.

Months later I walked out to the road to retrieve my *Register-Guard* on April 9. I opened the paper and a banner across the top highlighted that Rono had obliterated the 5000 world record. I threw the paper up in the air, yelled and jumped up, clicking my heels together. Inside at the breakfast table, I reviewed the details—13:05 in Berkeley—Nike's first world record!

I called Chaplin and invited Henry to come and visit us for Easter break. Henry arrived much to Tracy's delight, as they enjoyed playing "lion" with all the pillows and stuffed animals in the loft. After a good morning run, I made my favorite banana beer pancakes for Henry and drove him up to Beaverton High School where we met Hailu Ebba at the track. Henry warmed up, and then asked us to time him for 3000 meters on the Grasstex track. He sprinted the straightaways and floated the turns repeatedly for seven and a half laps. We clicked the watch—7:58 solo, doing it the hard way. He kept jogging as Hailu and I looked in disbelief at each other. "After I jog a 200, I'll drop my hand and time me for a quarter." He ran 56 seconds and pronounced himself "fit" with a big smile that was punctuated by the gap between his two front teeth.

That evening, Hailu and I took Henry out to dinner at Jazz de Opus. Henry was immediately recognized by the MC, who announced, "Ladies and gentlemen, we have in our midst tonight the great world record holder from Kenya, Henry Rono." The room full of diners, including three Portland Trailblazers, rose as one and gave Henry a standing ovation. Henry, not yet used to his new celebrity, stood quickly, smiled, and just as quickly sat down.

On May 13, in front of only a few hundred spectators inside the voluminous Husky Stadium, Henry struck again, dropping the steeplechase world standard to 8:05.4. I thought, "My God. My event. He could have lapped me."

I was on the phone often in Eugene, searching for those promising distance runners who were willing to relocate to be coached by Harry Johnson. Penn State steeplechaser George Malley and Villanova's Tiny Kane were interested. The lone exception to the distance rule was Mac Wilkins. Mac had student-coached for Harry. They kept in touch, "Mac can be helpful—he knows the meet promoters and the European circuit."

Mac stayed at the "Hollister Hilton" and could barely fit his huge frame through the opening at the top of the vertical ladder to the sleeping loft. Mac passed on my banana beer pancakes and Tracy sat there glued to Mac's bulging biceps as they moved while he spooned through his fruit and cereal. Tracy and I had just seen *Superman* with Christopher Reeve. When Mac left the house to return to California, 5-year-old Tracy turned to me and said, "Dad, Mac is just like Superman—he can do anything he wants!"

Athletics West was beginning to build momentum. Jeff Wells, a theology student who had won the Nike-OTC, liked Eugene and elected to move—he would be nicknamed "The running Rev." A sharp-tongued Easterner Jim Crawford joined. We called him "Craw."

Harry said, "We've got to get Virgin—he's a key. He's so good. And he'll push these guys."

Harry started planning the first European tour of the club with the same detail he put in to all his work. He decided that they needed a base that they could operate from—it would be Vaxjo, Sweden where everything was accessible by train, but where they had the country rather than the city to train in.

The NCAA meet was in Eugene and no one was a bigger celebrity than Henry Rono. Henry loved the Eugene crowd and wanted to reward them with his performance. He knew if he could run 8:05 in Seattle, he could go under 8:00 at Hayward Field. But Chaplin would have none of it, and told Henry "No world records here!" Chaplin hated losing to Oregon, and if Henry was going to set a world record, Chaplin wanted it to happen anywhere but in Eugene. Henry stewed.

I was sitting halfway up above the start of the steeple. One of America's best, Henry Marsh, of BYU, was at the line. The gun went off and Rono shot around the turn and down the straight, then settled into a sensible pace on the turn. But as he came to the straight, he took off. The fans responded with applause. Then he floated at the turn and cleared the first water jump. At the head of the west straightaway, he sprinted again, leaving the field in his wake. I said, "Oh my God. I've seen him do this!" I predicted to those surrounding me that he would do this the whole way. "I know he can. He's done it in practice."

Rono reached the finish in 8:12 with a smile on his face in front of an entertained crowd that realized they had just witnessed something special. They might never again view a race run so uniquely, and so easily won. Chaplin was running around like, "Did I coach him to do that?—of course I didn't—who would?—Henry's just Henry—he's from another planet."

It became obvious to me that Chaplin knew little of Rono's workouts, and perhaps less of what motivated him.

Later, Chaplin sat down with Strasser and me and turned serious at Roscoe Divine's house. "This is a big year. He'll do more in Europe. Then Henry has to attend the Kenyan AAA's camp and qualify in Mombassa, or he doesn't run the Commonwealth Games in Edmonton. Hollister, you've got to go with him or he'll screw it all up!" At this point John was right in front of my face and talking so fast he was spitting. I wiped my mouth and forehead off and looked at Strasser. A big gut laugh rolled out from under the reddish beard, "Okay, you're goin'—take care of him."

Strasser took me aside. "I've got another assignment for you— the Moscow games are two years away. Remember how we scouted Montreal? You scout Moscow a year earlier. We'll need it."

Hurdler Greg Foster showed up in our offices, asking for Nike products. He wasn't one of our athletes, and I knew he was with Adidas. When my secretary came in to announce him, I got my list of our athletes, and I went out to our reception area. "Greg," I said, "here's our list of athletes. Which one of these people do you want me to cross off our list so I can give you product?"

Foster just looked at me, speechless. We were eye to eye like that for a long moment, and then he just got up and left.

I departed the U.S. for Helsinki along with Mac and Al Feuerbach, and Harry's small contingent of A.W. runners. I sat between Big Al and Mac in what was left of my seat, awakening from time to time embarrassed to find my head laying on one or the other's shoulder. On arrival, Jaakko informed us of Rono's 27:22 world record 10,000 in Vienna the night before, with the crowd clapping and chanting "Rono, Rono, Rono."

Al Feuerbach set the world record in the shot put in 1973 with a mark of 71' 7".

Jaakko had arranged for massive Ilpo Nikila to drive in from Tampere, and "Mr. Tickle" went to work immediately on the Athletics West group, loosening the kinks from the long flight. Then I was off to Kenya via Frankfurt to rendezvous with Henry. The security at Frankfurt was the highest I had experienced. All the bags sat on the tarmac alongside the Lufthansa 747, dogs sniffed the bags, and security had Uzis as each passenger walked on board.

I spotted some big Adidas bags and looked closer at their tags—they read "Rono" and I thought, "Shit, they did it—they got Henry!" I sat down next to the door and waited. It would be thirty minutes before Henry and fellow Kenyan runner Joel Cheriyot arrived.

I wondered what the reaction would be when they saw me. They finally boarded, and to my surprise, Henry was excited to see me. He said he kept the bags only to carry all his things back to Kenya. He said Adidas really tried. He and fellow Kenyan Mike Boit were staying at a hotel in the country. Boit came out to the entrance as a big Mercedes whisked off with Henry in it—they kept him for a few days, trying to get him to switch shoes. He wore their socks, but stuck to his Vainqueurs in Vienna.

Boit won the bronze medal in the 800 at the 1972 Olympics. He ran a 3:49:45 mile in 1981.

Henry was now focused on Kenya and concerned about the Kenyan Amateur Athletic Association's officials, because he had extended his European tour, and was late arriving for the KAAA's training camp. I told him, "Your records will speak for themselves."

When we arrived, no officials were waiting, but everyone knew Henry. We came off the plane down to the hot tarmac and Henry grabbed my arm. "You took care of me—now you are in my country and I am taking care of you!" We pushed through the crowd, waved people away, and went into the terminal. The first newspaper we saw carried the headline "Where is Rono?" and listed the three world records he held, including the one he'd just set in Vienna.

It was my first look up close at the country I had heard so much about. Mombassa was an old Muslim shipping port on the East African coast, with unbearable humidity and heat. It seemed the most unlikely site for a championship. Henry and I split—me to my hotel on the coast and Henry to the training camp a few miles away. My taxi negotiated the potholes on the road through town, recently filled with rainwater from a thunderstorm. Businessmen also avoided the holes, carrying their socks and shoes, walking barefoot. I later told Henry that I didn't know if this location would work as a store site. Henry responded, "Don't judge it from where you have come from. Judge it from where I have come from."

My hotel had adobe spires, palm trees, and geckos that sang as the sun went down. I was up the next morning and out the front door for my run down the road, bordered on both sides by high grass over my head. I then took a cab ride to the training camp and was invited to go for a run on the beach.

"I've already gone."

"Where?"

"On the road in front of the hotel."

Their eyes got as big as saucers. "Oh! There are lions there."

I didn't know if it was true, but I didn't run on that road again. I found the Kenyan people to be the friendliest I had met anywhere. In the space of five days, I would meet over a hundred new faces. No one asked for anything. They simply wanted to meet you and welcome you. Fourteen miles outside of town on this beautiful beach, the best of Kenya's athletes gathered for the first time in history.

Kip Keino had never raced before his own people. Here I was at 2:30 p.m. on the infield looking for the best camera position, surrounded by thousands of Kenyans, the only white man. The steeple was about to begin on one of the worst cinder tracks I had seen. The water jump had been dug the day before. Burlap bags were spiked into the ground to form a bottom and a frog surfaced in the muddy water. I noticed the barrier seemed tall as the gun cracked and they were off. Despite the conditions, Henry ran an amazing 8:16. On a cool night in Europe with a fast track, he could have approached 8 flat. Henry came over to sit down on the grass, "Did you know the water jump barrier was two inches too high?"

Henry was right. The obstacles he overcame—I had to judge him by where he came from.

The next day Henry was recovered and ready for the 5000. He raised his hand as he was recognized by the announcer, "Rono the superstar." Henry's moves were quick, decisive, and surgical right from the beginning. He put away a talented field that showed that outside Kenya we had only seen the tip of the iceberg. "I think he is Superman" the announcer boasted as Henry came across in 13:32. The fans agreed as Henry ran a victory lap, stretching out his right palm to tap a long line of black hands just wanting to touch this 'superman' from Kenya, one of their own.

That evening the KAAA hosted a banquet for the athletes. I had a lengthy conversation with Phillip Ndoo, one of the first Kenyans to run on a U.S. scholarship, now with the *Daily Nation* newspaper. Phillip had great respect for my former teammate Kenny Moore, "He's the best."

A portly man standing behind me in the buffet line struck up a friendly conversation. When I finally asked his name, he responded, "Neftali Temu." I almost choked. "You're Neftali Temu, Olympic gold medalist at 10,000 meters?" Apparently, obesity is a sign of success in Kenya, and many accomplished runners end their competitive careers only to add girth to prove who they are now.

Not so for Kip Keino, who walked with a sense of pride and confidence. We spoke of his ITA days and early Nike connection and of his orphanage up in Eldoret in the Rift Valley. He joined Henry and me at the table. It was quite remarkable seeing those two together. Kip felt comfortable stepping aside for Rono, whom he called "the new shining star."

Henry, Joel, Chaplin and I flew the next morning to Nairobi. They drove to the Rift Valley where many of the good runners come from while I checked the retail sporting goods market in Nairobi, dominated by Bata with inexpensive footwear.

I flew to London and checked into the Sports Hostel at Crystal Palace. I had breakfast the next morning after running through a thick, cold summer rain—bloody awful and exceeded only by the entrée of bangers, eggs, tomato and toast, all fried in grease.

The next day was filled with securing my Russian visa, meeting Kiwi Dick Quax and talking shoes and promotions in New Zealand, and then going to the windy, rainy stadium to watch Brendan Foster run a gutsy 27:30 10k. This was a new European record. Rono jumped up and yelled at Bren, applauding his effort.

I met Andy Norman, a stout, gruff London policeman who moonlighted as a meet promoter and was admittedly the most powerful in the U.K. He wasn't impressed with Athletics West nor Americans in general. Over a beer, he said, "If it wasn't run in Europe, it probably didn't happen." He was looking for my reaction from the corner of his eye.

"Yeh," I said. "Rono was pretty pedestrian in his first two records in the States."

> *Rono set new world records of 13:08:04 in the 5000 in Berkeley, California, and 8:05:04 in the 3000 steeplechase in Seattle, Washington. In Europe, he went on to set world records in the 10,000 and the 3000, all within 81 days in 1978.*

Nyambui won the silver medal in the 5000 at the 1980 Moscow Olympics, and won the Berlin marathon twice, in 1987 and 1988.

The next day was another big qualifier for the Commonwealth Games, and Nike headlined the 5000, with shoes on the feet of Sulieman Nyambui, Nick Rose, Dick Quax, and Rod Dixon. Then my man Rono stepped out onto the track in Adidas. I couldn't believe it, and despite English Nike athletes qualifying for Edmonton in the 800 steeple, 5000 and 10,000, Rono was a big question.

Chaplin came running up, "You got a problem with Henry?"

"John, this is the first time I knew anything was wrong."

I spoke with Henry at Heathrow before we flew to Oslo. He said he didn't like the Adidas shoes, but their plans were more definite. I could only assume that meant immediate money. I asked Henry to trust us, remain patient, and to not jump to a quick situation while he was hot.

Our distributor Konrad Ystborg met me at the Oslo airport. We talked about business in Norway and then he drove me up to the Panorama Hotel to check in. The hotel sat on the side of a lake, and it was one of Pre's favorites. Bowerman had the American distance runners training here for a month prior to Munich. I immediately ran the loop trail, another run in Pre's footsteps, and returned for dinner with the Kenyans.

The following morning, I had breakfast with Rono and Mike Boit, making my final pitch to Henry on Nike. Fortunately, Boit spoke up in favor of our approach, the shoes, and our attitude. Boit had been with Adidas and had switched to Nike. He spoke to Henry in Swahili, and I can only assume he was telling Henry what the difference was between the two companies. His help couldn't have come at a better time.

Konrad arrived to take Quax, Dixon and me up to the Holmenkollen ski jump, left over from the Oslo Games. I spent more time with Dixon, learning about his frustration with

Adidas. "I had to pay for my TRXs and use my same spikes from '76. Why am I wearing three stripes?"

That evening I went to Bislet Stadium, nestled in a hilly residential district of Oslo. Local javelin throwers were showing up, carrying their spears and looking as though they just finished chopping wood in a forest. A crowd of 14000 sat snugly around the 6-lane all-weather track as meet promoter Arne Haukvik quipped in Norwegian and received appreciative laughter from the knowledgeable spectators. My eyes were on Rono as he sat on the infield grass to remove his training flats. He reached into his spike bag and I rose out of my seat. To my relief he pulled out his Vainqueurs, ran a few strides and then blasted even 60.2 second laps for 3000 for his fourth world record, 7:32! Nyambui and Rose trailed him. Later Henry told me that he didn't want to take a chance and would stay with Nike. Money was not a factor, he assured me.

At a banquet that evening a taped delay of the 3000 race was played on a screen. When Rono kicked the pace up from 60.2 to a higher gear with 300 meters to go, all eyes were turned to Henry in amazement, including Marty Liquori's. Nyambui broke out laughing. As the time was announced, everyone began to applaud, but Henry looked down to his strawberries and cream in embarrassment.

Strasser called my room at 3:45 a.m. After getting so excited telling him about the record, I couldn't get back to sleep, so I laced up my waffles and ran around the lake. As I returned to the hotel, Rono and Boit were going for their run, so I joined in for another 4 miles. We talked as we ran, and now I was confident that Henry was our man. I couldn't thank Mike Boit enough for the influence and mentoring he provided to Henry.

Rono and I flew to Helsinki for the World Games with Steve Scott, the American record holder in the mile. With Henry complaining of being sore, I had Jaakko set him up for a good rubdown with "Mr. Tickle." Even though he was sore and ran with poor barrier form, Henry still ran 8:16.

Tiny Kane, Athletics West's top 1500 meter runner from Villanova, had created his own problem. He had been taking out Finnish women in every little town the club competed in, and they were all coming to the big meet in Helsinki. Lasse Viren beat Jos Hermans at a 10k in 27:57. That night Tiny ran the fastest 1500. We thought it was just to get away from his adorers. Jaakko took A.W. 5000 man Ralph King and Don Clary, a teammate of Rudy and Alberto's from Alaska, out to a friend's home for a great sauna, beer, and sausages. So, this was what Pre was talking about. These Finns really knew how to live.

The next morning, Harry and the rest of us were waiting for Craig Virgin to show at the gangway of the ferry that would steam overnight to Stockholm. Craig never went anywhere unless his hair was perfectly blow dried, and this could take some time. The ferry left without him.

Harry and I talked about the progress of the club. The training program, which was basically Bowerman's Oregon program, was beginning to show results. A train ride to Vaxjo returned us to our base camp with nice trail runs around the lake. Virgin would show up hours later in disbelief that we had left him behind. He was in time for dinner, and Jody, Harry's wife, had prepared a big bowl of local strawberries and passed them around the table. Everyone took a reasonable portion, with Virgin and Jim Crawford being the last. The bowl came to Craig and he heaped his bowl and passed it on to "Craw." Jim looked over the edge of the porcelain bowl to spot four small strawberries at the bottom. "Gee Craig, thanks. That was big of you."

Virgin, totally oblivious, said "No problem."

Our distributor, Roy Ahnell, picked me up in Stockholm, and I delivered shoes to Quax and Dixon at the Boson Training Facility in the country. That evening in the beautiful Stockholm Stadium,

Dixon clocked a 13:17 5000 in his new Nikes, Doug Brown ran a U.S. best 10k for the year of 27:52, Feuerback and Wilkins won, Malley missed the American steeple record by a tenth of a second, and A.W.'s Virgin and Manke ran gutsy races, forcing the pace on their opponents. The next day I was running the trails just outside the stadium and hooked up with Poland's Malinowski—a great guy with good English skills. He loved Nike and wanted to wear them badly but said that his officials would force him to wear Adidas. "That's the way it is in our country—no freedom to choose."

> Bronislaw Malinowski won the steeplechase gold medal in the Moscow Olympic Games with a time of 8:09.7

Pre had spoken so highly of

Roy Ahnell picked me up at the stadium and introduced me to Linda Haglund, who at the age of 22, had just set a new world record for the 60 meter sprint. Adidas had been sporadically supplying her and she expressed interest in Nike. I went to work on it right away and traced her small feet. Tiny Kane was also working on her, so to speak.

After a stop in Amsterdam, I flew to Gateshead, England to visit Brendan Foster and try to iron out his issues with our distributor Mike Tagg and the apparel brand Viga. This proved to be a mess. Our American runners showed up in England wearing Nike from head to toe, but Tagg was only showing the English runners our shoes. I wanted to be able to take better care of these guys. Tagg was resistant. He'd been with Adidas and was very informed of their methods. He let me know that they bought more than just athletes, they bought entire national sports federations. Through Malinowski, I knew this to be true.

Foster loved the Vainqueur, and despite Adidas' efforts to recruit him, he was not switching. He would wear Nike at the Commonwealth Games. He was fit, and he was thinking of the marathon in the future and possibly even working for Nike.

Tagg took me to meet a young English 800 runner. At the age of 21, he had run 1:45.6 and seemed to have promise. Still a student at Loughborough, his name was Sebastian Coe.

Nike and Athletics West had a good showing at the Gateshead Meet, and Harry and I had a frank discussion on who I should bring to Europe in the future. Harry believed that between my distance people and his, we were over saturated—to Andy Norman we were just Nike.

On the train ride to England, I rode with England's top sports journalist, Cliff Temple. He wrote *The Brendan Foster Story* and was a big Nike fan. We agreed to spend more time together at the Commonwealth Games, in Edmonton, as he was impressed with our progress. Long before I ever heard the term "networking" I had stumbled on to this basic skill of how to grow a business.

CHAPTER 15: THE MOSCOW RUN-AROUND

Arriving in Moscow in 1978 was a confusing exercise. You could not book a hotel in advance. They book it for you. Then you line up for ground transportation. In my case, Nissho-Iwai informed me that Nelly Novikova from their office would be picking me up. I had dropped my Nike bags and gotten in line for lodging, looking around for someone with perhaps a sign saying Nike. At the same time, Nelly Novikova was looking for "a longtime Nike employee," which to her meant someone old.

Finally, I got my hotel assignment, the Hotel Russia on Red Square, and returned to my bags. Immediately, Nelly Novikova pounced on me, all 160 pounds of her stuffed into a leopard print dress. Her English was perfect and she directed me to a black car with a driver waiting outside. She sat in the front passenger seat, put a hefty arm over the top and looked back and purred as the driver headed through the streets choked with black smoke from trucks and buses equipped with failing mufflers. Women raked grass into large wicker baskets on the wide medians with what looked like witches' brooms—Soviet inefficiency at its best.

We arrived at the Hotel Russia, which dominated four city blocks. The hallways stretched that whole length with what must have been a 15-foot ceiling. Huge doors lined the hall—very impressive, until I opened the door to my room, which was surprisingly small. Workers were gilding the outside window frames for the 1980 Olympics. The frames however, were of a poor quality metal, and they were rusting from the inside.

As I was hanging my clothes, I heard a chime, "Da-da-da-da, da-da-da-da-da," again and again. There was a television sitting in the room and I listened closely to it, but the sound came from elsewhere. The window—no. Finally, I opened my door—it seemed to come from the huge hallway, but I couldn't pinpoint the source. A mystery, but I had work to do, so I let it go.

Nelly and Nissho-Iwai's Mr. Koito picked me up and took me to their office where we discussed our issues for the Olympics. One staffer who had lived in Moscow for nine years said, "Your first meeting will allow you to meet the people, the second will allow you to appraise the problems and Soviet mannerisms, and the third to solve the problems and bridge the gaps." I would meet with the Olympic organizing committee the next day.

In front of Mr. Kislov, Mr. Maslou and Mr. Roshpukin, I acknowledged their longstanding relationship with Adidas, gave them the history of Nike, our rapid rise, our top athletes, including Rono. I provided catalogues and recent issues of *Runner's World* and *Track & Field News*. They were quite impressed with the samples I showed them, but most of all with Bowerman's waffle. Kislov assigned Roshpukin to work with Mr. Koito for my lodging and tickets for the games, and then referred me to another man for the problem of bringing equipment into the country.

Then I met with Mr. Tartygen, who was responsible for ordering all sporting goods for the USSR. He started off with, "I am busy, we have 15 minutes. What are your problems?" I felt like throwing my notes over my shoulder, as I could tell that this would not be as cordial as my last meeting. Tartygen kept returning to "The official Olympic sponsor contracts" and said that we were late in our requests. I told him that Nike did not want to be an Olympic sponsor, but that we only wanted to bring in a small number of products for athletes already wearing our brand. He pledged support to those companies that provided the best support to the USSR during and after the Olympics. I could tell that we were going to have to get creative on how we serviced our athletes in Moscow. Mr. Tartygen would stand in our way.

I wanted to visit the Olympic site, so we drove by Lenin Stadium, and then out to the Village under construction. Our car stopped, Nelly and I got out and I started clicking photos with my Nikormat. Suddenly, a car drove up and men got out and asked for my camera. Nelly started speaking to them in Russian. They removed my film and took a few steps away, still talking. I realized they must have been following me the whole time. They returned my camera and we were free to go.

Nelly started crying. I asked her what the problem could possibly be—we weren't doing anything that could get you in trouble. Wiping her mascara streaks from her cheeks, she said, "You don't know, because you don't live here." I was beginning to get the picture.

That night Nelly took me to the ballet. This was something the Russians knew how to do. The music, the pageantry. I told Nelly that I thought it was a great love story, not understanding a word of Russian. She said, "Oh no, this is the story of the struggle for freedom in Chile!"

Mr. Koito and Nelly drove me to the airport, we discussed my list, and decided telex would be preferable to mail as a method to stay in close contact leading up to 1980. I almost thought I would not be allowed to depart, as a nasty agent questioned my dollars to ruble and back to dollar exchange rate. I was not to take rubles out of the country. "But I don't want your damned rubles!"

Finally sitting in my seat for a flight to Copenhagen, I wondered how American politicians managed to put such a fear of the Russians into our people. They can't even replace mufflers or collect grass clippings, their buildings are rusting, and that sound I kept hearing over and over in the hotel hall? I am not a musician—can't remember lyrics or sing a melody, but I have never forgotten those notes. When I repeated them to Nelly, she said, "Oh, it is our national anthem."

CHAPTER 16: RUNNING, FLYING, MARKETING

I was home by July 17, but only for a moment. "Vacation" would be a business trip to the Commonwealth Games in Edmonton. We drove our orange Volvo station wagon north, loaded with bags and kids stuff. We visited an old cavalry fort, stayed overnight in a log cabin, watched moose along the highway, and were stunned with the beauty of Banff.

We arrived at our not-so-hot lodging at the edge of Edmonton. I was walking around a corner in the lobby in my Nike La Villages, a color take-off of the Cortez, when a recognizable face noticed my shoes, and I saw that he was wearing the same model. "Ahaa!" we both said, and pointed at each other's feet. The other person was actor John Saxon who was in town shooting a movie about stockcar drivers. He had received his Nikes from our L.A. promotions team and was proudly wearing them.

I found Edmonton a difficult city for us to do what was now our customary hospitality effort. But our athletes were performing well, with Rono running away with the 5000 and the steeple, Foster with the 10,000, and David Moorcroft the 1500. We got strong performances by Nyambui, Trevor Wright, Quarrie, and David Chettle. Henry was so relaxed, we played one day with international sports photographer Heinz Klutmeier, Henry hoisting the huge bazooka sized lens above his Nike modified-block T-shirt. I snapped pictures back at a smiling Henry.

On the final day of competition, Prince Phillip stirred the closing ceremony crowd with his words, "...And in four years, the athletes of the Commonwealth will join together again in the spirit of sport." I ran down to the men's restroom for a pee, and Brendan stood alongside me. "Quite moving," I said, "left me almost wanting to join."

Bren responded, "You had your chance and you blew it in 1776!" We zipped up and laughed on the way out.

In Beaverton, Strasser called a summit meeting on track and field promotions, bringing together Nelson Farris, Peter Thompson, Todd Miller, and me. Rob steered us through the expanding opportunities and by the end, we had our priorities. We'd never had an Olympic gold medal—that was our first priority. More world records was our second.

> By 1978, Nike sales worldwide were $50 million.

The next day, Rob and I met with what was becoming our future apparel group. Rob had brought in an outside design consultant, Diane Katz. It wasn't only her off-base approach—she knew nothing about sports—that left me nicknaming her "the Katzepillar." The only item I saw appropriate for my athletes was the rain suit, which was a derivative of my promotions design. Diane had no history with BRS, but took credit for the look.

In three days, my staff member Peter Thompson and I were flying to Madison, Wisconsin for NCAA cross country. We immediately ran into Burch's Bill Combs of Eugene who decided if Phil Knight can do it, he could too. Burch's was the top shoe store in Eugene, and Combs started his own brand, naming it Osaga. He put money into Dellinger's scoreboard at Hayward Field, which we had turned down. Bowerman was irate at his successor's decision. Now Combs was at the NCAA meet, sponsoring a breakfast for athletes in an attempt to draw attention to his poorly built training flats.

Peter and I spent the two days meeting our top athletes like Sulieman Nyambui and other UTEP teammates like James Roetich. We checked the course for the best camera positions. Nyambui was looking forward to running the Portland indoor and seeing Nelson again. "Oh, that Nelson—he is a very funny man!"

The Oregon runners came to our room for proper length spikes for the course and Rudy Chapa hinted he might wear the Vainqueur spikes Nike shoe designer Dan Norton had modified for a narrow width. I went out with Rudy's father, *Register-Guard* writer John Conrad, and Duck supporter Ed Sullivan. Three pitchers later, I joined Peter for the Nike-sponsored spaghetti feed. Out of 218 runners competing the next day, 198 attended. It was good public relations and allowed for a rare opportunity to speak to a wide audience. With that kind of attendance, we must have been doing something right.

Afterwards, I went out with professional photographer Steve Sutton and journalist Marc Bloom of New York for more pitchers of beer. We talked of the amount of travel we do and Peter and Todd put a wager down on Salazar versus Chapa for the next day. It was only the following morning that Steve Sutton informed me that Marc Bloom was almost under the table trying to keep up with us.

Race day! It's 19 degrees out with a 15 mph north wind and slight snowfall as Peter, Todd and I jog the course with American record holder in the marathon, Kim Merritt, and coach Dixon Farmer. Back at meet headquarters, I had brief chats with Rono and several coaches from Indiana's Sam Bell to Penn State's Harry Groves, whose programs wore Nike. On the course, the majority of the runners were stripping down with long-sleeved shirts under their singlets, tights under their shorts and various combinations of gloves and stocking caps to keep warm. I shot off to the restrooms quickly, only to find John Chaplin's Cougars, mostly comprised of Kenyans, huddled for warmth and not wanting to go out to race. A good sign for Oregon.

Rudy Chapa pulled out his Vainqueurs and laced them up. Alberto had not tried his. The gun went off. I was positioned down the course with my Nikormat. Peter held the Polavision camera as 200 plus sets of spikes made crunching sounds on the hard, icy surface. Nike would have six of the top 10 finishers, and Alberto won the wager for Peter as individual champion. Don Clary, who benefited from a solid summer Europe experience, ran a strong seventh, Rudy came in 14th, Ken Martin 22nd, but Bill McChesney's 52nd gave Oregon so many points that they were outrun by UTEP 56 to 72.

The day after Thanksgiving Peter and I were on the Athletics West charter bus to the Holiday Inn by SeaTac Airport, on our way to the AAU cross country championships in Seattle. We distributed invitations to our "Watering Hole" celebration following the race. I noticed Craig Virgin poring over an Adidas catalogue—he would race in their shoes the next day. As nine of us piled in a car, I took the Colorado Track Club to dinner and Virgin stories filled the air. Now that Craig was no longer with Nike, no one held back. It softened the blow of the switch.

On the race course, Peter took the movie camera, and I positioned myself with my Nikormat amid photographers from *Sports Illustrated, Track & Field News, Runner's World,* and local photographers. Our runners came to us for longer spikes to handle the rain soaked golf course amid tight, confusing turns. We were all positioned to capture the pack on film in a beautifully framed uphill amid huge conifer trees, when suddenly, the leaders ran right. Only a lone runner from Maccabi Track Club correctly ran the course even though he was shocked by the clicking and whirring of the high speed cameras. Meet director Bill Roe of the host Club Northwest sprinted across the grass, commanding his officials to redirect the leaders back to the 10,000 course line. Greg Meyer would eventually win in Nikes, despite being a New Balance guy. He was having problems with their shoes and wasn't about to compromise. Don Clary had another fine race with fourth, Larry Cazzort sixth, Dave Murphy seventh, and overall Nike had 22 of the top 30, representing a broad geographic distribution. It was simple—we were getting product out on time. If we don't get the product out on time, nothing else we do matters.

The team from Mason-Dixon won the event, but Nike won the marketing game. We packed the "Watering Hole," and the New Balance-sponsored Greater Boston TC struck up a chorus of "Geoff, he's a horse's ass." I grinned and deposited another round of drink tickets at their table. Yes, 1978 was a very good year.

But the year wasn't over yet. At the end of November, I met A.W. marathoners Lionel Ortega and Tony Sandoval at the San Francisco airport for a flight to Tokyo, then on to the Fukuoka Marathon. We had checked into the Grand Hotel where Gary Bjorklund was in the lobby. BJ, as he was known, said he "had been 'niced' to death for three days" and hoped we were prepared.

Somehow, the Tiger people had already heard I was coming. I went up, changed into my running gear and went out the front door with Bill Rodgers, Tom Fleming, BJ, Randy Thomas, Ortega, and Sandoval. I suggested that with that much talent, we hold the race now. Cameras were clicking but little did I know one was a Tiger photographer. Their promotions guys would review the photos, see who was wearing competing brands, then knock on their hotel door and encourage them to switch. BJ said they wouldn't leave him alone, and offered $3,000 to switch just for this race. Fleming said they didn't understand that Americans have their own deals. Outside of Rodgers, they weren't getting ·anywhere. Kikuchi, a staffer for our Japanese distributor, took BJ, Randy Thomas, the Flemings and me out that night, and over Kirins, I heard Randy and Tom's frustration with New Balance.

The next morning, Tony and I were out the door for a morning run before breakfast, when we ran into BJ. He said the Tiger people woke him up at 1 a.m. last night, bringing cookies and fruit. That afternoon was the press conference, an amazing show with Bill Rodgers, Leonid Moseyv from Russia, BJ, Seko and Sou from Japan, Trevor Wright from England and Olympic gold medalist Cierpinski from East Germany—truly an international field. Then all the runners were given a physical, followed by opening ceremonies. Each runner was treated as a Hollywood celebrity. The organizing committee had a band, musicians, singers, flowers, and gifts. Getting on the bus, the runners were showered with photographers, autograph seekers, handshakes, and cheers. One runner stared blankly ahead, "I've gotta run well now."

Back at the hotel, New Balance CEO Jim Davis introduced himself, along with the *Boston Globe's* Joe Concannon. Randy Thomas joined us and we had a few beers, and Davis was complimentary to the progress the upstart Nike had made. I had returned to my room when the phone rang. It was Kikuchi, "Your presence is requested at the bar." So after a few more beers with Kikuchi and Concannon, I was certain my morning run would be fueled by pure alcohol.

The next morning I ran by myself around Ohbori Park, where the water was like glass. It was cool. No wind. Perfect for a marathon. I passed the Russians as they returned to the hotel, they waved, and to Moseyv I said, "Good morning Leonid." As I looked over my shoulder, he looked over his with one of those "Who the hell is he?" looks.

In the hotel lobby Mr. Shibuya, a man high up in the Japan Amateur Athletic Federation, asked if he could buy some Elites. I told him it would be easier to just give them to him. He mentioned that the Vice President of JAAF had a strong dislike for Tiger and their tactics. He mentioned that following complaints from athletes in the hotel. Tiger was asked to leave. "I like your approach," he said. "Low key and efficient."

On the bus to the stadium, the runners were silent. You could feel the tension as the competition drew closer. We were all ushered into a small locker room, where the competitors had a close look at each other. In a room that size there was no escape. Once the officials announced that the runners could now warm up in the stadium, Jerome Drayton, dressed all in black and sporting his sunglasses, was the first to leave. He had avoided socializing all week. That's how he was—he was with Nike for years, and he never said a word to us.

The stands began to fill as a flag flew from each nation represented. The fans all waved paper flags with the Japanese rising sun, and this created a fluttering sound around the stadium as 107 runners stepped to the start. Forty-four had run under 2:20. As the gun went off, firecrackers exploded and pigeons filled the air. An excited Ortega went right to the front to lead the two laps around the track. I zipped back to the hotel with Kikuchi and his staff to watch the excellent race coverage unfold on national television. Sou pushed hard in the early stages, maintaining a 2:09 pace. At 20km, he had a 200-meter lead over a pack of BJ, Rodgers, Cierpinski, Seko, Australia's Chris Wardlaw, Wright, and Ortega. But by the turnaround point on the out and back course, where rivals can stare into their competitors' eyes on the return, Sou's lead dropped to 100 yards, with Wardlaw pushing Kita and Seko. Rodgers followed with Wright, Cierpinski faded, and Ortega was jogging holding his side. Thomas and Sandoval were moving up and picking runners off.

At 30km, Wardlaw looked so good I thought he was going to win it, but by the time we ran back to the stadium for the finish, Seko had kicked past Wardlaw, followed by Kita and a tiring Sou. Seko's 2:10:21 displayed his strength and Wright PR'd in fourth with 2:12:31, then came Rodgers and Moseyv. Wardlaw PR'd next in 2:13:02, followed by Thomas and BJ with a PR and 10th place in the 2:13's. Reflecting on what I had witnessed, I felt Peter and I could put on the first marathon to have 30 men under 2:20. It would become a goal.

A year later the 1979 Nike-OTC Marathon would be won by Athletics West's Anthony Sandoval and Jeff Wells in 2:10:20 on a loop course.

Sandoval had reduced his mileage with pre-med finals coming up and ran out of gas. Ortega suffered stomach cramps but recovered and picked off 40 runners on the way in. Moseyv, as if having found a new friend, shook my hand like a wrestler, bowing at the same time and taking me to the ground! He must have been pleased with his performance.

> A total of 46 men qualified for the 1980 Olympic Trials that day, and 39 of them ran under 2:20. We called it 'A gathering of eagles.'

At the awards, with everything Seko received, it was obvious the Japanese value being first above all else. All of us received gifts and "happy coats," which were a cross between a coat and a kimono. There were a lot of speeches from important dignitaries, drinking and more speeches until national teams were encouraged to go on stage and sing a song—Fleming, BJ, Ortega, Sandoval, Thomas, and Rodgers sang a sorry version of Jingle Bells, as Drayton ducked out of the hall before having to join Canada's Houghson and Maxwell on stage.

I flew to Tokyo then Honolulu, where I met my family, who had flown in from Oregon. Nelson and I picked up Don Kardong at the airport and took him to dinner.

The next morning Carol, Tracy, Kaili and I were having breakfast at the hotel and I saw what I thought might be a touring basketball team, all decked out in Nike. I went over to ask them who they were playing. They responded, "You mean, where are we playing?" It was Lionel Ritchie and the Commodores—oops! Looking back on it now I realize that Nike had crossed a threshold. We weren't just a sports company anymore—we were a fashion company.

I went to the Scaffs' house that evening for what always proved to be a wild event. Jack warned me that Wally Larsen and his Adidas staff would be there, as they contributed to the American Medical Joggers Association convention. Wally had worked a year for us, but I don't think he transferred anything from Nike to Adidas. These AMJA guys liked to get together to share information and fill the bathtub with ice and beer. There must have been eight from Adidas there, not one looking like a runner, all mesomorphs with identical 3-stripe outfits, mustaches trimmed at the lower corner of the lip. Identical clones—it was quite a contrast when we walked in.

The next day, Nelson and old Long Beach State buddy Chris Smith lined up a sailing trip for us, followed by a gathering of about 100 we sponsored at Mateo's Italian Restaurant. It was a great evening thanks to Nelson and Chris' planning. I toasted Jack Scaff for putting on the best organized marathon in the world and pledged that as with this year, we'd return a strong men's and women's field from the 1979 Nike-OTC Marathon.

I spent most of the morning working out details to our athlete's post race Maui trip, then popped by the AMJA Pasta Feed to see Adidas TRX ads as placemats (3000 of them). Adidas banners hung on the walls and round stick-on Adidas decals were at each seat. I took one, stuck it on my chest, and went around shaking hands with my friends. I didn't eat and instead took Nike athletes Marty Cooksey, Nina Kuscik, Don Kardong, Benji Durdan, Jack Fultz, and tri-athlete Dr. Kent Davenport to one of my favorite restaurants. With the sun setting over the masts of the inner harbor, we closed the day in the open air of the Chart House Restaurant, excited about race day and building a challenge to Adidas.

The next day, we took a group of eleven sailing on a magnificent 47' ketch. Those on board included the hilarious duo of Nike employees Pam Magee and Kenya Strader. When they said "We're going whaling," I nicknamed them the "Harpoon Sisters." Everyone was doing fine as the canvas was up and we were churning along through beautiful green-blue seas at 7 knots until Ron Wayne came up and whispered, "Where can I sit in case I vomit?" He was looking a little green and I suggested he was in the best spot, at the stern. I was the only one to know Ron's secret and started looking at him as Chris Smith started telling this story of sailing to Catalina once, "Eating greasy salami sandwiches in the cabin, smoking cigars and smelling diesel fumes." Halfway through the story, Ron went "Bllaahh!"

Race time in Honolulu was 6 a.m. in an attempt to reduce the heat from the sun that rose in your face over the Eastern Pacific waters. It would be Carol's first marathon, as it would be Nelson's, and they picked a tough one. Nelson's wife Sharon and I were baby-sitters and cheerleaders. A Japanese runner set the early pace, followed by our Nike guys. Adidas was out of it by the 5-mile mark. Our guys were gutsy—first Chuck Hattersley went after the leader, then Mike Pinocci ran with him through 10 miles.

At 17 miles, Nike runner Tom Wysocki had a 200 meter lead over a closing Kardong and Durden. Kardong would end up running away with Jack Foster's course record, as the Nike men took 8 of the top 10 spots. The Japanese had the other two, wearing Tiger. Patti Lyons ran a course record to lead our women to the top six spots. Nike

> Lyons followed up her 1978 win with a 2:40:07 first place finish among women in the 1979 Honolulu Marathon.

had its logo on the finishers' T-shirts and Adidas had their logo on the finish banner and chute pennants. The press was building up the rivalry, but after looking at the results, I concluded that Nike was in the shoe business, not the chute business.

But where was my wife? It was 10 a.m., and she had a goal of 3:30. Finally, through the crowd gingerly walked a sobbing woman who slightly resembled my wife. When I asked her how she felt, she responded, spitting out, "I hurt in places you don't even have!" Nelson finished too, and Peter Thompson's 2:50 gave me a helluva challenge for my first marathon, the Adidas Marathon in Eugene.

Kent Davenport watched the race from the pace car. Impressed with the Nike runners, Kent remarked, "Not only did they run tough, they're great people. We really enjoyed having them over."

Our Nike runners all met at Honolulu International at 7:30 for the flight to Maui. There, we rented six VW convertibles, and wove like a centipede through the cane fields to the Intercontinental Hotel, where Chris Smith had arranged 50% off on everything. This might not seem like a big deal, but with my small budget, it made a huge difference. Kardong and Lyons were recognized everywhere they went, treated as celebrities, and constantly stopped for pictures. We went for runs on the soft golf course to restore the legs, swam in the surf, soaked up the sun, and that evening had a celebration dinner for 22.

The second day was more of the same with Wysocki saying, "The way I've been treated, Adidas doesn't have a chance." Patti said Adidas had offered her $1,000 just to switch for the race. At Scaff's party they asked Pinocci what it would take to make him switch. He didn't answer.

The return trip to Eugene completed the year. Tracy was sitting on my lap in the dark on the plane. In the middle of a movie, he threw up all over me. Scrambling around in the dark, I found an attendant with soda water and started mopping up. In San Francisco our plane was grounded due to fog in Eugene. Instead we flew into Portland, took a bus to Eugene and a taxi to the "Hollister Hilton," where we arrived at 2 a.m.

Still reeking, but so glad to be home.

CHAPTER 17: WE ARE NOT ADIDAS

In the late '70s, Nike was doubling and even tripling its annual sales. We had a runaway horse on our hands, and naturally, that gave us some problems. My operation, Track & Field Promotions, based in Eugene, was in frequent conflict with Jim Moodhe's international effort, based in Beaverton. Moodhe had been with the company a long time, but he didn't come from the culture of running. Of all things, Moodhe had been a furniture repossessor before Nike hired him, and to be honest, I'd never gotten along with him. The division he headed up was what became Nike International Limited.

I spent most of 1979 on the road, going to what felt like every track meet on the planet. I continued to work directly with athletes, supporting their efforts to perform better. It was what Nike was about—at times, we had more confidence in the athletes than they had in themselves. Moodhe was in charge of working with our overseas distributors. These distributors were not Nike employees. They were independent business people with established companies. Most came from the world of sports, and some were already in the apparel business. They recognized Nike's phenomenal growth as a business opportunity, and they wanted in. Sometimes their agendas matched up with ours, and sometimes they didn't, but Moodhe was the guy who should have figured that out before he signed them up. When he didn't get it right, the fallout blew in my direction in the form of athletes unhappy with what they were getting from Nike.

Under the circumstances, conflicts were bound to happen. Some of the responsibility has to be laid at Knight's door. He's never been a micro-manager, and he gives his top people plenty of freedom. You could make some big things happen with that freedom, but you could also make some big mistakes.

1979 got off in a rush with Mike Tully, a world-class pole vaulter, paying us a visit. Tully was with Adidas and one they would hate to lose. He had surfer/boy-next-door good looks, and what he wanted from Nike was a better set of spikes. He had world record holder written all over him, and we were more than happy to put shoe designer Dan Norton on the job of designing a better product for Tully.

Tully broke the American Record in the pole vault three times in 1984, and took the Olympic silver medal in the Los Angeles Olympics that year. His PR is 5.85 meters (19-2).

Don Quarrie was packing his spikes for a training trip to Australia and competition in Melbourne where DQ would "shock a few people" when he stepped out on the track in Nike gear. He expected a call from Adidas within 24 hours and had his answer prepared.

What had started out as a David versus Goliath battle between Nike and Adidas was now something a little more evenly matched. Adidas was still the leader, but we were cutting a bigger and bigger slice into their market. Rumor was that Adidas promo man John Pennel was under pressure and might soon leave the company. He failed to get Tully back and couldn't believe that we could be so patient as to allow Tully to continue to wear 3-stripes until we got his Nikes right. "No company does that!"

Nike did.

I let Knight and his top lieutenants fight the battle with Adidas in the corporate conference rooms while I concentrated on winning over the athletes. In Eugene, Harry Johnson was excited as the stud walls and ceiling beams were in place for the new Athletics West Club House, complete with weight room, offices, massage room and lockers. With a facility like this we could attract the best.

I'd been after Bill Rodgers for years. Bill had already turned me down for every invite to the Nike-OTC Marathon. I knew it was largely for the lack of an appearance fee, but Bill always wrote a reply, "I always look forward to reading the results in Monday's paper, because so many runners P.R. at Nike." Bill had asked the organizers of that year's Schlitz Lite 10km to remove Randy Thomas from the field to insure him an easy victory, but he ran head-on into Nike's Ric Rojas and Gary Bjorklund, who went 1-2. Bill was going to have to resign to the fact that he couldn't win every race.

That letter was my only possible salvation as Jon Anderson called me, saying that Bowerman was in his office under the old east grandstands and was hot. "He thinks you only invite Nike athletes to participate."

With Rodger's letter in hand, I entered Bill's sanctum. "Well, the son-of-a-bitch just walked in!" he snorted to someone on the phone and hung up. Then he tore into me and gave no mercy. I shook a little, but I took it, then said, "Well Bill, you're wrong—here's something for you to read." And I left. It wasn't often you had the pleasure of shutting the Old Master down. Bill never brought the topic up again.

England's Brendan Foster flew into Eugene with the BBC's David Cox, a former member of Eric Burdon's band before they became The Animals. David was now a filmmaker and doing a documentary on Brendan. We drove up to the McKenzie River Trail for some running shots in the snow, then drove to Portland for a clinic. Afterwards we met Strasser at Northwest Pub and over several pitchers of beer, Rob jotted the details of a contract for Brendan on a cocktail napkin.

Back in Eugene, we had a great interview in the *Eugene Register-Guard,* where the presence of one of the world's most versatile distance runners was truly appreciated. Track was popular in Eugene, and the *Register-Guard* was an important part of that track-friendly atmosphere. I made it a point to maintain good relations with their writers. Their coverage of running in particular was the best in the U.S., rivaling the coverage that track got in the European press.

The Prefontaine Foundation ensures the upkeep of Pre's trail in Eugene's Alton Baker Park.

We went on to a clinic in the Atrium Building above The Athletic Department store which had over 100 attendees. The clinic was a benefit for the Prefontaine Foundation. By the end of the trip, Brendan was contemplating resigning his position as Director of Gateshead Health and Recreation so he could devote himself full-time to preparing for the Moscow Olympics and then move on to working part time for Nike.

Brendan had some "zingers" for the clinic crowd, contrasting England's volunteer coaching system to America's paid system. "You should dominate as you do in tennis and basketball, but does a coach spend time improving his methods, or improving his job retention? Athletics West is a step in the right direction and ten years ahead of anything we have in Britain."

Brendan moved on to another topic, one of our former Nike athletes. "Then there's Craig Virgin, who doesn't know whether he wants to be the best cross country runner, the best outdoor runner, or the best paid runner."

In mid-January, Carol and I left on a trip that would take us to Bermuda and Puerto Rico. I brought 26 Nike runners to Bermuda to compete in a 10k and a marathon event sponsored by Adidas. Larry Defreides worked out of Adidas' Libco sales office and was not happy to see our small army on the flight from Washington DC. The excitable Defreides railed at an official for coming up to me asking if they could borrow the two Chronomix's I carried. But he had no power over the attractive, fit Debbie Butterfield who met us at the airport and provided transportation to our lodging.

Debbie, a 2:38 PR marathoner, was the wife of Bermuda Olympian Jim Butterfield. She delivered Carol and me to a guest cottage overlooking the bay on the Butterfield Estate.

When you travel to Bermuda, you notice the Bank of Butterfield and the Butterfield Travel Agency. What you don't know is that they import most of the food supply into Bermuda. The Butterfields go back to 1670 on the island when they were part of the original Forty Thieves.

With all of the housing, meals, parties, and transportation the Butterfields coordinated through their mid-Atlantic A.C., I figured we saved $5,000.

Local Commonwealth Games marathoner Peter Lever organized a dinner for our group at the very homey Henry the VIII's Restaurant on the opposite side of the bay from where we were staying. When the local runners found that we were coming, we had a total of 70 sitting down for good beer, better food, and introductions of our runners. This kind of community building event was invaluable. One of the unique things about the sport of road running is that at an event like this, you combine the best in the sport with average fitness runners. Roger Bannister told me once, "Running breeds very nice people, and the more they run, the nicer they get."

Through Libco, their East Coast distributor, Adidas brought in 10 of their top runners, including Craig Virgin. At a most boring clinic, while they showed two long films, our guys got up to leave so they could race the 10k the next day. Race director Clive Long came up to me at another rather tedious Adidas-sponsored clinic, beaming ear-to-ear. "See what you did for our event by bringing all your top runners?" he said. "Last year Adidas did nothing. This year, registration jumped from 100 to 500."

The Adidas sponsored Mid-Atlantic Athletic Club was in heavy attendance at the event, and they were far more organized than the Bermuda Track & Field Association. Yet this federation was relying directly on the Adidas promotions crew. Their overweight staff wrestled with the infield finish line banner that kept blowing over in the constant wind. They were more concerned with getting their logo up everywhere they could than they were with putting on a great race.

I had decided I was in good enough shape to do more than just watch this race, so on race day I was at the starting line for the 10k, wearing my Nike Elites, ready to run with our team of Nike runners.

BJ pushed a hard early pace, but Virgin caught our pack at three miles and sprinted in for the win to the obnoxious howling of Larry Defreides. Our guys took 13 of the top 15 spots. Not far behind, in 25th and 26th were Joan Benoit and Julie Shea, who thanked me for my words of encouragement as they passed me before I came through in 33rd. I didn't even remember speaking, as the hills and the wind gusts up to 40mph made the run most difficult. But I thought 33rd was pretty good for a guy my age.

The next day was marathon day. Despite Joan Benoit downing her share of Heinekens the night before, there she was on the start line, "To do a 20-mile training run." Carol and I rode our moped down to Front Street in Hamilton, had a coffee, and waited for the leaders. To my surprise, world-class runner Ian Thompson ran by with a group of fellow Brits in Nike Elites. A relatively unknown 2:34 marathoner was in the pack— red hair and a green and white striped singlet distinguished Andy Holden, a dentist from London. He looked strong as Thompson faded and Ron Hill's 2:26 course record was shattered with Holden's 2:18.50 P.R. Adidas was stronger in this race, as our men finished 6th, 9th, 10th, 11th.

Thompson suddenly emerged as a world-class marathon runner in 1973, when he won the first marathon he entered in 2:12:40.

Most of our guys were using the race as a training run because the course was filled with hills and they knew they would fight a brutal wind the whole way.

A hairy, bearded, Exeter factory worker, Tom Derderian crossed the line with something unusual on his feet—a racing shoe with air soles.

Julie Shea finished 26th overall in 2:46.42 for a new women's course record. Joan Benoit passed the 20-mile training mark, and decided she had enough left to finish her first marathon in 2:50:54 for 22nd overall, as Adidas' finish banner blew down for the final count. Their young hotshot finish line timer failed to provide a back-up system, and when the clock stopped at 50th place, none of the locals got a time or recognition. Not a nice thing at all for someone who's worked that hard.

> A guy named Frank Rudy, a NASA engineer, developed an airbag that he thought would make an excellent midsole cushion. It took Nike designer Joe Skaja months to learn how to encapsulate it with a urethane midsole. The shoes Derderian wore in this race were prototypes for the first Tailwinds.

I had dinner that night with England's Malcolm East, the only Adidas runner besides Virgin who broke into the top 15 for the 10k. Malcolm wanted in the worst way to leave Adidas—his coach, Neil Cohen, was a good friend of Nike. Malcom had recently run a 1:05 half marathon against Randy Thomas. I knew he had a future, and we signed him a few weeks later.

At the awards ceremony that evening, Adidas banners hung everywhere. Adidas was on each trophy and each winner received an Adidas product. Virgin stepped up on stage, then came BJ and Mike Slack, wearing Nike "billboard" rain suits they borrowed from other Nike runners. All night, our runners kept coming up, accepting their trophies, and giving their merchandise prizes to their hosts. Some, like Patti Lyons, were approached by Adidas representatives. The war was on, and those guys had no shame. She told them to leave her alone.

After a stop in Washington DC, Carol and I flew to Ponce, Puerto Rico. Ponce was the closest airport to Cuomo, home of the San Blas Half Marathon. Our contact in Cuomo was Angel Matos, an entrepreneur who owned a shop that catered to runners. A Donny Osmond look-alike, Angel informed us that the field was loaded with the likes of Miruts Yifter, Joel Cheriyot, Samson Kimombwa, Craig Virgin, David Cannon, Mohammed Kedir, and Brian Maxwell. I was roasting in Angel's car as he drove us over the course. His parents' home was right on it and would provide a welcome bit of hospitality before and after the race. From 15-20 km, we climbed hill after hill. These were going to be tough in the heat and humidity. Spectators were already staking out their spots, constructing tents and barbeque-ing chicken and pork. I actually started thinking about running, despite my low mileage base and poor history of running in the heat. Hey, the race was going to be run on my birthday. Why not make it an experience to remember?

Angel took us to his little running shop, and despite having sold a lot of his Nikes and Bill Rodger's running gear during the week, he was quite proud of his nearly empty store. He seemed to know all the runners in Cuomo. He started the store on the confirmation of his first order from Nike, and then it was cancelled without notice. Because he was my contact, he became a victim of Jim Moodhe's attempts to have total control over foreign distribution of Nike goods. When he informed BRS of his predicament, Lisa Wilson from the Beaverton office stepped in and saw to it that Angel was shipped Elites, Waffle Trainers, and Roadrunners. He said he thought the world of Lisa Wilson but asked, "Who is this Jim Moodhe?"

On race day, we left Ponce at 9 a.m. for the 4 p.m. start. By 10 a.m., Cuomo was so jammed with traffic, we were at a standstill. We arrived at the Matos house by 11 a.m. and they open their doors with big smiles. Eighteen of us entered as they were busy roasting two turkeys, making potato salad, and cooking rice for after the race. They acted as though this was the biggest event of the year.

With Carol Cook, a top 10k runner, and Patti Lyons deciding to run, I brought my gear with the thought of running their race as far as I could. A motorcycle club was racing up and down the street on big Harleys, each decked out with at least 12 taillights. Radios were turned up loud with Latin beats. People were dancing in the street in middle of the afternoon. This place was wild! I had to run.

I handed my camera off to Nike employee Todd Miller who conned a ride on the press truck, and I headed to the school buses for a ride to the start. I was scared to death. As I moved to the back of the bus, it was standing room only. We piled out at the starting line in the middle of a country road surrounded with jungle-like vegetation. The sun made slits through the steamy atmosphere. Last year had 200 entries. This year had 646, due to good publicity and national television. Virgin, Yifter and the Kenyans were off the bus, but Rono was absent. John Chaplin informed me privately that Henry would not run if he was not fit. The press was told that he was stuck in a snowstorm. The press didn't buy it and hammered on Chaplin.

First-time runners attempted to crowd the front for a downhill start, not knowing how dense the crush would be. The gun went off and the pack broke loose on a dangerous winding downhill. I nearly tripped two or three times and watched a guy out of the corner of my eye to the right who bit the dust hard, running into a parked Harley and knocking it into a van. After about 300 yards, the crush thinned out and I was striding evenly without having to sidestep. I found myself alongside Carol Cook and Patti Lyons.

I immediately realized what this meant, especially in this macho culture. One, it was uncommon for women to race, so they were going to draw a lot of attention, and two, if they were in front of a man, that man was not worthy. On this day, many a man would fall to Carol and Patti. "Hey muchachas, muchachas!!" men yelled from the sidelines, pointing and waving. The race was a real bitch—85 degrees, high humidity, rough road surface and tough hills, but I tried to soak up energy from the crowd. On top of that, since I'd entered the race so late, I was given a leftover low race number, which should have gone to someone who was seeded in this race. That alone was like running with a target on my chest, and it made running behind two women all the worse. Despite not understanding Spanish, I think I was insulted into finishing.

After I crossed the line in one hour and twenty minutes, Herm Atkins, a top American marathoner, was the first person I recognized. Herm had run the race of his life, just 59 seconds back from the winner, Yifter. Charlie Virgil was 5th, Ted Castenada 8th, Dave Babaracki 12th, Jim Schankel 14th, Jim Johnson 15th, and Bob Hensley 16th. Of our international people, Medina of Venezuela was 3rd, Dave Cannon of England 4th, and Vargas of Puerto Rico 9th. Patti and Carol tied for first for the women and beat Cheriyot in the process. Kimombua dropped out and Virgin was 72nd!

Herm and I walked to the Matos home. What a breakthrough. His 1:05:51 was under the most difficult of conditions. We ate, drank, and took turns in the one shower before the awards that night. As we talked, Todd Miller shared with us the run he had with my wife Carol and Angel. They cut through a property, dust and chickens flying down a ravine and just as Carol stepped down, she realized her foot barely missed the belly of a sleeping pig. She hurdled that porker and it was the talk of the day.

At 4 a.m. the following morning, we were up and returning home from the tropics to Oregon in January, a truly different world. It had been quite a trip. BJ told me that the Bermuda event was better than the Olympics and Europe. Todd Miller said, "This is the first time I've met a lot of our runners. Not only do they compete, they're good people."

Tom Wysocki said, "Adidas offered us money. Nike offers us opportunity." That opportunity came from the Athletes' Assistance Program, which gave them the opportunity to compete at an event of their choice.

As much as I could get excited with our athletes' performances on the road, my return to the Nike home office in Beaverton was full of frustration. I came back to a meeting with the Katzepillar, Diane Katz. She brought something to the table I didn't have—a professional background in outerwear. There was a growing realization among Nike's top executives that we didn't have the skills to keep up with the company's rapid growth. If we were going to be more than a shoe company, if our apparel was catching on with the likes of Lionel Ritchie and Chuck Mangione, maybe it made sense to consult with someone from that side of the industry. It made sense to Strasser, who hired Katz, and it must have made sense to Knight, who had brought Strasser in to help take the reins of this runaway horse called Nike.

With Katz we reviewed a wider range of warm-ups for our athletes. Katz drew them up in line art, as if she were designing for a New York runway model. "Add a little piping here," she'd say "It's cute, you'll love it."

I can just imagine what Bowerman would have said to that, and it isn't fit to print in these pages. We had prototypes made, but when we priced the garments out, we found they were too expensive to make. But there was an issue here larger than piping, larger than the production costs of a new apparel line. We were businessmen, after all, and when the opportunity to expand presented itself, what were we supposed to do? Cut the horse off at the knees because our core business was so precious? So reaching out for some help was something we had to do.

But not at the price of giving up our core values. And that was the issue—we had to recognize who we were and why people outside the track world, the running world, were drawn to our products. Our heart and soul was the culture of running. What people were buying when they bought Nike products was an identification with our athletes. Why? Not because they were celebrities—we were half a decade away from the Michael Jordan phenomenon, and our athletes were unknown outside the sports pages and the runner's magazines. But our athletes projected an image of fitness, of achievement, of the benefits of hard physical training. Health and fitness were becoming a preoccupation for people everywhere. Maybe it was a reaction to the hedonistic aspects of the '60s and '70s, but whatever the motivation, there was something that felt good about wearing the same clothes that athletes wore.

Bowerman taught us to reach out to the Eugene community that supported his track teams. We showed them how to be runners, not because they would compete at the level of national or world record holders, but because it was healthy and it felt good. Nike was in a position to bring that feeling to an ever-growing number of people. What we needed to do was figure out how to accomplish that without losing our authenticity.

It was a big task, and it required a huge effort by everyone on our team. I'm glad I didn't have to do anything more than my part, because dealing with the Katzepillars of the world drove me bonkers. I'm a designer, and it's not a big stretch to say I have an art head on my shoulders when I need one, but I was having a lot more fun working directly with athletes and watching some of the greatest running performances the world had ever seen. I was anxious to get back out on the road to do what I did best. But before I could go, we had to deal with one more big design issue.

Strasser had brought in a friend to deal with our logo issues. Peter Moore taught art in college and definitely had an opinion: there should be only one logo. That logo was the swoosh, combined with the word Nike printed in simple block letters. Our patent and copyright attorney Tom Niebergall agreed. This flew in the face of my love, shared by Harry Johnson, for the swoosh sunburst and my freewheeling T-shirt designs.

You know who won that argument. As Nike grew, there was less and less room for non-standard business practices. Yet a company that shuts down the creative impulses of its employees is a company that ultimately will wither and die. It's Phil Knight's genius that found a way to strike a balance between these competing interests. That's why he gets the big bucks, and I'm grateful for that.

Without Knight, I wouldn't have traveled to all the amazing places I've been nor worked with the people I've known.

I came back from the Boston marathon to Nike's International Meeting at Timberline Lodge, and a confrontation with Jim Moodhe. We gathered in the Nimbus parking lot to carpool up to the meeting. Moodhe pulled up in the middle of the parking lot in a white Chrysler with a white tonneau top. The door opened, and Moodhe stepped out in white boots and a stretchy white skin-tight ski suit. Somehow we all managed not to laugh in his face. After all, he must have put a lot of thought into his entrance—this is me guys, and I'm ready for the big sales meeting.

At Timberline Lodge, Nelson Farris and I had dinner with Nike's distributor in the Netherlands, Michel Lukkein, and his group. Michel had been through a year so tough he was checked into the hospital for exhaustion. We sat in my room and talked through issues until 1:30 a.m. After that, I still had slides to prepare for the next day.

Moodhe had requested that Nelson, Magee and I present what had worked successfully in the U.S. We knew that the foreign distributors were quite aware and excited about our momentum. What we didn't know was that prior to our arrival, Moodhe had informed the audience that our presentation had no understanding of their needs or relevance to their regions. His program did.

As the meeting proceeded, various distributors started objecting and listing demands. They wanted one organized track and field promotional program. They wanted involvement by my Eugene staff, communication of athletes' international movement, distributors' active participation in future Olympic efforts, an athlete's winter training retreat, and quicker response time.

Moodhe confronted me privately with what a piss poor job we had done with the German marathoners in Boston. I told him that we needed to know more than that they were running. We needed their flight arrivals and hotels. Jim informed me that they were staying with Tom Fleming. I informed Jim that Tom Fleming lives in New Jersey, not Boston, and the debate was over.

I could see that Strasser had some decisions to make. At the end of the day, the distributors' wish list would become the blueprint for Nike sports marketing that still exists today.

I was all over the U.S. and Europe in 1979. I watched Malcolm East, now a Nike athlete, run a unique 10k at the Long Beach California Gran Prix, with the runners running the same course that the drivers would race as soon as the 10k was finished. New Balance spanked us good in the Boston Marathon with five in the top ten. I spent a lot of time getting to know Rudy Chapa and working with Dan Norton to get him a custom set of spikes to fit his narrow, A-width foot. The payoff was watching Rudy run in those spikes against Alberto Salazar at Hayward Field. Pre's parents, Ray and Elfriede, were there too, as Rudy and Alberto went head to head for 3000 meters. They had a ten-yard lead over the rest of the field by the first straightaway, Alberto's stiff low foot action contrasting Rudy's beautiful toe contact and high back kick. At the bell lap, Rudy accelerated behind the scoreboard and closed with a 56-second quarter for a new American Record of 7:37. Alberto followed in 7:43. As if riding on a cloud, Rudy floated into the stands and gave Ray and Elfriede a hug. A great tribute to Pre from a class act.

At the Revco Marathon in Cleveland, Ohio, I watched as a field of 10,000 came to the finish line. Once again, Adidas was in charge, and they had set up only two chutes. Finishers were backed up for a quarter mile, losing whole minutes off what might have been PR's for many of them.

Brendan Foster had kept after me to develop a solid working relationship with English promoter Andy Norman, saying that British distance runners owed more to Andy than they did to the BAAA board. It was never a case of me not wanting to work with him, but Norman had to overcome his initial disdain for American track and field. By July of 1979, Nike had impressed him to the point that Andy was prepared to fly fourteen of our athletes to Europe and back.

The NCAA's, track meets in Stockholm, Oslo, Helsinki, Moscow, Montreal, the Gateshead Games in England, the list goes on and on. I watched the best of the best compete, many of them in Nike shoes and apparel. I ran on a number of trails that Pre had told me about, the trails that inspired him to have the city of Eugene build a similar trail. I was ever mindful that I was running, however humbly, in his footsteps. But more than any of those wonderful events, 1979 was the year of Sebastian Coe.

In Oslo there was a knock on my door. Young Sebastian Coe was rooming next door and appeared when I opened the door wide. "Do you remember me?" Of course I did, and Seb mentioned that the U.K. distributor, Mike Tagg, supplied him with Nike shoes, but for apparel he'd been given a competing line called Viga. Seb said, "I'd like to wear Nike."

I told Seb that I agreed, but that I only had a Nike polo shirt and my own warm-ups to offer. They were used, but clean. "It should fit, and I apologize for the hole in the elbow." He was such a young and gifted talent that I would have given him the shirt off my back. I guess I came pretty close to that as it was.

Quite satisfied, Seb was on his way when I asked, "So what's your plan for tonight?" He was running in the 800 at Bislet Stadium.

"I intend to come through the first lap in 50.5 and hope to hold up on the final stretch." He said all this very calmly, confident of the task. After he left, I sat down and did the math.

That pace would put him in position to set a new world record. He knew exactly what he had to do, and he was ready to go out and do it.

At Bislet Stadium that night I loaded my Polavision film cartridge into a movie camera. The atmosphere was electric in anticipation of the night's competition. It had rained earlier, clearing the sky and seeming to fill the air with oxygen. The flags had dropped. Perfect conditions. Meet promoter Arne Haukvik, with microphone in hand on the grass infield, started whipping the 16,000 crowded closely in attendance into a frenzy. They had a lot to look forward to, and they went wild when Henry Rono and Rod Dixon toed the line for the 5000. Dixon won, but not before Rono had pushed him to the limit in the final 300 meters.

Local Knut Hjeltnes unleashed a powerful discus throw of 65m in his Mac Wilkins designed discus shoe, only to be overtaken by East German Wolfgang Schmidt's final throw. Kasheef Hassan sprinted to a 46.13 400 win in his Vainqueur spikes, Tanzanian Sulieman Nyambui won the 1500 in 3:38.6 , and little Gunvar Hilde, all 4'10" of her, ran a solid 2nd in the 800 after almost getting knocked flat on the second turn. She sprinted from next to last in the final bend.

Then the sun began to set, the lights were on, the crowd quieted as the 800 men's field toed the line and the starter's pistol broke the silence. Coe bolted like a race horse out of the gate and all 16,000 were on their feet, stomping and clapping in unison to Seb's stride. By the end of the back straight, Coe had 20 meters on American Evans White, England's Gary Cook and Kenya's Mike Boit.

Evans would say later that after going out so fast, he thought Coe would come back to him. At 5'9", Coe's stride appeared that of a man 6' tall, yet he never appeared to over stride, and his turnover was so quick. As he passed us, he hit the 400 in exactly 50.5 as predicted, then kept his form around turn three. I had chills knowing that the record was already his. Coming off the final turn his head seemed to lift as he tightened slightly, but he crossed the line in 1:42.33, a full second ahead of Juantorena's world record.

The crowd had not settled by the time of the infield awards, and Seb took the stand in my chocolate brown and caramel warm-up, complete with the hole in the elbow, as he raised his Nike Triumph spikes above his head.

After a brief talk with Seb, I returned to the hotel to call Strasser in Beaverton with the news. The prior year, with the exception of Rono's 3000 in Oslo, I was in a different city every time Henry broke a world record. Tonight was the second time I had witnessed a runner in Nike shoes break through to set a new world standard. "Rob, it's impossible to express—the greatest feeling in the world. Sex comes in a close second."

Rob said, "Sign him."

I took my seat at the finish line the next day in London with Steve Ovett and his mother Gay. Steve launched into a serious discussion with me, sharing his concern over our distributor Reliance and Mike Tagg in particular. The night before, Reliance had taken out full page ads in a London newspaper, *Athletics' Weekly,* and *British Track and Field News*. The banner "Thanks for the record Seb" was followed below with the Nike and Viga logos and "for more information, contact Mike Tagg" and a phone number. This, of course, was still the era of "shamateurism," and England was at the heart of the reluctance for change. The ad was absolutely tone deaf to the public's impression that runners were pure and unsullied in their amateur status.

In 1979, when this meeting took place, Ovett had already recorded the world's best time in the 2 mile (8:13:51) although it was at an event not recognized for record purposes. He'd beaten Henry Rono in that race, one of the only defeats Rono suffered during his remarkable string of setting four world records in 1978.

The general public had little knowledge of the current realities, but Tagg's exploitation flew well above the radar. It was direct and tasteless, and I could tell Ovett was concerned. I had spent four hours with Tagg the day before to cover the Nike-Viga issue with our elite athletes, and never once did he mention the upcoming ads. I was embarrassed.

But later that day, Ovett did something that lifted my spirits. I had watched him toy with the preliminary field the day before, coming off the final bend of the 1500 and running a diagonal to the tape from lane 1 to 8. This was to spite the BAAA Board who not only forced him to run in this meet against his wishes, but insisted that he run in the qualifying heats despite his obvious superiority over the field.

Steve and his coach had built the season's training around an 800 in Dublin and a mile in Oslo. The BAAA Championships were right in the middle and Steve did not enter. The board said if he failed to show, they would not issue travel visas for Dublin and Oslo. This was exactly the problem Pre had with Olan Cassell and the AAU.

Now came the moment I had been waiting for, to see Ovett in a final. Ovett ran conservatively, staying at the back of the pack until the final backstretch. I didn't hear a cannon go off, but his acceleration was like an explosion. As Ovett crossed the line, he gave the board the finger and pointed to the track. Pre would have liked this guy Ovett.

Shortly after, I was sitting on the plane from London to Oslo, and a banner headline in the sports section read, "Time to get on the Gravy Train." The article went into the BAAA investigation into Reliance's use of Sebastian Coe. Seb's father, mentor, and coach, Peter Coe, called the incident "A bloody stunt."

Nike's Norwegian distributor, Johan Kaggestad, met us at the airport and he was embarrassed and pissed. I knew exactly how he felt. He drove us to his farm, where he had converted an outbuilding into his office. He pulled out the new Reliance catalog that used the names of Seb Coe, Brendan Foster, Dennis Coates and John Davies in its advertising. As Johan took me on one of Arne Kvalheim's favorite trail runs, through the woods, he told me I was right, and I had to confront Tagg. Only the best dinner on the trip, served at the Kaggestad table with fresh vegetables from the garden, calmed me down. The following morning, I drafted a 10-point message that I would deliver to Tagg.

Seb and Peter Coe arrived at my room, and over the course of an hour, it was made clear that the Coes wished no contact with Tagg and Reliance. They didn't want to even receive a pair of shoes. From then on, all contact for Coe would go through Oregon. I felt we repaired a lot of damage, but thought if every international athlete's relationship was similar with their distributor, we'd be in trouble.

The conversation turned to the evening's mile, to be run within a few hours. Young Seb was calm and collected, very matter of fact about what he was about to do and his place in history—the first man to hold both the 800 and mile world records at the same time since Peter Snell. He had prepared himself for a long time with a steady purpose. This was his moment. He was all of 22.

The Coes left, and when Carol returned to the room, I called Tagg. She said she had never heard me be so frank: the advertisements were totally against Nike policy as outlined at the Timberline sales meeting. Reliance was not in line with Nike's low-key image. He had overtly exploited the athlete. The ads were an embarrassment to the Coes and Nike. He performed without the Coes'

Coe claimed his second world record later that night, turning in a 3:48:95 mile. Later that year he set the world record in the 1500 meters in Zurich, Switzerland—3:32:03 knowledge, and I demanded a letter of apology be sent from Reliance to the BAAA and Seb Coe.

There was silence on the other end of the line until, "But Adidas has used similar tactics."

"We are not fucking Adidas, Mike!" And I hung up.

CHAPTER 18: A SEA OF CHANGE, PART ONE

For Nike, phenomenal growth continued through the early '80s. For me, 1980 was another year of airplanes and track meets, and the constant travel was both a lot of fun and a lot of work. My long absences from home placed stresses on my family life that would come to a head in 1980. But I had a job to do, and I continued preparations for the 1980 Moscow Olympics. I did so under the cloud of President Jimmy Carter's threatened boycott. What the Russian occupation of Afghanistan had to do with the Olympics was beyond me.

In 1980, Nike sales were $269 million. By 1982, they reached $500 million.

Given Nike's growth pattern—doubling and tripling annual sales in the late '70s, and adding more and more employees to help carry the work load, a couple of things were probably inevitable. One, Nike was going public, and two, we weren't going to be able to solve all of our growth-related problems at once.

Nike went from around 800 employees in 1978 to 3600 employees in 1982.

The early '80s were watershed years for the whole sport of track and field, which was about to throw off the constraints of "shamateurism" and become a sport like any other, where a gifted athlete could make a living commensurate with his skills. Nike had a large part to play in that transition, and, as always, we would align ourselves with the athletes.

Early in the year, I was back in England, first visiting Sebastian Coe in Sheffield. I spent a lovely evening with the entire Coe family, all home for the holidays. I was right on the heels of

Kenny Moore's visit. Kenny was writing an article for *Sports Illustrated* on Seb's record setting summer and Peter Coe kept accidentally calling me "Kenny."

The next morning there was so much ice on the road, Seb and I scrubbed the morning run and walked carefully down the street a few blocks to the gym. There I witnessed the secret to Seb's success. The proof of his strength showed during a one-hour weight workout. This little guy could do straight leg repetitions with the pin positioned in the plate next to the bottom. Astounding. No wonder he could bound along with such a high knee lift.

A quick train ride from Sheffield to Newcastle, and Brendan Foster was waiting at the station. Bren took me out for a bastard of a 45-minute run in the cold, freezing rain. Then we warmed up over hot Indian curry at one of the Fosters' favorite restaurants. Bren expressed his interest in working for Nike after 1980 and living a few years in the States.

Filmmaker David Cox came over to Bren's house, thanked us for the Coe connection, as he was the only person to acquire any footage of Seb following his four world records. David had just received his second national award for sport documentary and expressed how much he would love to do a piece for Nike. I asked how much, and he replied, "For some people, I work for a bottle of wine." I've always felt that people were the most important part of Nike's business, and when you get that kind of response, you know you're doing something right.

Then I was off to London by train to meet Andy Norman and Steve Ovett. We were in the heart of London's antique row, and Steve looked with astonishment as I rummaged through boxes of old woodworking tools—chisels, hand planes and measuring tools. "These are beautiful—can't find them where I come from." I bought a bunch, much to Steve's amusement.

Andy Norman and his wife joined me at the Heathrow Holiday Inn, and then Henry Rono flew in from Kenya. The four of us met for lunch.

"Care for a beer, Henry?"

"No."

Good, I thought. He's focused, doesn't drink.

We were sitting there and I saw this guy walk by with a big diamond stud in his ear, "Henry. Know who that is? It's Elton John."

"Who's he?"

After lunch, I was waiting for the elevator and Elton John walked up to wait. I reached into my pocket and pulled out a business card, "You probably don't remember this, but in 1975, I built you some custom Nikes."

Elton looked at the card, "Yes, I do."

"Well, if you ever perform in Portland, Oregon, give us a call." We talked about his running and tennis and his soccer team, who were staying at the hotel. He was a sports nut and admitted he had to exercise to stay in shape. We didn't mention music once.

The following year, Elton John would perform in the Portland Coliseum. I was back in Europe, but he called the home office number anyway and was invited out. In exchange for concert tickets for our Nike staff, Elton and the band loaded their shopping carts at the promotions warehouse with $16,000 worth of product. When I heard this I said, "Oh shit! I'm losing my job!" Well, I didn't lose my job. That evening, in full Elton John plumage, he approached the piano and announced, "This first song I'd like to dedicate to all my good friends at Nike." At the same time, he raised one foot and put it atop the piano, sporting one of his new shoes from the warehouse. I've said more than once, "Now, wasn't that worth sixteen grand?"

Moments like that were fueling Nike's phenomenal growth. All we had to do was figure out how to turn a runaway horse into a race-ready thoroughbred.

Steve Cram challenged Steve Ovett and Sebastian Coe for supremacy in the middle distances in the '80's. McLeod won the silver medal in the 10,000 meters at the 1984 Olympics in LA. Cram won the silver at the same games in the 1500 meters.

I flew the London-L.A. portion of Andy Norman's flight to New Zealand with a group he had organized for winter training down under during their summer. It gave me plenty of time to speak with Mick McLeod and young Steve Cram, a quickly emerging teenage miler from Gateshead. In L.A. Strasser and Farris joined Andy and me in a "state of the sport" discussion. A shift towards professionalism was percolating under-neath the surface of track and field. Athletes wanted professionalism, but the federations were against it. The time to take a stand was coming.

In Eugene, the new walls were going up in our office suite, one more sign of our growth as a company. I had shown Strasser the new River Place office building earlier in the year and argued that this location would be more appropriate for our athletes to visit than our basement on Pearl Street. Strasser bought in and we signed the lease.

Runners were beginning to arrive for the International Cross Country Trials, and I was working the phone with the factories producing this year's Olympic T-shirts and warm-ups. I delegated John Gregorio to accommodate the athletes and rent a van for transportation. A few short years before it would have been me doing that job. Olan Cassell and The Athletics Congress (TAC) were doing nothing for their own event. Same old story—in order to preserve the illusion that track and field athletes were pure amateurs, unsullied by money, the organizations that put on these events left it up to each athlete to fend for themselves.

I predicted on race day that six Nike athletes would make the National Team. We would have seven. Boston's Dan Dillon would brazenly lead Craig Virgin by 20-30 meters around the duck pond at the midway point. As Craig scratched his way to

Brendan Foster and I run over the snow-covered McKenzie River Trail.

Tom Derderian—need I say more?

Wysocki and Schankel give me the runner-up Team Trophy at San Blas.

Geoff Hollister

The Nike Billboard and Sunburst designs on Dutch distance runner Jos Hermans and girlfriend Bebka.

Geoff Hollister

Ovett signs autographs for school children following his 1500 final at Crystal Palace.

Knight and I look at Sebastian Coe at a 1979 party in Building 19. Moodhe is going for the buffet chow in the black leather jacket.

Tinker Hatfield's illustration of "Don't slay the dragon in his own backyard."

Geoff Hollister

Tracy is ready for a bike ride.

Tinker's illustration of the "Hollister Hilton."

Tracy and Kaili in front of the "Hollister Hilton."

Steve Ovett on the track with manager and European meet promoter Andy Norman.

I assembled the highly talented group of Nike athletes for a team photo at the 1982 Commonwealth Games in Brisbane, Australia. Jamaican sprinter Donald Quarrie is sitting to my right in his USC maroon polo.

Joan Benoit flanks Betty Jo Springs early in the first U.S. Womens' Marathon Trials.

The best track and field promotions team ever assembled–1984 for the Los Angeles Olympic Games. Nike archives.

Al Joyner proudly displays his gold medal in the stands of the L.A. Coliseum.

the lead, Dan would hold a close second. Guy Arbogast, Mark Anderson, Jon Sinclair, Steve Placencia, Don Clary and Ken Martin would follow. Duncan MacDonald, who would make the team in Adidas, said afterwards, "I want back in Nike—get me a narrow shoe." We got him the shoes he wanted, and he was back in Nike in a couple of weeks.

I spent all day Sunday discarding old letterhead, business cards, and files as I boxed up for our impending office move. Every once in a while, I'd pause at something that had extra meaning or had consumed a lot of time—we had come a long way from 1976 to 1980. I took time out to watch the Super Bowl and was impressed with the success our man Bill Keller had putting Nike shoes on the big guys.

Nike in the Super Bowl—you gotta love it.

That following morning I flew to Columbia, South Carolina. I had placed an Olympic order for hats for our athletes, and the factory had not responded to my requests for updates. So I decided to show up unannounced. Somewhat embarrassed, they assured me they would be on time. During a tour of their factory, I didn't see any of my hats, but I did see Nike rain suits for retail in production to the tune of 600 dozen per week. That's a lot of rain suits, and it made me think that maybe the apparel division would someday pay for itself after all. The owners admired the new design I was wearing—the Windrunner, now a Nike apparel icon—and expressed interest in absorbing all the business we could give them.

In Bermuda that year, the Nike team took second through eighth place in the 10k behind Craig Virgin's first place finish for Adidas. I finished 40th out of

> *Nike sold $4.75 billion worth of apparel in the fiscal year 2006-2007.*
>
> *Andy Holden finished first, lowering his course record to 2:15:20, with Jim Dingwall finishing second at 2:18:14. Patty Lyons broke Julie Shea's course record with a 2:46:52 run.*

500 and beat my previous year's time by two seconds, despite the fact that I'd hoisted a few too many beers at the bar the night before. The Nike team finished 1-2 in the men's marathon, and Patty Lyons took the Women's honors for us.

We stopped in Washington DC on our way to the San Blas Half-Marathon. My sister Laura was now managing the DC Athletic Department store. Over dinner at her home, I met with Nike lobbyists Jay Edwards and Tom Carmody, as well as Jeff Darman and Phil Stewart of the *Running Times*. The lobbyists would be meeting with White House staffers within the week, and the message I wanted sent to President Carter was this: a boycott of the Olympics would be a major setback for amateur athletes who make huge sacrifices in order to train for the Olympics. If you take that rare opportunity away over politics that have nothing to do with sports, you can't expect them to just sit back and say 'Oh well.' A boycott was going to accelerate the open track and field movement. From my perspective this was a plus, although the damage to athletes training for the Olympics far outweighed it, but had the President considered this unintended consequence of his boycott?

> Nike runners Mark Anderson, Jim Schankel, Mike Layman, and Ted Castenada finished 3-4-5-6 in the 1980 San Blas Half Marathon, with five more runners in the top 20.

Back in Eugene, the world was marching on. It was becoming clear that Jimmy Carter's boycott of the Moscow Olympics was unstoppable. Nike was going to make a public stock offering. Track and field was inching toward professionalism. The plague of sports agents, something we hadn't had to deal with before, would soon be upon us.

I met with Rob Strasser and told him I was $50,000 over budget in 1979. Fortunately I had nine world records by our athletes to show him, as well as pages and pages of media reports and photos of their successes. With Nike's phenomenal growth, Rob had one answer for me—"Keep going."

I had become so swept up in all the change that my personal life was not keeping pace. I had no balance, and I made an abrupt decision. I was leaving my family. Carol had struggled with my travel and the commitment I had to the athletes and my job. I loved what I was doing so much, I didn't see a choice. When I informed Strasser he ensured I had an apartment close to the office. I had to tell my son Tracy, and I brought him up to my office over the Willamette River on a weekend when the office was empty. I explained that I was moving into an apartment nearby. At age seven, he looked up from under his blond mop of hair and asked, "Does that mean we won't ride bikes together anymore?"

Yes, we will, Tracy. Yes, we will.

A large number of our athletes had gotten word to Strasser how upset they were by the prospect of the boycott. Strasser responded—he made it his mission to pull every string he could think of to try and change Carter's policy. His best shot was former Portland Mayor and Oregon Governor Neil Goldschmidt, who had been appointed Carter's Secretary of Transportation. As mayor, Neil was the vision behind the Tom McCall Waterfront Park, development of the Pearl District, preservation of the historic downtown sector and construction of the Max light-rail system. And Goldschmidt happened to be a big track fan. I remembered sitting with him at the 1976 Olympic Trials, high in the east grandstands at Hayward Field as he watched in a white T-shirt and chewed on one of his cigars. With Neil, we had an 'in' with Carter's cabinet.

Strasser sent a delegation of athletes to meet with Carter's people. Not all were Nike athletes, since Strasser was more than shrewd enough to see that sending all Nike athletes would have sent the wrong message. This wasn't about Nike, it was about treating gifted athletes fairly. It was about not mixing politics with sports. The delegation proposed options to Carter's "no show" position. One was to compete, but not attend the award ceremonies—an excellent way to send a message to the Kremlin. All options were turned down. The U.S. stayed away from the Moscow Olympics, and the Russians stayed in Afghanistan. Worse, the Soviet Union returned the favor by leading a boycott of the 1984 Olympics in Los Angeles. Carter's policy didn't change a single mind in the Kremlin, and American athletes suffered because of it.

There was one bright note that came from Strasser's efforts. The delegation he assembled included Jane Frederick, the American record holder for women in the decathlon. Jane Frederick was so impressed with our gesture that she left Adidas and joined Athletics West.

One provision in Carter's boycott also eliminated American corporate involvement. If an American employee was caught promoting his product within the USSR during the period of the games, that employee could face prison time. In a meeting with Strasser, it was decided that we would not take the risk.

We had two options. If we trusted the Nike distributor in a country, we sent them one large shipment for dispersal to our athletes. If we didn't, we sent shipments to the individual athletes' homes. Early preparation of sizes and addresses were key. We would have to speed up production for our international athletes. Then there was the issue of loss or potential theft of competition shoes prior to any athlete's competition.

A back-up plan was hatched. We would ask key athletes to hand carry into Moscow a Nike "body bag" full of back-up spikes. These would go to guys like Foster, Coe, Ovett, and Quarrie. We then notified our athletes worldwide of their personal shipments and which athletes would be in possession of the back-up shoes in the Athletes' Village. "Project Trojan" was born.

"Project Trojan" worked like clockwork. Our athletes got their gear, not one athlete was lost to the competition, and we were never in Moscow.

As BRS moved closer to going public with its Nike stock offering, a couple of facts became obvious. First, Phil Knight understood that he had a brand. The corporation would be changed from BRS, Inc. to Nike, Inc. Second, some people were about to become rich. Knight had always risked everything and deserved to be rewarded. Over the years, others, like Bob Woodell's parents, risked their family savings as debenture holders. The Woodells took that risk as a thank you to Phil for the opportunity afforded their son. You had to be happy for them. Contrast that with another debenture holder, Abe Johnson, who walked into the Nike Eugene store and crowed to the staff, most of whom were making a little something above minimum wage. "I'm going to be a millionaire," he said, "six and a half times over." I told Phil, "I don't care if this asshole never returns."

Knight recognized that certain individuals had made significant contributions to Nike's success, and decided to reward them accordingly. Jeff Johnson, Bob Woodell, Harry Carsh, Del Hayes and Ron Nelson were choices that I respected because I admired their work. They had been responsible for overseeing large chunks of the Nike business, and they had done so skillfully and with integrity. They immediately became millionaires, and the value of their stock would only go up from there.

The final choice, I took issue with. Jim Moodhe, whom I had multiple battles with, apparently pleaded with Knight to be included, and Knight relented. Like Abe Johnson, Moodhe was intolerable with his new-found wealth. For personal transportation, Knight had always driven what could best be described as "a wreck." When associates suggested he drive something more becoming a corporate CEO, he splurged and purchased a Porsche 924, perhaps the first new car he ever owned. Moodhe went out and bought a new Porsche 928. He started wearing white suits, and telling everybody he was going to retire to the south of France. He'd always had a big ego, and this just made him impossible to deal with.

If Moodhe had done a better job at Nike, I might not have cared that he made the list of instant millionaires. His one contribution to the business was a program called "Futures." If a Nike retailer could predict what they wanted to order in a particular shoe model six months in advance, our Japanese trading company, Nissho-iwai, would treat it as a sale and finance the production as though we had cash in the bank. This helped our forecasting and eased our tight relationship with the Portland banks. "Futures" became a reliable barometer of growth. A pretty neat deal all the way around.

But Moodhe locked Nike into a number of contracts with foreign distributors that caused us a lot of grief. Once we made the jump into the sportswear business, we found we were saddled with distributors who had competing lines of apparel of their own. Our carefully nurtured relationships with athletes suffered, because the athletes wanted to wear Nike head to toe, and our foreign distributors insisted on giving them outerwear made by other manufacturers to go with their Nike shoes. Several of the distributors he signed deals with were flat out incompetent. In countries with good distributors, like Norway and the Netherlands, the distributors wanted the products, programs, and sports marketing coordination I had developed in the U.S. Moodhe repeatedly got in the way. From back room conversations to sales meeting speeches, he stabbed us in the back whenever he could.

Farris, Gorman, Magee and I were left out when Nike went public. I have no quarrel with that—I understood Phil's position and accepted it. Looking back on it now, I see that most of the people who got the big money left the company within a few short years. Moodhe was gone first, fired, but Jeff Johnson, our first employee, was the first to leave on his own. The more the company grew, the less it felt like the place where those people loved to work when they started.

What I got was another twenty years of working with athletes I admired, traveling the globe, working alongside thousands of

Nike teammates around the world. I'd have made a terrible retired person, and I wouldn't trade those last twenty years at Nike away.

Someone—I suspect it was Phil—did tell Moodhe that he would have to take a small portion of his stock and divide it evenly among the four of us. At the 1980 First International Sales Meeting Moodhe told me, "I did that purely out of the kindness of my own heart."

There he was, next to a 6-foot-tall margarita fountain, a man without color. He was dressed all in black—black leather jacket, black shirt, black slacks, black boots. Bald, goateed, the top two buttons on his polyester shirt open, he gave me the most sincere, picking-up-sticks-is-just-my-job-so-don't-take-it-personally-look a former repo man could muster.

"What heart?" I said.

At that same International Sales Meeting, Rob Strasser took me aside. He reviewed the points that the foreign distributors had made at the meeting the previous year at Timberline Lodge. "Geoff, I want you to write all this down," he said. "We'll get it out to our distributors as a blueprint."

I thought about Rob's assignment and the difficulty of communicating something that seemed almost personal. As Pam Magee said, "Promotions is an extension of our own personalities." Rob wanted a chronology of events, and I could do that. But how do we reach beyond that? I thought of a young Oregon athlete who had graduated in architecture and whose graphic skills had impressed me, especially with a pencil rendering he had completed as a tribute to Pre. I hired Tinker Hatfield to illustrate the book for $1,500. That was his first job at Nike.

What would become "The Nike International Promotions Handbook" was filled with facts and explanations, and punctuated with Tinker's drawings. For my explanation of Bowerman's message, "Don't try to slay the dragon in his own backyard," he drew a small sword-wielding soldier with Nike running shorts and shoes and a shield in front of a large dragon, wrapped in three stripes. Tinker's architectural skill captured my home in Eugene with a "Hollister Hilton" sign on the street. The handbook would guide our distributors through the "how's and why's" with patience. It would identify where our philosophy came from, like Bowerman's preference not to recruit. He preferred the athlete who came to him.

At the end, I felt a warning was necessary, and I wrote:

Let's assume you have been a total success: you have surpassed your short-range goals, exceeded your long-range goals, and slain the dragon. What do you do now? And what does the consumer think of you? Are you now the dragon in their eyes? Are you perceived as just another obese corporation, making lots of money, not listening, not caring, not promoting anymore? Could it be possible to come so far, go full circle, and have to start all over again? Look at yourself. Being number one does not have to be so ugly. Try the following:

- *Maintain a sense of humor.*
- *Know when to back off when pressures get to you.*
- *Keep listening and caring.*
- *Don't ever forget your basic operating principles.*
- *Don't quit promoting.*
- *Strive always to put something back into the sport.*

Separately, I drafted a letter to Knight, Woodell and Strasser, saying that we had been very lucky so far with the band of "rag tags" we had hired. Somehow, we managed to survive in spite of our mistakes. My message was simple. Hire better people and make it a priority.

Two months of living alone proved to be a hollow freedom. As much as my love of work consumed me, sleeping on a mattress on the bedroom floor, eating mostly out of heated up cans of food, and the occasional bike ride with Tracy on the trail beside the Willamette River did not match the warm environment at home. I returned to the "Hollister Hilton."

Not long after, Rob Strasser told me he wanted me to move to Amsterdam. Nelson Farris was already living in Europe, and Strasser had been living there. Rob wanted me to drop everything, leave my family, and get my butt over there right now to work with Nelson. I was in Strasser's office, and I don't mind telling you that "Rolling Thunder" didn't get his nickname for nothing. He could be pretty intimidating, and he knew it, and he wasn't above using that intimidation to get what he wanted.

Strasser wasn't used to hearing the word "no," but I had to say it to him. I just couldn't leave my family again. I had two young kids and a wife who wanted me back home. There was a lot of hurt between us, and if I was going to save my marriage, I didn't have a choice.

Strasser was so mad he picked up a book, a big heavy leather- bound book, and hurled it as hard as he could at me. I ducked, and the book hit the wall behind me. I'm pretty sure it left a sizeable dent.

Another shock was the removal of Harry Johnson as coach and administrator of Athletics West. Harry had been my pick, and with the success of all the distance runners, especially the marathoners, who could do it better? Nobody worked harder. Caught by surprise, I saw it as a classic "a few rotten apples spoiled the barrel." Craig Virgin was gone, and despite his continued success, his teammates saw his departure as an improvement. Why was Harry being held accountable for that loss? I had warned Strasser about adding Paul Geis because I didn't trust him, but because Paul had married the daughter of a Nike debenture holder, my concern was overruled. Henry Marsh caused problems by asking Bowerman to coach him, a violation of Athletics West's club procedures, and on top of that he tried to use Bowerman to get his contract sweetened.

At least Strasser recognized Harry's strengths and asked him to move to Beaverton to head up the Cleated Division. With Harry's work ethic, knowledge and skill as a coach, he would become a strong mentor to future Nike standouts like Dave Taylor, Bill Keller, Bill Freshette, Bob Wood, Peter Rupe and Ralph Greene. Cleated Division was in good hands.

Two more smart personnel moves came when Nike hired Tinker Hatfield and Peter Moore, the college professor who had advised us to stick to a single version of the swoosh. No two people would have a greater influence on the graphic impact of Nike's signature logo.

With Jimmy Carter's ban on any American corporate involvement in the Moscow Olympics, I couldn't even watch the Games on TV. I had to rely on newspaper accounts of what, for me, was the most memorable event of the entire Olympiad.

All through the run-up to the 1980 Olympics, Steve Ovett and Sebastian Coe had carefully avoided running in the same races. They were both medal contenders in the middle distances, and both wore Nike. It was a dream match-up.

I had watched Ovett train in Illinois earlier in the year. He was running the turns with both arms out in front, his forearms parallel to the track and his fingertips touching. Not an easy thing to do at sub-4 pace. When I asked him why, he explained that in competition, if he got boxed in, he could use the space his arms made to avoid getting tangled with the runner in front of him. Ovett always sought every advantage and tried to anticipate every contingency.

The two first went head to head in the finals of the 800. Coe still held the world record and was favored to win, but a strategic error cost him the race. He waited too long to make his move and got caught in traffic, and it was Ovett who thundered down the final straight in front of Coe for the first-ever Olympic gold Medal in Nike shoes. Fittingly, Ovett had provided valuable feed-back to the Exeter team for the design of those Zoom Distance spikes. Coe picked up the silver.

They met again in the finals for the 1500, but now the bets were on Ovett to take the gold medal again. Coe had spent the months before the Olympics nursing a pulled hamstring, avoiding Ovett and training in Italy. Even though Coe's loss in the 800 was due to a tactical error as much as Ovett's speed, the pressure was on Coe. With Ovett's string of 41 straight 1500-meter victories on the line, Seb now had to gather himself, find confidence and run at the peak of his ability. He found himself free and flying on the final turn, Ovett on his shoulder. Looking over and swinging wide, Coe held Ovett, unleashed a punishing kick to catch the leader, East Germany's Jürgen Straub, and then ran out of gas. The expression of anxiety on Coe's face at the finish said it all. If anyone would have come to him at that moment, the gold would have been theirs. No one did, and the gold was Coe's.

Further back in the pack was a young English 19-year-old to be reckoned with in the future. The tall presence who finished eighth on this day was young Steve Cram.

CHAPTER 19: A SEA OF CHANGE, PART TWO

President Jimmy Carter left office in January of 1981 following his loss to Ronald Reagan. Transportation Secretary Neil Goldschmidt was out of a job as well, but his subsequent job search was brief. He had close friends at Nike, like Bob Woodell and Dave Kottkamp, who had been his city manager in Portland. Not long after Nike hired Goldschmidt to head up Nike International, my phone rang in Eugene. With absolute confidence, Neil Goldschmidt said, "You're coming to work for me and moving to Beaverton."

After turning Strasser down and having the literal book thrown at me, I decided I better accept the offer.

Soon after, there was a shareholders meeting in Beaverton. Jeff Johnson and I were standing in the back. Goldschmidt was standing behind us writing on the back of a small business card. Phil quickly dispensed with the old business, moved to the new business, and announced, "With great pleasure, I am introducing the new Vice President of Nike International." Neil stepped up to the podium, worked the room with his eyes, and delivered a machine gun speech filled with expectation and goals in faraway places. Johnson looked at me following a thunderous applause and said, "We just watched him write that thing on a business card."

In private conversations later, Goldschmidt discussed my salary and job responsibilities. With Nelson Farris and Strasser responsible for promotions in Europe, I would cover the rest of the world out of Beaverton. Sticking points for me were the sale of my old house in Eugene and the salary. Eugene was in a recession with a big dip in the timber industry. Over 2000 homes in Eugene/Springfield were on the market. Men were leaving and seeking employment in the Texas oilfields. Selling our home looked bleak. The salary increase I was offered was a fairly standard percentage and I argued for double, with the provision that I would not get a pay raise for two years after that. Goldschmidt agreed to the deal. I would later learn that Knight was not pleased.

But there were firings in the early '80s as well. Nike's offices were housed in Building 19 of the Nimbus Business Park at that time, and most of Building 19 was a big open space—no cubicles, no half walls, just a lot of desks in rows. In 1981 word spread quickly through that room—Moodhe had been fired. Despite our differences, I was surprised. It's never been my way to wish ill upon other people. Still, I couldn't keep myself from asking, "Did anybody 'key' his 928 on the way out?"

At the same time, I had a firestorm brewing in Eugene with Bowerman. Nike's U.S. road racing budget was under me, and Nike had decided it was time to issue a challenge to the status quo of the sport. With Strasser and Knight's approval, Nike provided the financial backing for the Cascade Runoff, managed by Portland attorney Chuck Galford. We planned to present the top runners with a check, above the table, and based on place. Olan Cassell of TAC was furious, and sent his attorney Alvin Chriss to argue for a change. Galford and Nike would not bend, and the line had been drawn in the sand. The brave toed the line under the watchful eye of the TAC. Nike-OTC was scheduled to follow The

The Athletic Congress (TAC) was the body that governed amateur track and field in the U.S. after the break up of the AAU, which Cassell also headed. At this time, there was a fledgling organization of professional track and field athletes called the International Track Association (ITA), and this was headed up by Michael O'Hara.

Cascade Run-Off in its September time slot and would be the first marathon to offer a Gran Prix system for the competitors. The Oregon Track Club Board was so nervous about accepting a payment schedule that they had us remove OTC remove from the name of this year's event. TAC threatened the competitors by invoking the Contamination Rule—any runner competing in our event, then competing in a subsequent event, contaminates the whole field. Alvin Chriss flew to Eugene to argue the point with me. In addition, he claimed we had to be sanctioned, meaning that every participant had to be a card-carrying member. "Alvin, do you really think a 4-hour marathoner gives a shit if he or she carries a TAC card? What are you giving them in return? What are you giving us for signing them up?"

"Okay then, I'll fly back out and sign them up myself."

Then Bowerman called. He was livid, "God damn it, I taught you to bend the rules, not break them!" I informed him that the runners, including one of his favorites, Jon Anderson, were committed to running for cash, no matter what Olan Cassell said or did.

Chriss scrambled, and between long distance meetings and back door meetings around the country, he cobbled together a face-saving plan. Through the Bank of Boulder, a trust was devised where monies earned from competition would be placed in full into an account in the athlete's name. The athlete then could withdraw funds for "legitimate training expenses." It became obvious that Cassell would not scrutinize the transactions that carefully. Perhaps he had finally seen the handwriting on the wall.

The trust fund not only created a solution under the watchful eye of the International Amateur Athletic Federation, but Cassell and Chriss would steal the maverick concept and establish the Mobil Gran Prix for Track and Field, with Mobil Oil as the sponsor. The IAAF would quickly follow with a Gran Prix schedule of selected meets in Europe. The sport was changing quickly. Pre would have been proud.

However, if Pre were alive, would he have been a member of O'Hara's ITA? They were now struggling with a limited event format and far fewer athletes. They had some marquee names like Ryun, Wottle, Keino, Seagren and Stones, but the Mobil Gran Prix proved a powerful competitor.

Now crippled, ITA competitors were exploring reinstatement in TAC. ITA high jumper Dwight Stones had additional issues. In the shady dealings of "shamateurism," an athlete could successfully hide taxable income, as the meet promoters would contend that compensation did not exist. O'Hara's books were more open. In any case, the Internal Revenue Service claimed that Stones failed to claim income and took him to court for delinquent taxes.

In October 1981, Alberto Salazar, having just graduated from the University of Oregon, returned to New York City for the NYC Marathon, this time representing Athletics West. As I watched the press conference, I remembered back to the previous year when the young and inexperienced Salazar was asked by a reporter, "What do you expect to run?"

The dark eyes of Salazar looked seriously at the questioner as he responded, "2:09." He drew laughs from the supposedly knowledgeable press, but they failed to recognize Alberto's many miles of track experience with Chapa under the watchful eye of Dellinger. But more than that, they underestimated the fire that burns within this Cuban-born competitor. The last laugh was on them, as Alberto won in 2:09:41.

This year, the same press came armed with expectations, and they had also been covering the movement and change within the sport. It was understandable that Fred Lebow, organizer of the New York City Marathon, was not prepared to follow suit so closely with Nike-OTC and offer a Gran Prix finish schedule. Lebow already had commitments, the way he had in previous events. It was painful to see Alberto face the reporter's question, "I heard you've been paid $50,000 to run in New York—any comment?"

Knowing how religious Al is, it had to be hard for him to sit there and deny it, to protect both himself and Lebow. Al responded, "Whatever the amount is, my agent will deposit it in my trust account." I could only hope this would be the last such conflict with New York.

With my move north to Beaverton, there would be a lot of change. John Gregorio would head the U.S. sports marketing effort. Goldschmidt was having a large building next to the Greenwood Inn renovated for Nike International's Headquarters. Carol and I spent days looking for a new home, finally settling on an old bungalow above the Willamette River in Lake Oswego. With Salazar's incredible 2:08:13 in New York, Nike athletes held every men's world best from the 800 on up. Salazar had given us the cherry on top that made Nike synonymous with excellence in running.

Someone at Nike came up with a way to solve two problems at once. Alberto's contract was being renegotiated after his win in New York, and Nike included our Eugene home as part of his compensation. Alberto and Molly Salazar, the former Molly Morton, would move out of their apartment in Eugene and start a family in the home that I was desperate to sell so I could move my family to Beaverton. Talk about a win-win situation—this was it.

Prior to leaving for Beaverton I hired former Oregon sprinter Don Coleman. Don would join the already competent staff now under John Gregorio of Athletics West: steeple-chaser Ron Addison, Mikki Gehlhar, Carolyn Brown, and our three full-time shippers Glenn Owen, Scott Krause and Chris Haun.

What do you do when Nike runners hold all the middle and long distance world records? You go after the sprints. Don Coleman brought the highly talented Carl Lewis into Nike. Don knew Carl personally because they had been relay teammates and roommates on prior tours. Once again it was the personal connection between a Nike employee and an athlete that made the deal happen. Don Quarrie had been one of our few world-class sprinters up to that point, and his most recent accomplishment was bringing the bronze medal for the 200 home to Jamaica from Moscow. But the addition of Carl Lewis gave Nike a big credibility boost in the sprints.

With the Eugene house sold to Alberto Salazar, I felt comfortable now turning my attention to Asia and Latin America. Goldschmidt was hiring talented young people in International. They were multilingual, and many had lived overseas. Neil often joined me for a light jog down Allen Boulevard before lunch. Despite a bad knee, Neil was making the effort to keep his weight under control.

A kind of reserved guy joined us in our runs. Bill Hall had worked for Evergreen, an aviation contractor out of nearby McMinnville. It was well known that one of their clients was the CIA. I heard that Bill's father was in the State Department in Washington DC and that Bill grew up living in far away places like Pakistan. The fact that Bill didn't talk about his experiences left us filling in the blanks. Rumors circulated that Bill himself was former CIA, but if you said that to his face, he'd dismiss it with a laugh.

Somehow, I must have gained Bill Hall's confidence. Perhaps it was the fact that I was coached by Bowerman, because one day Bill confided in me that he was a nephew of the Bowermans, and his mother was Jane Bowerman Hall, one of Bill Bowerman's two half-sisters. When Bowerman called for the Marines at the U.S. Olympic compound in Munich, that phone call was placed to Bill Hall's father.

I didn't know it at the time, but Bill Hall himself would one day make a decision that would greatly affect my life.

A telex was delivered to me soon after moving into my Nike International Limited (NIL) office. It was from the office of

Coca-Cola Brazil. They were sponsoring a talented 17-year-old 800 runner who had run 1:47. Would we be interested in equipping him with Nike product? I requested sizes and then spoke with Nike attorney Kevin Brown. We decided to add a stop on our impending South America trip and meet this young Joaquim Cruz.

In Mexico City, I followed up with an acquaintance I had made at a meet in California. Tadeusz Kepka had left Poland around the Mexico Olympics, married in Mexico, raised a family and become the Mexican National coach. Mexico now had some of the world's top race walkers and a few good marathoners.

Tadeusz showed me his facilities in the smog-choked air of the high city, and then drove me out to their secret, forested trails that attracted world-class runners from around the globe. This is where gold medalists from Eastern bloc countries came for high altitude training. Trails were named after them.

When we returned to the Kepka home, his wife and daughters were busy in the kitchen wrapping Mexican delights in banana leaves to be baked. Tadeusz broke out the tequila before dinner. We downed a few shots, and Kepka told me about a couple of very promising race walkers training with him—Ernesto Canto and Raul Gonzalez. We talked about the possibility of Nike support for his athletes. Maybe it was the tequila, but there was a warm glow between us that I thought boded well for the future.

From Mexico City, we flew to Caracas where we met our distributor, one of Moodhe's acquisitions, a former baseball great who owned a small sports shop filled with just about everything but Nike. It wasn't a long meeting. He couldn't speak English, and we were stuck with him due to the contract that Moodhe had signed, even though he was useless to us.

We were informed by Coca-Cola that Joaquim would be competing in a meet outside Caracas. His competition was "El

Caballo," Cuban double gold medalist Alberto Juantorena. We learned that the location was a few hours drive away in a country we knew nothing about. Somehow, we had an offer from a man who had a jeep. He would drive us out and back for a fee, and off we went.

It seemed over two hours by the time we arrived at the small stadium. I pulled out the large body bag filled with gear for the young Brazilian. Inside the stadium, Agberto Guimares recognized me. He had run the 800 for BYU, his English was excellent, and he pulled us over. We met Carlos Alberto Lanceta, Chief of the Brazilian Delegation, but I would learn later that it was Luiz de Oliveira who coached a younger Cruz in basketball, discovered he had running talent, and then started coaching him in a new sport.

Joaquim Cruz was the quiet but imposing 6'3" boy in tattered old gray cotton sweats who joined us next. He had a quick smile but no English. We shook hands, and I handed him the bag. He was quite surprised, but I told Agberto to let him know he didn't have to wear anything now. He needed to get ready to race.

Cruz took off with a loping easy stride. On the other side of the track was the even taller figure of "El Caballo." I was already excited well before the gun went off, fully expecting the Cuban to drag the young Brazilian around the track for a P.R. To my surprise, Cruz tucked in comfortably behind Juantorena, matching stride for stride through the first lap and on through the third turn of the second lap. Then, just as Bowerman coached us, Cruz showed great tactics and burst past the Cuban on the back stretch. Extending his stride length with an uncharacteristic upper body lean, he looked slightly back going into the turn and sped to the tape. He had broken Juantorena.

Afterwards, Cruz returned to us in the stands with a broad smile, the air filled with cheers. Carlos, Agberto, and Joaquim communicated in Portuguese as Cruz now returned to the big bag and unzipped it. Inside was our full Olympic package—three or four pairs of training shoes, two pair of spikes, a rainsuit, a warm-up suit, several T-shirts, running shorts, and a small travel bag. Joaquim stared at it all in disbelief. His gray warm-ups were ragged and full of holes, and I could tell this kid came from real poverty, probably worse than anything there is in the US.

"All for me?" he asked through Agberto.

I nodded my head and said "Si." The wide grin he gave me was something I will never forget.

We continued on to Buenos Aires, and I was stunned with how gray and drab the buildings were, almost lifeless. Then we met our Argentine distributor, Mancini, another failed effort by Moodhe. Mancini's only connection to sport was as a member of the local tennis club. He had a son who was a promising player. Mancini himself was in the dumpster business and showed a quick temper if you disagreed with him. I immediately thought of the mafia and decided I didn't want to end up in one of his dumpsters.

From Buenos Aires, we were off to Sao Paulo to meet with a potential manufacturer who was building a new factory and receiving all new machinery for his lines. Well connected, he got us into the locker room of the Sao Paulo football club. When he heard that I had a son who played the game, he had the staff present me with a jersey to give to Tracy. Nike meant nothing at the time to the world's most popular sport, but that would change, and especially here in Brazil.

Back home on the Willamette River, the old bungalow Carol and I bought became the site for occasional Nike meetings. In nice weather, we'd sit out on the lawn, overlooking the river. We knew that Mary Decker and Alberto Salazar had acquired an agent, or should I say the agent acquired them. This was a sure sign, and not a welcome one, that the age of "shamateurism" was coming to an end. Agents are in business for the money, and while their entry into track and field signaled that the athletes were worth pursuing, they could be a royal pain in the ass to deal with. Up to this point, Nike's deals with our athletes were handshake deals, typically done in a bar. Strasser was notorious for jotting a few notes down on a cocktail napkin and then going back to his office to type up a very simply worded contract. Our athletes trusted Nike enough to do business this way, and that trust was a precious thing. The step into professional sport meant that never again would a handshake be enough.

Mary and Alberto's agent was Drew Mears, a young lawyer who worked for IMG. At Nike, we saw two sets of contracts—IMG's, and Alberto and Mary's. But something was amiss, because the numbers didn't match. Someone was getting the difference. It wasn't Nike, and it wasn't Alberto or Mary.

I don't know if Mearns thought we wouldn't notice the discrepancy, but one of our riverside meetings was interrupted with a phone call from Mearns. He was in town and wanted to meet with me immediately. I told him it would have to be at the house.

Mearns drove up, left his wife in the car and walked over to join us. He started right in talking, and I let him. From the way he talked, he probably didn't know I was aware of the discrepancy in Mary and Al's contracts. He went on for a while and I just let him talk. Finally, I took him aside and let him know we had discovered the difference in the contracts. He returned to his rental car, drove off, and I never saw Drew Mearns again.

Although I wouldn't see Mearns again, it wasn't the end of IMG. One of their agents, whose background was working with hockey players, called to say "We have a $100,000 offer on the table from Adidas for Sebastian Coe. The Coes consider you as family and hope you will match." I was stunned and immediately called Peter Coe who denied any IMG contract other than their original attempt at the Coe-Ovett mile series.

I then went to Strasser and Knight. I told them that I believed IMG was bluffing and if they were not, we should let Coe go. I followed with, "Look, I've spoken at some length with Edwin Moses, he's been undefeated for years, and is the highest paid athlete in the sport at $40,000. Edwin would like to go with Nike."

I was serious about letting Coe go and argued, "If you do it for Coe, then you have to be fair to Ovett, Salazar, and Decker." As much as I objected, Knight showed why he is the master at sports marketing. The guy you rarely saw, he surveyed the playing field, knew how much money he was holding and how much to bet for a return on investment. Years later it would be Michael Jordan and Tiger Woods. But now it was Sebastian Coe, and Knight authorized the $100,000 contract. "The Golden Swooshes" were born.

Too rich for my blood. I was more excited about the young Brazilian, Cruz. From the day I watched Seb's weight workout, I thought the only runner who could beat him would have to have the same turnover, but be much taller with a longer stride length. Could that be Joaquim? I learned later that when Cruz won the World Juniors in Italy, Adidas approached him prior to the race with cash to wear their shoes. It was tempting for a young man so poor that he caught bugs around his home in Brazil, fried them in a skillet, and ate them for protein. He met a Nike European representative and there was no financial match, only a "Your time will come." Joaquim could only look back and remember the guy who brought the big bag to the meet outside Caracas. It was a leap of faith.

The phone rang, and I heard broken but improved English on the other end, "Geoff, it's Luiz. Luiz de Oliveira. We are in Provo, Utah. I have Joaquim and a few other athletes. Joaquim is studying English to take his entrance exams for BYU. But, we have a problem. Joaquim is hurt and not running well—a lot of pain. Do you know a good doctor?"

I told Luis that the best orthopedist for runners is a good friend of mine in Eugene. Luis said they would fly to Eugene to meet with Stan James. It didn't take long for Stan to diagnose the problem. Joaquim had a 2cm leg discrepancy, creating a pelvic tilt when he ran. Stan believed that adding that much to his shoe would correct the problem. We immediately went to Bob Newland in Bowerman's downtown shoe lab for the correction to Joaquim's training flats.

The weather was quite pleasant during the Brazilians' visit to Eugene. Luis added, "The snow in Provo is above our heads as we run on the roads. The ground is covered. We are not allowed to drink coffee. Joaquim doesn't drink coffee anyway, but, no Coke, and he's been sponsored by Coca-Cola!" And Luis laughed, "I like Eugene."

After returning to Provo, Luis called again. He explained that he and the athletes had talked and decided that they wanted to move to Eugene. I told Luis that entry to Oregon would be no different than BYU. A potential student would have to have enough English comprehension to pass the entrance exams. But the Brazilians were on their way.

CHAPTER 20: TO SEOUL,
OR NOT TO SEOUL

In 1981, with the IOC selection of Seoul as host for the 1988 summer games, Korea immediately became a focus for Nike International strategy. We already had influence in South Korea with our footwear production and a reasonably aggressive retail plan. I had never been to Korea, but it wasn't long before I was off to Seoul for my first exploratory trip.

Arriving in Seoul, it did not take long to identify a significant difference between the general mannerisms of the Korean people and the Japanese, with whom I had some experience. The Japanese rarely display their emotion. Angry or happy, the Japanese face reveals no reaction. Koreans were quick to laugh and if provoked, just as quick to almost get in a fight with you if they disagreed. Whereas you came out of a meeting with the Japanese saying, "I wonder how they took it?" you knew where you stood with the Koreans. I found I liked the latter.

To help me find my way, I relied on a young Nike Korean hire by the name of Chris Cho. Chris and his sister Susan went to school at Beaverton High School at the suggestion of their parents, who were well connected to Korean politics. I soon began to think everyone in Korea is politically connected. Politics is taken seriously, and an early observation in 1981 was the changing attitude of the younger generation. Young Koreans were aggressively seeking a new identity and a break from the norm. A high percentage of Koreans lived in apartments rather than stand alone homes. When you traveled the roads, you noticed that you got your choice of an automobile, as long as it was black. If you had money, you did not show it.

Chris Cho opened a few doors on my first visit that gave me some insight as to a potential plan for 1988. In addition, I was happy to reconnect with Harry Johnson and Neal Lauridsen in Pusan. Harry's long-time knowledge of track and field provided a quick read. Lauridsen, who in a white tux could pass for Roger Moore's 007 portrayal, had a broad experience of Asian culture and had helpful suggestions. Neither indicated it would be easy.

On the flight home, I sketched out some simple thoughts—how Nike might provide a unique partnership with Korea to prepare them for hosting the 1988 games. It would require a strategy that our competitors would be hard pressed to match. It would also be outside the capability of IMG, who was now eyeing marketing opportunities at the IOC level. Basically, Nike would have to utilize its extensive network of athletes, coaches, and the sports medicine community to bring the Korean sports program out of cultural isolation. To avoid total embarrassment, Korean athletes would need to compete at their highest possible level in front of the home crowd.

The problem of Korean cultural isolation was exemplified by the organizers of the first Seoul marathon, and their misguided translation of "sponge station." The lead pack approached the first sponge station, anticipating a water soaked sponge to run over their head and down their face to remove the salt from their eyes. To their surprise, they hit their head with a gooey, sticky mess crumpling and oozing down their forehead. Precisely laid out on baking sheets was row after row of sponge cake.

The big event for 1982 would be the Commonwealth Games in Brisbane, and Brisbane would be at the front end of a five-week Asia swing for me. To commemorate the Games, I designed a T-shirt for our athletes, sporting a kangaroo whose tail extended into a Nike swoosh. This was just the sort of thing that drove our patent attorney Tom Niebergall nuts. Tom's concern was that we would not be able to defend our trademark in court unless we restricted ourselves to a single recognizable version. But I couldn't resist the kangaroo design, and the fact is, Nike has had no issues in this area.

The athlete gear was shipped in advance, leaving only the T-shirts sitting at the airport. I took one of our vans to pick them up. In the process of moving a heavy box over a seat with minimal headroom, I felt my back go. I could hardly move. We had rented a couple of homes for our staff and Don Steen, a former teammate of Phil Knight and father of Dave Steen, Canada's promising decathlete. Somehow I managed to pull up to our house—a quaint tin-roofed home sitting on stilts, and surrounded with lush vegetation filled with chattering exotic birds. Don, Nelson Farris and Bill McIntosh started unloading the boxes. I told Bruce Palmer I could hardly move. Bruce went to work on me immediately, massaging my back and trying to loosen me up. It was going to be a long week.

A highlight of the week was watching Don and Dave Steen. Dave was named after his uncle, one of Bowerman's NCAA shot put champions. Dave was good looking, gregarious and talented, And you could see a father's pride on Don's face. Dave Steen would go on to win the decathlon, one of 18 Nike gold medals compared to Adidas' 12.

The surge in Nike athlete competitiveness did not go unnoticed. I was sitting in the upper rows of the Commonwealth Stadium one day with the Kenyans, led by Mike Boit, and the Tanzanians, led by Gidemas Shihanga. Sitting several rows in front of us, with no spectators in-between, was a slimy Australian athletics promoter named Murray Plant. Plant and the man sitting next to him turned, and Plant pointed with his finger, saying "That's him!" I looked left and right before realizing the finger was pointing at me. Donald Quarrie would later identify the other man as

Mike Boit won a bronze medal in the 1500 at the 1982 Commonwealth Games. Gidemas Shihanga won gold in the 10,000.

Dieter Weiss, Adidas' Head of International Promotions. I felt like I was on some kind of hit list. Adidas was tied to all the important federations, had full accreditation at events, and survived well with cash payments in an amateur world. They could make life miserable for you and we had obviously caught their attention.

The 1982 International season closed with a few surprises. Young Steve Cram, who raced as a teenager in the Moscow 1500 final, won the Commonwealth gold in the same event, and he was now becoming a contender with countrymen Ovett and Coe. Countryman David Moorcroft experimented and moved up to the 5000, and lowered Rono's world record to 13:00.41 in Oslo. He followed with a Commonwealth gold in the same distance.

In 1983, the IAAF held the first World Championships in Athletics in Helsinki. My good friend Jaakko Tuominen was ecstatic, as the world was coming to his city and stadium. We went to work immediately on our plans. Jaakko had been captain of the Finnish Olympic team, was well connected with the Finnish Athletics Federation, was meet promoter for the World Games and now worked for Stockmans, our Nike distributor in Finland. Helsinki would prove to be a good test for our upcoming efforts in Los Angeles.

Just as I had done in Eugene, I made Jaakko's house the nerve center of the Nike effort. Jaakko and Kati Tuominen would make their home available for our staff meetings, product inventory and nightly celebrations following the competition. In addition, Jaakko's brother owned The Captain's Table, an incredible restaurant on an island in the middle of Helsinki's harbor.

Things got off to a bang with the arrival of the Chinese team. Their top entry was the new world record holder in the men's high jump, Zhu Jianhua. Nike had signed the Chinese

Athletics Federation, and Nike footwear developer Rick Lower accompanied them. When the Chinese arrived at Jaakko's and saw all the product lined up in the yard in large boxes, they dove into each box, extracting two or three of this, and more of that. Our international diplomacy was tested as Rick and I tried to communicate, "One each for each athlete."

It must have worked. We still sponsor the Chinese team.

Our athletes got off to an impressive start, when relative unknown Marianne Dickerson from the state of Illinois ran the race of her life in the women's marathon. Coached by John Goodridge, she finished second to Grete Waitz in 2:31:09.

Perhaps the tequila with Tadeous Kepka paid off, as Mexico's Ernesto Canto won the 10km racewalk in custom racing flats, built at Nike's Exeter factory. Carl Lewis again put his speed on display, powering to a 10.06 gold medal in the 100. Young Joaquim Cruz proved that he was no longer a junior, dropping his 800 time to 1:44.27 for the bronze. He would have another 12 months of hardening and sharpening under Luiz de Oliveira prior to the 1984 Los Angeles Olympic Games.

But not all went well. While Italy's Alberto Cova unleashed a startling kick on the homestretch of the 10,000, propelling him from 5th to 1st, Alberto Salazar struggled in last place, 48 seconds behind. I rode on the bus with Salazar back to the village. His eyes burned, he was so upset he could barely get a word out, but he uttered, "I didn't work hard enough, I didn't work hard enough!"

I told Al, "No. You worked too hard. You need a break. Take a month off."

When I saw Al's wife, Molly, I reiterated what I had told Al. She said it wouldn't be easy to hold him to it. Later, Molly told me Al took two weeks off, then began training for Los Angeles.

That night at Jaakko's, the Nike staff gathered to celebrate Cova's victory. Food, beer and wine fueled the party. England's John Caine stood on a chair to get everyone's attention, lifted his glass on high to toast Cova, and promptly fell through the woven wicker chair seat to the floor. Jaakko never had the seat repaired. Instead, he had it framed, and kept it as a memento of a great victory.

Carl Lewis continued to roll, leading Nike athletes Jason Grimes and Mike Conley in a sweep of the long jump. Mary Decker controlled the 3000 for the gold, then Lewis returned to anchor the Americans to gold in the 4x100 relay. For Lewis, that was three events entered and three gold medals won. Carol Lewis, his sister, added to the family medal count with a bronze in the women's long jump.

On break day, several of us went out with England's Steve Cram for a game of putt and run on a public golf course. Each carrying a driver, a wedge and a putter, we'd run between each stroke to where our ball lay. "Crammy" proved to be not only one of the world's fastest runners, but a good golfer as well.

That night we gathered at The Captain's Table for a truly unique evening. First off, you arrive there via a small ferry that motored out to the island. The building itself is made of stone, the weather was perfect that evening, and the midsummer sun was high enough in the sky that it never really got dark. The restaurant itself is a series of rooms, and with the stone walls it felt like we were in a magical cavern. There is so much pressure on the athletes at these events. Anything we could do to give our Nike athletes a break from that pressure was a plus, and it often paid off with outstanding performances coming after the break day.

Mary Decker doubled back with a gutsy 1500 performance, outlasting a dive at the tape by Russia's Zamira Zajtseva for a second gold. To finish off a great competition for our Nike athletes, Steve Cram led a tactical 1500 over Steve Scott, Said Aouita, Steve Ovett and Jose Abascal.

Jaakko was pleased, but promised me, "In Los Angeles, Arto Bryggare and Tina Lilak will be wearing Nike. We will get better. Trust me."

> *Arto Bryggare took the bronze medal in the 110 hurdles at the Los Angeles Olympics. Tina Lilak took the silver medal in the women's javelin.*

Jaakko was prophetic. Far from Helsinki was Seoul. I had some strong recommendations to present to the proper people. At Nike headquarters, I proposed an exchange of information and talent prior to the Seoul Olympics. We should bring our best people to Korea and create opportunities for their athletes and coaches to train and learn outside their own country. To coordinate all this, it was proposed that I would move to Seoul.

Before we could move forward, we would first have to come to an agreement with the sport federation. You learn quickly that Korea is very political—politics, corporate conglomerates, and the military are all fused together.

Chris Cho had introduced me to a most interesting character. Dr. Kong was a gray haired, enthusiastic, quick-to-laugh Korean guru of fitness. It might have been a stretch to call him their Bowerman, but he seemed to have a sense of the issues, and he had the respect of the Vice Minister of Sport, Young Ho Lee. Kong provided an introduction to Lee, who graduated from the University of Georgia. His English was excellent, and he was a skilled politician. He listened carefully to what I had to say, but he gave no immediate indication of acceptance. I could only hope that dealing with the Korean government would not parallel my Moscow experience. Lee strongly recommended that I received input from others.

Chris began arranging meetings. I met with the Minister of Defense, Mr. Yoon. An old friend of Chris' father, Yoon had considerable control over Korea's future in sports. I learned that there is a mandatory draft in Korea, and all men are eligible at age 18. The various branches have sports teams and they compete against other countries' military teams. Yoon was most interested in education, testing, and invitations for his runners.

We went to the Olympic training center, where you saw a disparity in their programs. The Koreans seemed skilled at boxing, wrestling, and volleyball. They had a great interest in baseball and basketball, but track and field appeared to be a weak spot.

I had already met with Kwan Soo Hur. Kwan Soo's family owns the Lucky Group, a giant conglomerate that manufactures everything, including Goldstar Electronics and Nike shoes. For a different perspective, Chris arranged a meeting with the head of Hyundai. Hyundai was not yet known for their automobiles, but was already one of the largest manufacturers of container ships and supertankers in the world. Here I received a lesson in the competitiveness of the Koreans, who had an eye on Japan's success and beyond. To a man like Kwan Soo, the Seoul Olympics was all about Korean pride.

I felt that I was now armed with enough information that I could draft an acceptable presentation. In addition, Carol was flown over and we had toured possible schools for the kids and choices of homes to lease. We seemed to be on our way, but when we returned to Oregon, Strasser called me in.

I met with Strasser and Knight at the Beaverton headquarters. Knight questioned why we were rushing to 1988 when we still had 1984 in front of us. I responded that Seoul was far more complicated. Rob said to me that the problem in the U.S. was more immediate. Since my hiring of Don Coleman, Don had become the target of racial remarks from within his own office—the same office I used to manage—and the Track and Field Department was in disarray. Mikki Gehlhar moved over to Athletics West. Tom Sturak had been elevated from master's coordinator to overseeing both the men's and women's programs from Beaverton. In an attempt to monitor and control the men's program, John Gregorio and staff were moved to Beaverton. Strasser was disappointed in the improvement.

There had been a shake up in my absence. Strasser informed me that Gregorio was gone and that the same would happen to Sturak for not controlling the situation. I argued that Tom may not have been the best manager, but he was an excellent editor and we should keep him onboard for projects like *Running* magazine. Rob didn't agree—he'd made up his mind, "We're bringing you and Nelson back to run the L.A. effort." I was stunned and couldn't speak. As I approached the door to leave, "Rolling Thunder" put a big hand on my shoulder and looked down. "Hollister, it's going to be okay. Hey, we're going to have a lot of fun with L.A." That big hand was a lot better than a book hurled in my direction, but Strasser left me feeling unnerved. I've always known that his primary motivation was to get all of us to perform at our best, but sometimes his methods made me uncomfortable.

Still, we had made inroads into the Seoul '88 effort, and I was allowed to go back to push the ball forward a bit more. Nike would come up with someone who would continue what I had started. Knight had not committed to a dollar amount, but it seemed appropriate to at least open a dialogue, so I was on my way to Korea to solicit feedback on some ideas. It was arranged that I would speak to a group of Korean movers and shakers about Nike's ideas for the Seoul Olympics.

Young Ho Lee sat in the back of the room as I stepped forward to the podium after being introduced. My words were being translated into Korean, so it wasn't comfortable. I shared my observations with suggestions for assistance. First, Nike had just produced a complete series of track and field International tapes with top Oregon athletes like Salazar and Wilkins, and we would ensure translation into Korean and make these available. Second, Nike would bring its best coaches and doctors in sports medicine to Seoul for a seminar. Third, Nike would recommend an athlete and coaches exchange—ours would come to Korea and theirs would go to the U.S. for extended training periods. Four, Nike would provide its best products to the Korean National Team. And five, Nike would provide international competitive opportunities at competitions like Nike-OTC and the Prefontaine Classic.

The less supportive stood up and walked out, right past a smiling Young Ho Lee, who later said, "I like your ideas." But this was very different from dealing with the Japanese, who never would have tipped their hands by leaving.

Lee not only sent athletes to train in Eugene and compete in the marathon, he himself made the trip to observe. He and Kong set a date for the medical seminar. I felt like we were almost there, and we didn't even have a budget.

Knight and Strasser wanted to know what we were going to get out of all this. At the top of the list for Knight was visibility in 1988. Strasser felt 1988 should be a retail opportunity. I felt we could have both, but in Korea more than perhaps any other country other than Russia, the government would be in control of many of the decisions. The government had a lot to say about its sports programs, and I felt that this was the strategy to pursue. If we wanted traction for our Seoul '88 goals, we needed to build relationships through the government-controlled Korean sports structures. We weren't just buying our way in, which anyone else could attempt. We were going to show our commitment by starting early and staying.

The medical seminar was scheduled at the Sheraton Walker Hotel in Seoul. I was accompanied by my replacement for the Seoul Olympics project, Ian Campbell. Ian was Australian and had competed at Washington State against Don Coleman. An outstanding triple jumper and sprinter, Campbell was jumping well in the 1980 Olympic final. To his dismay, large doors in Lenin Stadium were opened when the Russian and East German jumped, admitting a tailwind down the runway. When Campbell approached for his jumps, those doors were closed.

Ian got a quick education in what it was like to shadow the master. Carol drove me to the airport and upon arrival, I realized I didn't have my passport. Carol and I raced back to the house while I told Ian to board. We raced back with passport in hand and I flew through the airport. Arriving at the gate five minutes late, the crew was waiting for me and closed the plane door behind me. I settled into my seat next to Campbell and rolled my eyes, still shaken from such a stupid mistake. Ian showed he could bullshit with the best of them. "I told the pilot, 'You need to hold the plane,'" he said, in his best Aussie accent. "There is a 'Voey oey poey' that must be on this flight." At the moment, I didn't feel like a V.I.P.

If there was a V.I.P. within Nike, it was Knight. But always reluctant to show his cards, Knight kept you guessing. He was making his own trips to Seoul and using his own contacts to learn how to deal with the Koreans. Upon arrival at the Sheraton Walker, I found that we had a meeting scheduled with an expert on Asian affairs by the name of Richard Holbrook. Knight called me at the last minute and said he had a change of plans, "You go." I immediately thought, "What the hell am I going to ask Richard Holbrook?" Knight was traveling in very different circles from the ones I traveled in.

Holbrook would go on to become an effective international adviser and negotiator for President Clinton and Secretary of State Madeline Albright.

Knight wasn't my only problem. Chris Cho informed me that the legendary New Zealand distance coach Arthur Lydiard had packed his bags and was returning to Auckland before the seminar even started. He claimed that the Korean Amateur Athletic Federation reneged on his guaranteed honorarium. I followed up and asked some pointed questions of the officials. They claimed a misunderstanding, and that Lydiard would be paid. I asked for a guarantee and got it from a man I trusted, Young Ho Lee.

It was early morning when I rang Lydiard's room. I had only met Arthur once before and knew he wouldn't remember me, so I used Bowerman's name and informed him that I had run for Bill. "Will you join me for breakfast Arthur?" He accepted, but he was still hot and didn't have the kindest words for the Koreans. Much like Bowerman, Lydiard was a very direct man and wasted little time. I asked, "If I could guarantee your honorarium, would you accept it?" Quite taken aback, Arthur responded, "That's quite kind of you Geoff. Most thoughtful. Okay, I'll speak and then get the hell out of this bloody damn place and back to Auckland where I belong."

I offered to give Arthur a ride in my car to the seminar, and we talked the whole way about mutual acquaintances. "You know," Arthur said, "Prefontaine should have won the 5000 in Munich. I counted the number of laps he ran in lane 2 and 3. He ran a much longer distance than Viren, who ran most of the race in lane 1!"

If only.

CHAPTER 21: I LOVE L.A.

I never really did love L.A.—from attempting to run in the smog to not seeing the hills surrounding the City of Angels for months while I was in the Navy. A city of excess. A city of nothing. Yeah, if you had the money, you were safe, most of the time. But Los Angeles was the chosen site for the 1984 Olympics, and Nelson and I would have to be there. The Athletic Congress followed the IOC's lead and decided it would be a benefit to hold the U.S. trials in the Los Angeles Coliseum, so we were going twice.

Strasser loved the challenge and the obstacles, and his approach was as big as he was. Strasser once said, "Anything worth doing is worth doing to excess," and Rob was himself an example of certain excesses. Strasser was also a master of what Woodell called "running for daylight." When it was announced that Converse was an official sponsor of the Olympics, what might have been our best option was off the table. We had to come up with a new approach. How could we own the games and the city of L.A. without being a sponsor?

By now, Strasser had Peter Moore working full time. It was quite a show, with plenty of theatrics—name calling, throwing whatever was handy, and walking out of meetings. But along with all the theatrics they embraced each other with big bodacious thoughts. Peter Moore did his design work in a room with music on all the time, and Nike's "City Campaign" was hatched from the lyrics of Randy Newman's "I Love L.A."

I was already working on the athlete's package, as the apparel lead times were so long. Knowing that L.A. would be hot and that the coliseum would block any breeze, I looked at what the athletes could wear as a defense against the elements. The centerpiece would be nicknamed "The Marshmallow Suit." Predominantly a light blend of 85% cotton and 15% white nylon, the jacket had a full zip into a stand-up collar, and both the pant and jacket had vertical navy nylon mesh panels on the sides to provide cooling air flow. Thin red piping on the edges gave a nice accent to the lines. A matching cap completed the ensemble. The warm-up suit I designed used a different color scheme— sky blue and mocha—and was made of a very light and stretchy fabric to flex with the athlete's body movement.

Peter Moore was also at work. Peter thought the product should tell a story and, with Strasser, we discussed options. To evoke the presence of the Olympics in California, Peter came up with a horizontal band of racing oranges and stars with legs and shoes. For the T-shirt design, I took my "Nike 1" license plate, changed it to a California plate, and put it on the shiny chrome bumper of a 1950's Buick.

So who did we have competing in L.A.? Who had the chance to medal? We had to budget ahead for the cost of success. Contracts were now common in track and field, Athletic West was now the most powerful club in the world, and globally, Nike had several of the world's top performers. On April 16, I brought Knight and Strasser into a room in our Murray Boulevard office. Laid out on a table were our athletes' names listed event by event, from Cruz of Brazil to Finland's Tina Lilak in the javelin. I took my best guess as to how we'd fare. Our contracted athletes had bonuses written in, topping out at $40k for Olympic gold. What were we to tell the non-contracted athletes, the up-and-comers who wore Nike and had our support? Any one of them just might have their big day in L.A.—it had happened before, and it was a possibility we had to consider.

The IOC threw an interesting curve into the equation. Prior to the start of the Olympic Games, each athlete was required to declare his footwear sponsor and sign to that effect. Then they were required to wear their sponsor's footwear throughout the competition. Companies could no longer bid under the table for athletes between heats. For us, this was perfect, as we never participated in that game.

John Gregorio had signed a large group under the guidance of UCLA coach Bobby Kersee. UCLA was an Adidas school but Kersee also had a post-graduate group that included, among others, hurdler Greg Foster, the same Greg Foster I had earlier denied product to, knowing his Adidas connection. In my mind, the queen of this group was Jackie Joyner. Talented and a real lady, Jackie is the sister of one of our Athletics West members, Al Joyner.

I'd been shocked at an A.W. meeting in Indianapolis when this athlete with a huge smile came up to me and asked, "Remember me?" I didn't, but there was something familiar about that smile. "I'm the guy you picked up at the Austin airport and gave a ride to the dorms." Now I had it. Young Al Joyner, or "Sweet Water" to his friends, had been a hurdler at the 1980 NCAA's. By 1984, he'd switched events from the hurdles, and now with A.W. teammates Willie Banks and Mike Conley, provided a solid 1-2-3 punch in the triple jump.

We were fine, and then that spring, I received a letter from one of Kersee's athletes. This letter was followed by another, then another. With the exception of the name and signature, they were identical. Each athlete was requesting release from his or her contract with Nike.

I called Nelson after the first letter. Nelson called Kersee and it was decided we needed a face-to-face. Kersee flew up to Portland and we met at the airport Sheraton. I let Nelson talk while Kersee listened and barely said a word. I can't prove it, but Kersee must have gotten a kickback from Adidas—nothing else made sense.

Nike was in an impossible position. To publicly announce breach of contract held no positive outcome for Nike, and it wouldn't be good for the athletes either. As I watched Kersee, I thought, "we are better off—we'll miss a few athletes, but we don't have to deal with him anymore."

With the Kersee mass exit, Knight and Strasser agreed to go with the bonuses across the board. If the athlete wears the shoes, we keep our promise whether it's written down or not. We had budgeted $1.6 million for L.A. I told them the bonuses could bump us up another $600,000.

We communicated the bonus structure to our athletes, but then, in a staff meeting on May 8th, a bomb dropped. It was announced that the Eastern block nations were boycotting Los Angeles. You could start doing the math, but without the Soviet Union and thirteen communist allies pulling down their typically substantial number of medals, there was no doubt that our budget would be hit with additional increases.

Beyond the budget, one of my greatest concerns after touring the University of Southern California was security. We had decided on renting a fraternity house and a sorority house across the street from each other to accommodate our staff, guests, product, and to host our athletes. During my visit, I learned that the fraternity house was vandalized, in daylight hours no less, and that cars were broken into. It was believed that those responsible lived right behind the house and had a clear view of the occupants' coming and going. To deal with the security issue, Nike brought in Eric Moroney, a neighbor of Knight's, and a member of the Portland Police Department.

Former Nike debenture holder Chuck Cale, the same Chuck Cale who once slept on my couch during the 1972 trials, was now a member of Peter Ubberoth's Los Angeles organizing committee. We received a complete tour of the facilities and a briefing on what access restrictions we faced. The key thing was that we had a reliable line of communication for the first time at the Olympic level.

The clock was ticking on another personal athlete story. Joan Benoit was struggling in April with a knee problem. We were so proud of Joan's progress since her high school days in Cape Elizabeth, Maine. She had met Jeff Johnson early in Exeter and was a member of the Nike family by the time she discovered her event, the marathon. If there was ever to be a beneficiary of Strasser's hard fought battle with the IOC to bring women's competition to the Olympics above the 1500 distance, it was Joan.

Now she was training in Oregon in pain. Joan had switched coaches from John Babington to Bob Sevene, known by everyone as "Sev." Bob was a Vietnam vet. He had fallen some distance out of a helicopter once, ran the 800 during his competitive years, and cracked us all up with his enthusiasm for his athletes. With his raspy Boston accent he'd say "I tell ya, the kid's got grapefruits for balls—wait and see!" Like Bowerman and any good coach, Sev was tempering Joan's workouts, but the first- ever women's marathon trials was closing in.

Help was offered by Jack Scott, the same Jack Scott who'd been entangled with the Symbionese Liberation Army and the Patty Hearst abduction. Scott had developed an electric stimulation device, and he tested it on Joan. Dr. Stan James was consulted, and a decision to try arthroscopic surgery seventeen days prior to trials was approved. A scope would result in the least damage and leave some hope for competing on May 12th.

Olympia, Washington had won the bid for the first-ever women's marathon trials. Laurel James, a friend of mine and a friend of Prefontaine's, was a sincere mother of five boys who had opened a specialty running store in Seattle. She campaigned doggedly to get the trials to Olympia. Her toughest competition came from New York City and L.A., and she had to fight all the labels of "someone who had never done it before." Well, guess what, neither had anyone else. Laurel would secure the first women's trials with tenacity, grit, and a never-say-die attitude. Nike liked her style.

On race day, I loaded up the van with Carol, Tracy (now 11 years old), Kaili (now 7), and Bob Sevene. With stopwatches in hand, we waited at the 5km mark for the leaders. Sev's Boston rasp rang out, "I told her the goal is to be in the top

three—she doesn't have to win this. It's about making the team."
We waited, and I stood with my hands around Kaili in front of
me. The lead car turned the corner blocks away. Small figures
became recognizable as they drew closer, their strides matched.

One was a surprising North Carolina runner, Betty Jo
Springs. Then Sev exploded, "Oh shit, she's up there." Joan
Benoit emerged with her recognizably efficient stride. Now
committed, Sev was careful not to say anything negative. "You
look smooth Joan," he called out.

Kaili locked eyes on the passing Benoit, and I sensed her
interest in this young female athlete. We hopped in the van, and
I drove to the 10k mark. Again Joan and Springs zoomed by,
and now Kaili had a name to cheer for, "Go Joanie!" We kept
moving, up to 15k and 20k through the streets of Olympia,
looping west of the I-5 freeway and back. As the other runners
fell back, we kept losing contact with the leaders' progress, and
we realized we better head to the finish and park.

We found a clear vantage point and waited for the lead
vehicles. They came around a corner and down a long straight
to the finish. Now we waited for the lead runners to appear. A
small figure rounded the corner and was immediately
identifiable in her Athletics West uniform. All alone, it was
Joan. Kaili jumped up and down and clapped for the person
she had already viewed six times on the course as though she
knew her. Without another runner in sight, Sev said, "Shit. I
hope she's alright. She didn't have to do that."

Back at the Holiday Inn, I went to the swimming pool with
Kaili. The water felt relaxing after the hectic drive on back streets
to stay off the course yet catch the kilometer splits. Kaili was
swimming away to the deep end as Joan arrived, slipped into the
water, and slowly moved with a breast stroke in the same
direction. Kaili turned, and from my vantage point, it looked like
two crocodiles meeting each other. Looking straight ahead, Kaili
recognized Joan's eyes, turned to me, and through the gap in
her missing teeth, spit out, "Dad! Ithh's her!"

This was a pivotal moment for Kaili. She was face to face with greatness, and she would remember this moment for the rest of her life. Joan Benoit would inspire countless women with her remarkable journey, and Kaili was among the first.

Call it destiny. Call it timing. Joan Benoit was setting her course in history.

The men's trials would follow two weeks later in Buffalo, New York. Alberto Salazar was Nike's best shot at an Olympic medal, but if Joan had physical problems, Salazar had them in spades. Ever since his win over Dick Beardsley in the 1982 Boston marathon, Al had been plagued with nagging leg injuries. Always tight, he seemed to get tighter after he and Beardsley reached so far into their reserves to win in Boston.

Even with all his injuries, Salazar was the favorite going in. Pete Pfitzinger, a relative unknown, broke away from the pack at about the halfway point and opened up a 150 meter lead. He was overtaken by John Tuttle in the last mile, and then Salazar passed both of them. The finish was thrilling, with Pfitzinger finding another gear in the last 400 meters to win. Salazar took second, and he would run in Los Angeles.

Strasser and Moore had been busy with what was later labeled "Guerilla Marketing" by the USOC and the IOC. As part of the "City Campaign," the sides of buildings were leased where L.A. freeway traffic would have the best vantage point. Huge images of Nike's athletes in action were painted on those buildings—Mary Decker, Joan Benoit, and Carl Lewis were joined by local hero and all-pro Lester Hayes of the Los Angeles Raiders. Hayes' eyes peered out from his helmet as he crouched in his defensive position facing the cars.

Nike Westwood went through a complete remodel. A precursor to the future Niketowns, the remodel pulled Nike retail out of the financially restrained dark ages. Nike Westwood went state of the art, with a giant Swoosh that appeared to have crashed into the roof, complete with smoke. Nike Entertainment scheduled celebrity appearances in the store to add to the buzz.

Back at the USC campus, Eric Moroney counseled our staff on safety precautions and awareness. His staff was even checking under our vehicles with mirrors. I thought, "Shit, this is serious stuff!" A young Nike employee named Skip Lei was assigned to run day-to-day operations so those of us in promotions were free to do our jobs. Housekeeping, grocery shopping, and operational rules would keep us on a smooth course throughout the games.

An invitation had gone out to our promotion teams around the world—if they chose to come to Los Angeles to support their athletes, they had a place to stay. The pace was guaranteed to be fast and furious, but one of the best sports marketing teams in the history of track and field responded. Among the many were Jos Herman of the Netherlands, Carlo Grippo of Italy, Jaakko Tuominen of Finland, Jacque Noe of France, Konrad Ystborg of Norway, and the now-famous massage therapist Shiarishi of Japan. Letterman's jackets were ordered for each member of this highly motivated team, and the work we did together in L.A. formed a lasting bond. This was the moment we lived for.

Our athletes began arriving at the house. We had shipped their Olympic packages to them already, so the main attraction was simply meeting with our staff, sharing a meal, and getting away from the crush of the media and the Olympic village. The only exception we made on media access was for Ahmad Rashad, the former Oregon Duck and Minnesota Viking. This was his breakout moment in sports broadcasting—couldn't have happened to a nicer guy.

Carl Lewis was one of the first to show, and Joan Benoit and Mary Decker were regulars. Cruz and the Brazilians arrived, and

I met Europeans like French pole vaulter Pierre Quinon for the first time. Despite seven years of solid and increased support, we never saw Sebastian Coe once during the games except from the stands when he was racing on the track.

Our alarms were set for 6 a.m. If our staff wanted to go for a run, our rented vans were ready to go, and we'd drive to Santa Monica where we could run on the grass under palm trees or hit the sandy beach. Then it was back to the house for breakfast, and an endless stream of coaches and athletes stopping by for some hospitality or to visit with old friends and to make new ones.

The new IOC sponsor declaration was already creating problems for some. One of our top female sprinters, Merlene Ottey of Jamaica had a conflict. A Puma promotions rep by the name of Cubi had signed Ottey to a contract, but she had failed to meet the deadline for her Olympic shoe sponsor declaration. She wanted out of her Nike contract. She was not the most pleasant person in the world, and I wouldn't have minded letting her go. I thought she and Cubi deserved each other's company. Even though she was under contract to Puma and wore their product, by IOC rules, when she appeared with her credentials to check in at the practice track prior to being admitted to the coliseum for her event, an official would inspect her footwear and check it against her declared sponsor. She was like a hissing cat as I informed her that there was nothing I could do to influence the IOC in her favor. In fact, given the less than professional way she dealt with us, I didn't feel compelled to give her a bonus if she medaled. If her future was with Puma, let Cubi pay her bonus. Ottey would sprint to bronze medals in both the 100 and 200 wearing Nike spikes. I don't know if Puma paid, but I do know that Nike didn't.

Danny Harris, our top prospect in the 400 hurdles, appeared at the house soon after. Wearing Adidas shoes and hanging his head low, Harris was accompanied by Larry Ellis, head coach at Princeton and head men's Olympic coach. Ellis had already informed Danny of the issue. Other than that, I didn't ask what role he had played.

What happened was that Harris showed up for his preliminary heat in Adidas even though he had declared Nike as his sponsor. The officials would not allow him to run, but Carl Lewis had just completed a round in the 100 and was leaving. Harris asked if he could borrow Carl's shoes, and Carl obliged. Although Carl's spikes were a size and a half too large, Danny advanced and now, embarrassed, was asking for shoes in his size. I let Danny know how displeased I was with all of this and told him that even if he medaled, I might not honor his bonus. He said he understood and just wanted to race. Danny Harris went on to win the silver behind Olympic champion Edwin Moses. We paid his bonus, and he remained with Nike the rest of his career.

The games got off to a bang for us on the first day. Nike's Mike Conley was undeniably one of the most talented athletes in track and field. World class in the 200 and long jump, his best event was the triple jump, and Mike was having a good day. But not good enough for the gold medal. Al Joyner, the young man with the big smile in Austin, was hot. Al would hop, step and jump to gold. Mike took the silver, and Nike had a 1-2 finish to start off the Olympics.

Arriving at the Nike house in his singlet, Al was beaming with his gold medal hanging around his neck on a ribbon. Two Nike vans full of staff were ready to take "Sweet Water" Al to the Hard Rock Café to celebrate. As our vans drove side by side, the theme song for the popular movie *Ghostbusters* came on the radio, and we turned it up high. Both vans were bouncing up and down as everyone inside jumped to the rhythm and sang, "Who you gonna call? Sweet Water!"

When we arrived at the Hard Rock, we informed their staff we had an Olympic gold medalist with us and could they please play "Ghostbusters." As the music blared, Don Coleman put Al on his shoulders. Al's head just missed a ceiling fan as we snaked through the crowd to our tables, "Who you gonna call? Sweet Water!" Once we settled down to our table, this bodacious blond ran over and asked what Al's event was. "I just want to touch it," she said, then bent over and gave Al a kiss. A smile that just couldn't get bigger did just that.

In my kitchen I still have the Hard Rock Café menu from that day, framed, and signed "Al Joyner, gold Medal, Sweet H2O."

On that same day of competition, under clear blue skies, Carl Lewis began his trek towards the Olympian status of "King Carl." The media buzz going into the Olympics, fueled in no small part by Lewis and his agent, Joe Douglas, was that Lewis was out to equal the four gold medals won by the legendary Jesse Owens at the Munich Games in 1936. Lewis got the first one in the 100, running just under 10 flat. There were those who didn't want this to happen, turned off, perhaps, by the perception that Lewis lacked humility. But Lewis came to the Nike house often, and what you saw was a calm, unflappable competitor with a quick sense of humor.

The question was, could anyone stop him?

The following morning we were up early for breakfast and down to Santa Monica for a midpoint view of the women's marathon. Again, I had Sev in my van, but unlike the trials in Olympia, Washington, the crowds and the traffic made the L.A. course far less negotiable.

It was a long wait on a street near the beach that was filling up with spectators. Finally, the motorcycle escorts arrived with sirens and lights flashing. Then there was a gap and another wait. Then more police on motorcycles and you could see little figures moving in the distance in a large pack. But closer in was a lone figure by herself. It was Joan. She had broken free surprisingly early and no one was covering her move.

Sev recognized her, "Shit. She's going for all the marbles. This is it!" There was no holding back now. She had committed herself. We ran back to the van and raced back to the house to watch the finish on television. The Nike staff filled the room as the network helicopter camera beamed an image of a lone figure running on an L.A. freeway. What stood out from that angle was an oversized white painter's cap, protecting the small figure from the sun. You could see the white shoes stepping out below in an even rhythm. Joan's legs had an almost piston-like action, and she was well in front of the Norwegians Waitz and Christiansen and Portugal's Rosa Mota.

We could see it on the screen, but when Joan appeared out of the tunnel and on to the track, we heard the crowd erupt from the packed coliseum blocks away. Born of tough Maine stock, taught to ski by her father, a member of the 10th Mountain Division in WWII, Joan was a girl who would quickly stop to pick the flowers alongside the road she ran on when a car approached, because women were seldom seen running back then. Yet only boys could test her in a workout, and here she was, alone at the finish. She had her place in history—the first woman marathoner to win a gold medal in the Olympics.

Decades later, when he was asked if he had a favorite moment in sports, Phil Knight said "Yes, when Joan Benoit emerged from the tunnel in Los Angeles. It was so emotional."

As Joan ran all alone down that Los Angeles freeway she passed her own image painted so much larger than life on the side of a building, and this underscored one of Nike's proudest moments. From an early relationship with Jeff Johnson at the Nike Exeter factory when he himself was a high school coach, to her eventual employment at the Exeter Sports Lab, to being placed on our Athletes Assistance Program and then Athletics West, to her American record at the 1982 Nike-OTC Marathon, to Nike's push for inclusion of the marathon in the Olympics and finally Nike consultant Stan James's successful arthroscopic surgery on a problem knee, Joan Benoit symbolized what can happen when you combine Nike's effort with an undying spirit of determination and grit. That run through the coliseum tunnel in Los Angeles was packed full of emotion and pride. I still am brought to tears every time I watch it.

August 6th marked a banner day for Nike. Carl Lewis added his second gold with a solid performance in the long jump. Italy's Alberto Cova, who had attended one of our training camps on the Algarve, ran away with the 10,000. England's Mick McLeod added a silver. Stepping to the line in the 800 was perhaps the most talented field in Olympic history. Steve Ovett was there to defend, Sebastian Coe was there to redeem himself, and then there was Joaquim Cruz.

Cova's time was 27:47:54, and McLeod's was 28:06:22. Martti Vainio of Finland finished in 27:51.10, good enough for the silver, but he tested positive for drugs. His silver medal was awarded to McLeod. Nobody ever asked McLeod to return the bronze.

The Cruz family was watching with nervous anticipation around a small television in rural Brazil. With only two laps to race, Cruz quickly gave not only the Cruz family, but an entire nation, a reason to express their joy. It was a crushing performance by the young Brazilian. Ovett could hardly breathe from an earlier bout of bronchitis. Coe was fit, but unable to match Cruz stride for stride. At the NCAAs earlier in the year, Cruz had won the 800 and helped Dellinger's Ducks to an NCAA record 113 team points, and he was race ready. He stormed home in an Olympic record 1:43.00 and would go on to be voted the most popular sports figure in Brazil, topping even the magnificent Pele.

With Adi Dassler's passing, son Horst had assumed the leadership of Adidas. During the '84 Olympics, I attended a conference at the Hilton Hotel to learn more about this man. Sitting at a panel table up front, Dassler fielded questions as I sat halfway back in the crowd. I thought, "Here's the guy that works from within the federations, exerting as much control as possible to keep the three stripes in front of the consumer's eyes. And here we sit quietly, eating his lunch."

Nelson and I were on our way to the coliseum for another big day of competition when we had a celebrity sighting. I nudged Nelson with my elbow as two men were approaching from the opposite direction. One was dressed in a baseball cap, red silk jacket, white baseball pants, striped baseball socks and Nike running shoes. It was Mick Jagger.

Nelson gave me a look and then danced down the sidewalk, singing "I got me some—Satis-fack-shun."

The pole vaulters were warming up as we took our seats in the stadium. They would have a long day under the sun, waiting for their attempts, and I was pleased to see our Nike athletes wearing the "Marshmallow Suit" for protection. The other option for the Americans was the suit issued by the Olympic Committee from Roba de Kappa. Because they fit so poorly that athletes had to have them retailored in order to wear them, some athletes called them "Roba de Crappa."

We were stunned in the women's 400 hurdles when Nawal El Mouta-wakel, a diminutive Moroccan woman who won the event in the NCAAs, overpowered Athletics West's Judy Brown to win the gold. This was quite an achievement for a young woman

In a cat and mouse game of passing heights, France's Pierre Quinon (5.75 m) outlasted the U.S. contestants Mike Tully (5.7 m) and Earl Bell (5.6 m) in the pole vault.

Nike runner Said Aouita brought home Morocco's other medal in the '84 Olympics. He won the gold in the men's 5000 with an Olympic record time of 13:05:59.

who in her own country is required to keep her body fully clothed in public. Carl Lewis continued his march into the record books with an Olympic record of 19:80 in the 200. Athletic West's Kirk Baptiste would also dip under 20 seconds with a 19:96 for the silver.

Much to my dismay Henry Rono was gone from International competition by now, a sad story of alcohol and denial. He had taken up residence in Eugene and at times was found in the gutters. Don Coleman and I arrived in Eugene one day with a one-way ticket for Henry to Spokane and a round trip for Don. Henry had done his best in Pullman, and we were going to bring him back. He refused, already drunk in the morning, lashing out and telling us we were not his friends.

On August 10th, I was excited about the final in my event, the steeplechase. Two members of Athletics West were competing against the Kenyans, who had dominated the event for years.

Kenya's Julius Korir would glide over the steeple barriers deer-like, just as the great steeplers Keino, Biwott, Jipcho, and Rono before him. The gold seemed to be his after only a few laps. Behind, Marsh would run his customary conservative tactic, loping along behind the pack, but this was the Olympic final and he could not delay as long. Korir prevailed, and in a mad final kick, the lesser-known Brian Diemer would outlast American record holder Henry Marsh for the bronze, 8:14.06 to 8:14.25. France's Joseph Mahmoud took the silver medal in the 3000 steeplechase.

On the track was another women's first time event, the 3000 run. Mary Decker was poised to repeat her 1983 World Championship effort in the 1500 and the 5000, especially with the Eastern block boycotting. Mary was fit and healthy and ran with her natural grace in the middle of the pack.

Much had been made of the South African Zola Budd, who now ran barefoot for Great Britain. Despite all the hype, it seemed like a normal walk in the park for Mary—sort of "ho hum." Then it happened. A slight misstep, Budd in front of Decker, a tangle of feet, a hand on the back, and Decker was down hard on the rail, rolling over on her hip and off the track. Looking up at the fleeting pack, disbelief and emotion filled Mary's face as we stood horror-stricken and watched.

A billboard on a building with her image, an appearance in Nike's television commercial set to Randy Newman's "I Love L.A.," a dream from childhood, after meeting Steve Prefontaine, of being not only an Olympian, but a champion. All for naught. Numerous boyfriends, a failed marriage with marathoner Ron Tabb, and Mary lay all alone on the infield grass as officials ran to her aid. A large figure emerged from the stands—Richard Slaney, an English discus thrower, who scooped Mary up and, hiding her tearful, pained face, carried her off the field.

The men's 1500 final had been tossed up like a salad. It was Seb Coe's to defend, and his countryman Steve Ovett, who had come so close to beating him in the 1500 in Moscow, was still suffering from a bronchial infection. Joaquim Cruz, considered by many a favorite, was hit by the flu following his 800 gold medal performance. I had no idea of Coe's state of mind, as we had not spoken, but I clearly remember him telling me about the pressure he felt from the British press. "They put you on a pedestal, then they relish knocking you off!"

Young Steve Cram came in eighth in the Moscow final, but this time he was a player. Steve Scott moved boldly on the first lap, then Spain's Abascal and Kenya's Cheshire made their moves, while Coe stumbled twice but maintained his footing. Ovett ran off the track on the east turn and stopped, dropping to the infield. The race was over for him. Cram shadowed Coe. Abascal's split time after three laps was faster than anyone in Olympic history—2:53.1, and the race was on. Cram started to jump Coe on the backstretch with his long grinding kick, but Coe took one look to the outside and would have no part of it. He was off and past Abascal before the final turn. Coe's 52-second final lap carried him home to defend his title in record time, with Cram less than a second ahead of Abascal. By then Coe was on his knees, totally spent, hands and head extended down to the track. He took a moment to gather himself, and then he was back on his feet. Coe looked to the British press and, with left and right index fingers extended in their direction, jabbed at them. "I told you so!"

In the 400 relay, Jamaica's Don Quarrie teamed up for a silver medal in his third Olympics—this time in what had become his home after his marriage to Yolanda. The talented American team of Graddy, Brown, Smith, and Lewis obliterated the Olympic record and lowered the world record to 37:83. That made four gold medals for Lewis, tying Jesse Owen's feat.

Lewis went on to win a total of nine Olympic gold medals, last competing in the 1996 Atlanta Olympics.

The men's marathon was run on the last day of the Olympics. Alberto Salazar's injuries and surgeries had accumulated over the past couple years, and he would finish in fifteenth place. Portugal's Carlos Lopes took the gold with a 2:09:21 finish, ahead of Ireland's John Tracy (2:09:56) and a surprising Charlie Spedding of Brendan Foster's club in northern England (2:09:58).

The Los Angeles Olympics finally marked a moment of domination by Nike track and field athletes. Forty-nine medals in total, seven were with Athletics West, 21 were U.S. athletes, and 28 were foreign. One question loomed—in the retail war with Adidas, would all that Olympic gold make a difference?

CHAPTER 22: THE DUMPER

Strasser and Moore had taken the "City Campaign" national, painting the sides of buildings in key cities with local Nike sports heroes. Back in Beaverton, Strasser smiled through his beard, almost as if he were baiting you. "What did we create?" His question was leveled at what for us at the time was an expensive effort in Los Angeles. He underlined the word on the flipchart, "Demand—did we create that?"

You could see that Strasser wanted it to be true, that we at Nike knew who we were and what we stood for. He believed that Nike should be involved in real sports, and we had to quit chasing competitors' business. We were now spread into business areas called "Duty" and "Freestyle." We were starting to explore golf and soccer and even looking at creating a second brand.

At this time, two critical facts escaped us. First, running remained by far our largest category, and we believed that runners, joggers, and walkers bought our shoes to run, walk, and jog in. We were the number one athletic shoe retailer in the world by this time, and we thought we knew our business. We discounted the idea that Nike running shoes were the consumer's casual shoe of choice. But the truth was different. A much larger

The Duty line was aimed at people in service professions: nurses, firemen, policemen, etc. Freestyle was a line of men's and women's casual shoes with an emphasis on comfort. Both lines required a unique approach to marketing that was outside of Nike's core business. Duty customers typically shopped through specialty magazines and stores devoted to their particular professions. The Freestyle line was sold through normal consumer shoe shops rather than specialty athletic shoe shops.

portion of our business than we realized consisted of average people who bought our shoes to wear for everyday use. They wanted comfortable shoes to wear to the supermarket or the mall. They liked Nike's product, but these consumers were a lot less loyal than our athletic customers.

Second, aerobics was in its infancy and the male-dominated management of Nike was not even listening to its wives. This cost us big time. Reebok was a company that was barely on our radar screen as a competitor in the mid-'80s. They received a bad shipment of soft leather in Asia, leather that was unsuitable for athletic shoes because it was too stretchy to stand up to the lateral stresses that athletes put on their footwear. Reebok decided to dump the inferior product in L.A., and no one at Nike took notice.

But the women who were just starting to get aerobics off the ground took notice. The Reebok shoe was supple and provided immediate comfort from the first time you tried them on in the store. No breaking in period like there was with a more rigid athletic shoe. No blisters. And these shoe buyers were quick to abandon Nike because they wanted comfort and didn't need all the support that a competitive athlete demanded from his or her footwear. For Reebok, one of the oldest sports footwear brands, aerobics became a wildfire.

In the midst of all this, Nike continued to hire new people. Strasser seemed to prefer attorneys, apparently for their organizational skills. Some of them made positive contributions, like the congenial Dave Smith, who was hired to handle legal matters at Nike International. Some, like Cascade run-off founder Chuck Galford, were good people who were given difficult assignments. Galford had the unenviable task of cutting back on department staff, and he ended up firing people that I had hired and worked with for years, people who were let go not because of poor performance but simply because profits were down.

And then there was Jack Joyce. Joyce was hired to head up all footwear development he seemed a bad fit to me. Joyce loved irritating people, and he became Strasser's henchman. He made me think of the old Will Rogers quote, "It's not what you pay a man, it's what he costs you that counts."

I lined that comment up with an L.A. Olympic effort that I was proud of. Yet in my review after that effort, I found myself defending 1,300 athletes and my staff of 20, 15 of whom I hired. Despite this successful effort, profits were down, and Nike took steps to turn things around. One such step was the dismantling of the track and field program—my program, and a program respected by athletes and coaches. Nike was heading for a net loss, our first since 1973, and Reebok was soaring into the number one position globally. The shake-up was inevitable, but whether Nike was making the right shake-up was an open question.

In September, Peter Moore instructed me to design a new distinctive look for Athletics West. The goal was to have the athletes in uniform by spring. In addition, I was to put Carl Lewis in a new look. Lewis' performance at the Olympics, combined with the fact that these were the first summer Olympic Games on American soil since 1932, prompted a sea change in the visibility of track and field athletes. Lewis achieved 'rock star' celebrity status, and Nike was out to capitalize on his success.

After the Olympics, Nike was contacted by a Los Angeles entertainment agent by the name of Sid Craig. His client, Mitch Gaylord won four medals in Los Angeles as a member of an impressive U.S. gymnastics team. Sid Craig was convincing enough at selling us on the future of the handsome, boy-next-door image of Gaylord to get Nike excited about entering the gymnastics market.

Gaylord won a gold medal as part of the U.S. gymnastics team, and three medals in individual events: silver in the vault, and bronze medals for the rings and the parallel bars.

With the gymnastics footwear market dominated by our old rival Tiger, we turned to my wife Carol's old gymnastics coach, Dick Mulvihill. With input from Mulvihill, we designed and produced an apparel line.

Mitch Gaylord was a great guy, but we might as well have been trying to jam a square peg into a round hole. Here we were with a male gymnastics hero trying to break into a market dominated by pre-pubescent females, the vast majority of whom wouldn't stick with the sport. We might have done better if we'd used Mary Lou Retton, but frankly, we were all a little tone-deaf at Nike around the issue of gender. The whole effort proved to be an exercise in futility.

By the end of the year, Carl Lewis knew what he wanted in a uniform. The idea of a lycra full-body tight was bold, and it was initially deemed controversial by many in the sprint community. But that's where Carl wanted to be. In an apparel meeting where we searched for direction, I suggested we start with the "Muscle Tite." The Muscle Tite was developed by Tom Derderian and designer Tracy Cottingham, but Tom and I had different visions, and this was the beginning of what would become an internal battle.

Even though Derderian was involved with the Muscle Tite, which gave functional and aesthetic body lines from the ankle to the waist, he was arguing that the upper torso lines need not relate. Derderian favored horizontal lines above the waist, while I wanted long vertical lines from head to toe. Rather than cut the body up horizontally, I wanted the feel of a ballet dancer reaching upward from the toes. I compared his view to a butcher's drawing in a meat shop. "We're dealing with athletes—not cattle!" I'd argue, and I saw quickly why Bowerman wanted to throw Derderian out of his lab. In collaborating with Cottingham, he was making her a poorer designer.

The long vertical lines of the Muscle Tite became a design clue as to how to design the rest of the athletic apparel line, and most importantly for me, the new Athletics West uniform. But by January of 1985, I was having a hard time moving forward with the Athletics West project. Tom Derderian was hanging out on his own, "in charge of innovation." As designers, Cottingham and I reported to Peter Moore, and Jim Gorman had now moved back from Exeter and would head up production.

I made repeated trips to Eugene to meet with Athletics West, starting with drawings, then prototypes, sewn in the sample room. Decker and Lewis in Santa Monica were the primary models. Immediately Joan Benoit said, "You'll have to do a short for me." So we began creating a parallel look in optional styles. Lewis liked the yellow and orange of Santa Monica T.C. and Athletics West would be red, white, and blue.

In the uniforms we designed for Athletics West, the torso lines followed the vertical muscle lines from the waist and continued to the highest point of the body, over the shoulders, maximizing and accentuating body height. I was working out of the 17th Street location, home to Peter Moore and Michael Dougherty and what we called "The Vidiots," the beginning of Nike film and video. Sitting next to me at his drawing table was Tinker Hatfield. A key element for the A.W. look was the embroidered badge that identified the club. I asked Tinker for help and we started with my earlier Oregon Track Club designs. The result was a green conifer in front of a snow-capped mountain. Without words, it said, "Oregon."

An external battle came at the end of the year, as well. I attended the track and field coaches' board meeting. I formed the original board as a forum for Nike to communicate with key "movers and shakers" in the world of track and field. With my promotion to Nike International, the responsibility for the board had passed to Chuck Galford. And now, I was designing apparel, but these folks were the people I had carefully nurtured relationships with for years. There was outrage over poor communication and linkage to their programs, slow service, a poor team sales program, and lack of stability in who they were dealing with at Nike. There was disbelief that we were not capitalizing on our successes in L.A. "Where's Carl?" was a constant question. One coach said "Just because it's raining in Beaverton, it's not raining around the world." The shake-up that ousted many of my hires, combined with the cutbacks that were driven by our 1984 net loss, had produced a program that simply wasn't working. One coach put it succinctly. "You are doing less," he said, "but you aren't doing less better."

There was not a whole lot of commotion over the signing of a new Nike athlete, even though Strasser and Moore were involved in the negotiation. North Carolina's Michael Jordan was drafted by the Chicago Bulls and neither Nike nor Chicago could predict his future impact. Everyone knew he was a terrific college player, but plenty of terrific college players went on to ho-hum NBA careers.

But Jordan was special. He proved to be one of those very articulate athletes who could tell a shoe designer exactly what he wanted in a shoe. Chicago's red and black gave Peter Moore a starting point. Sketching and coloring away, Peter was not aware of one critical point as to what an NBA player could or could not wear. The NBA at that time required that all of its players wear white shoes on the court. But Peter Moore was thinking well outside the box, and the first edition Air Jordan shoe was born, with its utterly distinctive red on black color scheme.

Peter's ignorance of NBA shoe rules turned out to be the source of a huge marketing opportunity. Jordan wore the shoes in every game, simply paying the NBA fines while he began to dazzle the league with his incredible moves. Every time he paid a fine it was news, and Nike got a ton of free publicity. When the shoes were released to the public the following spring, everyone wanted to "be like Mike." We sold $2.3 million worth of Air Jordans in the first two months.

Jordan's high-flying style on the court and his work ethic began to drive a market that would combine shoes, apparel, and accessories in one look. The NBA eventually changed its policy and allowed NBA players to wear shoes in team colors. Kids on the street, the ones who drove the leisure market, began color coordinating their shoes and their warm-ups. It didn't really matter if you had a crossover dribble or could dunk. Jordan became so popular that his on-court shoe choice became an off-court fashion choice for millions, from die-hard fans to casual onlookers.

Peter Moore was quick to see the opportunity and, with Strasser piping in and occasionally prodding and bullying, Nike ran with it. Out of the Michael Jordan phenomenon came a new core Nike marketing strategy: the Collection. The fundamental lesson of Nike's association with Jordan was the importance of a single athlete. Jordan was charismatic, lived a clean life, and was a phenomenal athlete. With a foundation like that, you didn't have to stop at the shoes—you could build a whole line of apparel.

After a successful wear test of my one-piece jumpsuit for A.W. and Carl Lewis, I was asked to design and build a prototype for Jordan. Acting more like a Skunk Works, we kept it out of the Nike sample room. I had the patterns for the 6'7" Jordan drawn up by a freelancer in East Portland, then Carol sewed the black and red crushed nylon into what we called "The Flight Suit." Prior to shipping it to Jordan for his feedback, 12-year-old Tracy climbed in and walked about the carpet, looking every bit like one of the seven dwarfs.

One of Phil Knight's favorite athletes was John McEnroe. Similar to

> *Skunk Works is a term used in engineering and technical fields to describe a group within an organization given a high degree of autonomy and unhampered by bureaucracy, tasked with working on advanced or secret projects.*

Prefontaine in temperament, competitiveness, and attitude toward the establishment, McEnroe would have his own Collection. Based off the green and purple of Wimbledon, a checker pattern was the signature of the first Nike collection in tennis. The colors and pattern were radical in a sport known for conservative white apparel, and that edginess fit McEnroe's image perfectly.

With Air Jordans booking $2.3 million in two months, half the McEnroe line selling out, and 10,000 pair of Georgetown's gray/navy sneakers booked by Foot Locker, the pressure was now on. In this new direction, you either kept up or got left behind. I wanted to change the white panel in the A.W. collection to black for a better retail look, but it was too late. We were committed.

Georgetown, led by 1985 NBA Number 1 draft pick Patrick Ewing, won the NCAA basketball championship in 1984, and lost to Villanova in the final in 1985.

That spring, in a staff meeting, Rob listed what I would call "Strasser's Rules," 10 principles that would guide Nike back to the number one position for good:
1. Our business is change.
2. We are on offense all the time.
3. Perfect results count, not a perfect process. Break the rules, as it is about the business.
4. It's as much about the battle as it is about the business.
5. Assume nothing. Stretch the possible.
6. Live off the land.
7. Your job isn't done until the job is done.
8. Dangers:
   —Bureaucracy
   —Personal ambition
   —Energy takes vs. energy gives
   —Know our weaknesses

9. It won't be pretty.
10. If we do it right, we make money damn near guaranteed every time.

Strasser thought in military terms often, and item 6 on his list was straight out of a military textbook. "Living off the land" was exactly what I had done all those years I traveled the track circuit. What Strasser meant was that we should be opportunistic. Take the moment when it appears. You strike, rather than have a bunch of meetings and bump everything up the chain of command. It was the freedom I had to add a world-class athlete to our shoe list that gave us the edge we needed to beat Adidas.

This attitude was famously exemplified in what may be Nike's signature ad campaign: Just Do It.

Back on the home front, I followed up on a flyer pinned on a message board at West Marine, where I purchased most of my boating needs. I arranged to meet the contact at a boathouse on the Columbia Slough near the town of Scappoose. Owned by a retired Saint Helens dentist, the 1940 30-foot Owens cruiser was built of $7/_8$"mahogany planking. With a plumb bow, classic lines and dual steering stations, we took her out for a sea trial and I fell in love with her. A sailor since 16, I was buying a "Stinkpot," complete with boathouse. I would rename her *Bogie*, because if Bogart ever had a powerboat, it would have looked like this.

Nelson Farris, who had been with Nike since almost the beginning, was fired on a Friday. Strasser must have approved it, which was a surprise since they had worked well together when they were both in Europe. But the company was trying to turn itself around, and the cuts were getting closer and closer to the bone.

Nelson went home, moped around not knowing what to do for the weekend, then out of habit, simply returned to the office as usual on the following Monday. Knight rescinded the firing, and Nelson was told to go work in Nike's T-shirt business.

I had been traveling between the 17th Street design office of Peter Moore to the new Nimbus design building. Strasser had his office in front, dominated by a ping-pong table as the conference table. Jack Joyce now headed up footwear production with a unique leadership style in the same building. He ordered sleeping cots to be placed next to each workspace, apparently to emphasize Strasser's Rule #7 "Your job isn't done until the job is done."

Tinker who also was commuting between locations and not having a lot of money, bought a moped to travel on nice days. But Tinker realized his most creative work was done at home. At one point, watching Tinker leave the parking lot on his moped, Joyce commented, "I don't mind you people taking vacation. Just don't take it around my people!"

Jack obviously didn't understand Rob's Rule #3: "Perfect results count, not a perfect process." Plus, Jack was an asshole.

I didn't get fired, but I found myself without a job. One day I was told to move to an empty cubicel at the far south end of Nimbus. No job, but "You report to Harry Johnson." One meeting with Harry and he said, "I don't know what you're supposed to do." I thought back to my defining moment with Bowerman, when he said "You can leave, or stay and be the best you can be." In fact, I drove to Eugene and met with Bill in his home overlooking the McKenzie River.

As was typical, Bill confessed that he didn't know if any of his advice made any sense. It always did. His advice this time was simple. "Hold your powder. Things always change."

Back at Nimbus, I couldn't stand sitting at that desk with nothing to do, so I went home. It was summer now, starting to warm the chilled Willamette River and the sandy beach. I spent the time with Tracy and Kaili on the boats and bought a long board windsurfer. Tracy and I started windsurfing across the river and back, and with the Willamette being tidal, we noticed a problem. Rocks and sticks once visible disappeared from sight when the tide went up. Coming in on the board, it was not unusual to step on a rock or stick, cutting or bruising the foot. I pulled out a pair of Nike racing flats, a model called the Sock Racer that sported a nylon mesh upper. They allowed the water to flow in and out, which was good, but the molded urethane sole was slippery on the board or boat deck. So I went to work.

With nothing better to do, I started sketching some ideas, then drove to Eugene and met with Bob Newland in Bowerman's lab. It felt good to get back to something that I had learned to do as a young man. We looked at material options and Newland was eager to make a prototype.

Windsurfing was taking off in the Columbia Gorge, as the wind passing over the river built up speed through the high and narrow passage. The stretch of the Columbia at Hood River was known as one of the top windsurf spots on the planet, right up there with Ho'okipa Beach on Maui. Lewis and Clark paddled these waters below the falls after portaging their canoes. Now the brightly colored sails of windsurfing boards dotted a river made wide with dammed up water.

I visited the first shop for "boardheads" in Hood River and, to my surprise, the owner was Doug Campbell. Doug grew up in Eugene and graduated two years ahead of me at South Eugene High. A good skier on South's team, he had followed in his father's footsteps and became a doctor. Doug married a member of the Stevenson timber family and settled in White Salmon, Washington, a small town on a high rock ridge looking out to Mount Hood. He started out on a big board in the Hood River Marina, where the water was calm and protected by the docks. But gradually, with experience, Doug ventured farther out on the Columbia and gained a reputation. By the time I met Doug again, he had quit practicing medicine, opened Gorge Windsurfing, had a popular launch site named after him, and ran a windsurfing school. I found Doug to be full of enthusiasm, but also capable of a strong, well-informed critique of my design work. I would be back.

At Nimbus, Jack Joyce controlled what product was developed in the sample room with a "green light/red light" response. I needed some help and had gone to a Nike pattern maker named Peter Dillon. From Boston, Dillon was a young, willing contributor to the design process. My challenge was figuring out how to replace the Sock Racer outsole with a lower profile, perhaps die cut like the Waffle Racer.

Joyce didn't have authority over Bowerman's lab in Eugene. If he had tried, Bill would have handed Jack his ass on a silver plate, but he had no problem giving me the red light. Peter and I had gotten far enough to make a rough sample marrying the Sock Racer upper to the Waffle Racer bottom and midsole. I put this in front of Doug Campbell alongside the prototype Newland sent up from Eugene.

By then, Doug was so good he wouldn't even go out on the water unless the wind was blowing at least 40 mph. He knew enough to explain the lateral forces at play and the reason most people go barefoot. You need to feel the surface of the board, and going barefoot gave you a huge tactile advantage. I was struggling with how to combine proper lateral support with the low profile that would give a sock-like fit, and if I could get it right, the Aqua Sock would give windsurfers who wanted more foot protection a choice.

In frustration, I drove to Eugene to meet with Bowerman. He toyed with the prototype in his hands, looking at it from all angles. "You're trying too hard," he said. "Follow the KISS Method—Keep It Simple Stupid," and he laughed. Bill knew of Doug Campbell. One of Doug's teammates on the South ski team was Dave Lafferty, son of Frank Lafferty. Bowerman had carried Frank over his shoulders in Italy when Frank had

Nelson Farris

Joan Benoit has broken from the pack early in Santa Monica. She was running free for the gold.

Geoff Hollister

Carl Lewis walks out on the Beaverton High School track to test the muscle look unitard and jumpsuit. Manager Joe Douglas prefers the trenchcoat.

Farris and me in a typical meeting with "Rolling Thunder."

One immaculate "Kookaburra" remains dockside while another is towed to the race course.

Jeff Johnson, Geoff Hollister & Jeff Galloway—"the 3 Jeffs" at a Running Design Resource meeting.

Nike Archives

Nike Archives

Geoff Hollister

Tracy has his arm around me following his state championship win (top), and is buried in a hug from his grandfather (above).

Fred Stolle controlling the doubles court.

Geoff Hollister

Wendy Young with her hand out in Macau. She never let go.

Jaakko Tuominen

Erich and I prepare Lasse Viren for his Fire On The Track interview in front of Prefontaine Hall on the Nike campus.

I'm squinting into the cold wind near the Scottish border, while the tough Englishmen Brendan Foster and Ian Stewart are wide-eyed.

With Dana Carvey and the film crew after the Fire on the Track interview. It was impossible to keep a straight face as the interviewer.

Geoff Hollister

"Kaili" churns through the water under threatening skies.

Nike Archives

One of my last times with Bill Bowerman, with the wonderful Barbara Bowerman between us.

The "1940's" Bowerman athletes lead the rest of us past the Bowerman Building on the track before the fans assembled for the 2000 Prefontaine Classic.

Sharon Young

With our yellow lab Sam as a puppy. He would become my constant companion during my biggest challenge.

jumped into a foxhole and a German hand grenade went off. He said "Keep working with Doug."

To do what Bill suggested, I had to get around Jack Joyce's red light. I talked Peter Dillon into coming into Nimbus on a Saturday, and we worked on the changes and stripped the prototype down, eliminating the support straps and foxing, minimizing the heel cup and lowering the midsole

Foxing is a narrow strip of reinforcement layered between the mid-sole and outsole at the heel and toe. It is typically made of suede or a synthetic, and it helps hold the glue that binds the various parts together.

crepe. On the outsole, we'd use Bill's waffle from the javelin boot. Strasser got involved, and with Rolling Thunder's insistence, we turned the red light into a green light.

I returned to Hood River with the prototype and a birthday present for Tracy—short board lessons for the two of us. Now on the water next to the launch site, Tracy was fearlessly picking up water starts while I proved a hopeless student, the cold water cramping my leg muscles. The prototype still received mixed reviews from Doug Campbell.

Back at Nike, I began showing the green light prototype to a few confidantes. Tinker Hatfield was into sailing and had built a small, flat bottomed boat called a pram from a kit. He would launch it at the Sellwood Bridge close to his home and sail it on a north wind upstream on the Willamette to our beach. Another sailor was Nike's new Public Relations manager, Chris Van Dyke. The son of comedian Dick Van Dyke, Chris owned one of the best blue water cruising sloops, a Valiant 40 named *Windsong*. I showed him the prototype outside Knight's office, where we talked about possible uses, and discussed the Campbell connection and what was happening in The Gorge.

"Can you get other colors?" Chris asked. Peter and I returned to the sample room, and turned out the still unnamed shoe in six colors.

I showed the prototypes to Nike's "Dean of Sales Reps," Al Miller. Al had known my uncle Elzie, who was a sales rep for the Brown Shoe and the White Shoe companies when I was just a boy, and I had great respect for his input. Once, in a meeting at Nimbus, I witnessed Jack Joyce ripping into Al with a slew of obscenities. It was totally uncalled for, but Al sat there looking professional as always in sport coat and tie, not responding. I told Al afterwards, "You have my apology—that was not necessary."

"Don't worry," Al said. "But I tell you, you've got a winner in this little product. Price it right and I can sell a ton of them."

This was all Van Dyke needed, "Hey, maybe there's a job for both of us here." I was traveling to the east coast and Chris and I arranged to meet with the Northeast area sales reps at the LaGuardia Marriott. Headed by New York's Sam Siegel, they loved the simple product laid out on a coffee table in a rainbow of colors. "Under twenty bucks retail? I can sell plenty."

Nike had hired accountant Ron Nelson to manage our footwear orders from the factories. Initially cautious, Ron Nelson informed Chris and me that the original factory order would be for only 40,000 pair. Undaunted, Chris and I met with a guy I dealt with at my local West Marine store, Jeff Sleight. Jeff introduced us to the big cheeses at their home office in Watsonville, California. Chris and I were still struggling with coming up with a name for our simple little footwear product. While sitting outdoors during lunch with the West Marine guys, Chris excused himself to go to the men's room with, "Well, that's aqua under the bridge." When Chris returned, I said, "I've got it. I've got the name for our product—the Aqua Sock."

The Aqua Sock it would be, and the first 40,000 pair were gone in two months, leaving Ron Nelson and the production team scrambling to fill the hole. In the meantime, Chris and I were on the road talking and promoting. Dave Kottkamp was in Hong Kong at this time and left a message, "Hollister, I don't know how you did it, but you pulled a rabbit out of your hat again." More like a shoe from out of nowhere, but coming from Dave, the comment was appreciated.

The response to the Aqua Sock surprised even Chris and me. Al Miller informed us that the older generation used the Aqua Sock for water aerobics to avoid cutting their feet on the edge of pool tiles. Sailors, paddlers, and power boaters used them. We got requests from parents for children's sizes for beachwear. While manning our booth at our first Seattle Boat Show, one consumer spun the Aqua Sock in his hands, laughed, and said admiringly, "The guy that came up with this must be cooling his heels with a piña colada in the Caribbean right now."

"No," I responded, "you're talking to him."

Doug Campbell, however, was not satisfied. His complaint? "They don't work for short boards." It was part of the Nike way to try to please the most demanding and knowledgeable customer because doing so led to excellence. So, I went back to work on what would become the Aqua Sock Too. Doug thought that a wide strap over the instep would help. We also designed a new cup sole to help hold the foot in place.

I never did win Doug over. Even though he's sold quite a few pairs of Aqua Socks out of his shop, as far as I know he's still riding barefoot.

Tom Niebergall, Nike's patent attorney, told me that the Aqua Sock was not patentable. I had incorporated a variety of materials and techniques that were known throughout the industry, but the Aqua Sock lacked that essential patentable new idea. What we did do was create a large new footwear category, and Nike soon had dozens of competitors. Twenty years later sales are still strong enough to keep the Aqua Sock in the Nike product line.

CHAPTER 23: THE AMERICA'S CUP

In July of 1985, a phone call came in from out of the blue, all the way from Australia. The call was from Kim Grist, who ran track at Oregon State with Nike footwear developer Dan Fulton. After he returned to Australia, Kim started a small marketing company called GBW.

Kim was looking ahead to the America's Cup races in 1987. An Australian businessman named Kevin Parry came forward to challenge Alan Bond for the right to the defend the cup against the Americans. Parry built three racing yachts, named *Kookaburra I, II* and *III*, all designed by Iian Murray, and he'd just hired a top young skipper named Peter Gilmour. Kim Grist put us in touch with Murray and Gilmour to discuss their product needs and to see if Nike would be willing to design and build apparel for their crews.

> In 1983, Australia II, owned by Australian Alan Bond, ended 132 years of American dominance in the America's Cup. Beset with mechanical problems in the first two races, Australia II came back from a 3-1 deficit with three straight victories in the final three races.

Shortly after that call from Grist, I met with Strasser. With my wife Carol partnering with a Lake Oswego couple to open a retail sporting goods store, I was seriously considering leaving Nike and joining them full-time. I felt the company was changing and that perhaps I was no longer a proper fit. I don't know if it was the flood of orders for Aqua Socks or the call from the Aussies and Rob's willingness to meet with them, but Rob argued that I should be patient. "Let's get these Aussies up here and then go see Knight."

Chris Van Dyke was really getting stoked about the possibilities. Public Relations remained Chris' day job, but with his boundless energy and enthusiasm, he was ready to take on the challenge of working with the Australians. "Imagine going sailing and getting paid for it," he said. "It's almost like cheating."

Meanwhile, I had been working on a line of windsurfer apparel to go with the colorful Aqua Socks. The footwear was creating some concerns with top windsurfing competitors like Alan Cadiz and Laird Hamilton, so I went to Maui to meet with them and gain insight into what was needed. We had some good contacts in the Gorge with Kay Kuchera, Pat Dougherty and Jane Parker. Kay and a hot high school competitor from Fresno, Brent Pederson, swore by Aqua Socks. But we were not windsurfers ourselves, despite the fact that we had both been taking lessons, and we were setting ourselves up for a fall.

We were really just spectators, and we made a classic error. Observing all the bright colors of sails, we took that as a design cue for the apparel line, called "Aqua Gear." The problem was that really serious competitors other than Kay wore mostly black and gray, and we underestimated their resistance to change.

Iian Murray and Peter Gilmour sat down with Strasser, Chris and me over beers, and you could immediately see Rob liked these guys. Murray was definitely the experienced visionary, while Gilmour possessed this childlike enthusiasm and a broad grin. Rob, with his typical enthusiasm, jotted notes on a cocktail napkin—his answer to a legal pad. We weren't close to being there, but Rob was willing to check into the difficult Australian import quota issues and have both sides determine an apparel line list so we could set a total cost.

With the Aqua Sock approaching unit sales only seen in the Jordan shoe, and Rob thinking this Australian America's cup effort had potential, Knight sat down with Chris, me and a group of Nike V.P.s. Knight delivered a message: Van Dyke would move over full-time from public relations to the marketing of this new category, I would design, and "they are to be left alone." When asked where we would work, Phil said, "I don't know, put them in a metal shed somewhere." We ended up next door to Nike headquarters.

One of the first things I pursued was what the conditions would be like in Australia for the crew. Van Dyke made the first trip down to visit the operation and explore the needs. It was becoming obvious that it was going to be expensive and we'd be negotiating small production numbers out of Asia.

I followed up with a sketchbook of ideas and a long flight to Perth. The Cup would be conducted out of Freemantle, a port town just a few kilometers from Perth. Freemantle was full of beautiful old brick buildings from an earlier day. Now neglected, they were going through a major transformation as this was where the action would be for the biggest event in yachting. A combination of the Olympics, the Super Bowl, and Wimbledon, the America's Cup would attract everyone from the simplest enthusiast to the wealthy, arriving in their personal jets to stay aboard their crewed mega-yachts, transported there for their pleasure.

I stayed in Perth but was invited out to spend as much time with the *Kookaburra* crews as I needed. The morning started early, and I camped out with my workout gear to join in their 6 a.m. run through the streets, which I handled with ease. Some of these guys were huge, and not so quick on a jog. Then we hit the weight room. I followed them on their circuit and the big guys kindly reset pins lower on each machine, "'Ow 'bout that mate?"

We didn't waste much time getting to the chow hall. Parry's yachting syndicate had thought of everything from the visually shielded pens the boats were lifted into, to apartments nearby and huge metal work sheds with high security and meeting rooms. Following a hearty breakfast fit for a lumberjack, we entered one meeting room. I joined the crews for *Kookaburra I* and *II* who would be sparring that day off the coast. Weather buoys sent real time feedback into the room on the tides, wind, water and air temperature—the latter expected to hit a high of 90°F that day.

I eyed the ragtag collection of gear the guys were wearing. Most of their shirts, pants, and shorts were a dark green. A locked gate opened for us in the closed compound and there sat the magnificent gold-hulled *Kookaburras*. They sparkled. I would join the after guard behind Laurie Smith, the helmsman on *Kookaburra II*. Smith was a long, blond haired Englishman and a highly regarded helmsman. He was hired to sharpen Murray and Gilmour.

Large inflatables with high-powered outboards pulled the motorless 12-meters from their bays out into open water. As the sails went up, the crew on the inflatables raced off to set markers for the day's course. As the wind blew up, *Kookaburra II* heeled and my first impression was how noisy a 12-meter could be. Metal on metal growled and banged at every adjustment and each tack. Orders had to be barked loudly over the din and the wind noise that slapped the side of the hull and the Kevlar sails.

A typical 12-meter racing yacht crew numbers 11, including 2 grinders, 2 tailers, 1 bowman, 1 foredeck man, 1 sewerman, 1 navigator, 1 tactician, and 1 helmsman. The after guard consists of the helmsman, who stands at the wheel, and the tactician and navigator, who stand behind the helmsman. While at sea, crew members are quick to assist each other and are not confined to their nominal tasks.

Once up to speed, we were sailing—practically flying, really—parallel with *Kookaburra I*, and we tacked and looped and jibed in a swan dance to the start line. The practice session would run 9 hours and, from my position on the stern, I could view each crewmember at work, from the gymnastic, nimble bowmen to the muscular grinders. The sewerman seemed to have the unenviable job of emerging from the windless, shadowed forward hull, lugging a sail change up into windswept 90-degree heat, then hauling the old sail back down to leave the deck unencumbered. With the salt and the sun and the wind on top of the strenuous physical work the crew did, I could see that apparel design was going to be a challenge.

I learned three other lessons that day. About one hour into the practice, we tacked as a powerful wind gusted, and my ball cap landed in the sea yards behind us. Not that I hadn't witnessed caps coming off the crew, but they all had tethers connecting their caps to the backs of their shirts. They'd simply turn and smile as they retrieved the flyer and plopped it back where it belonged.

Sometimes you can use an extra set of hands when things get hairy, and Laurie Smith, moving as fast as he could, accidentally flipped a good sized chrome winch handle overboard. He shrugged at me, smiling, and with both hands palm up, said "150 bucks—we have more." Second lesson learned—even the best yachtsman can make a mistake.

Peter Gilmour kindly offered his apartment for me to shower after the sparing sessions. Looking in the mirror, I desperately needed it. Capless, sunburned, and covered in salt with the low freeboard, this was just one day in the life of a professional sailor. I did not grind, trim or hoist one sail, but I stood there, beat-up with a jagged split atop my head, as though someone had used a can opener. The sun, wind, and salt exacts a toll, and that was another lesson learned.

Over the next few days, I collected more detailed information on the crew's apparel needs from the syndicate heads, but I focused more on the guys on the boat like bowman Donny McCracken, sewerman Tony Bellingham and a guy nicknamed "Fresh." I laughed at that, as "Fresh" was usually covered in grease and sported a ratty beard and hair. But as Gilmour offered, "He's experienced, and he gives you the straight scoop. No ego here." In fact, the crew handled any egos when they surfaced with this gentle put-down—"Yeah, he's a legend in his own lunchbox."

To mount an America's Cup challenge, one must be consumed by some measure of ego and ambition. Alan Bond began as a sign painter and built an empire that would include a communications company. It was huge news when he wrestled the cup away from the Americans and brought it to Perth. Rival Kevin Parry must have eyed the Cup at some length before announcing his multi-million dollar gamble to challenge Bond. But here they were, full of bluster and bravado, the smaller Parry and now a heavier Bond, toe-to-toe.

When I returned to Beaverton I was pleased to see that the Aqua Sock had maintained its momentum. They were catching on with campers and being used on jet skis and for bringing dinghies ashore. Kids wore them to school, and they were a popular choice for everything from reef walking to wearing in public showers.

Another unique call came in—this time from a banker in Wichita, Kansas. Peter Zandbergen was high up in the U.S. Rowing Federation and commented on how popular the Aqua Sock had become with rowers. He inquired as to Nike's interest in outfitting the 1988 Olympic team with the sock and uniforms. We arranged to meet at a rowing event in Los Angeles.

With so many directions spinning off one product, it became difficult to prioritize. Chris and I decided to focus on the needs of the *Kookaburra* crew. They would end up in a globally televised spotlight if they successfully advanced and we had a tight timeline. Delivery was needed by June 1. Once we had that out of the way, we could deal with the rowing team's needs.

We sent some initial samples to Freemantle for testing. I was surprised by the response I got. These guys had been wearing rugby shirts and shorts on deck for years, and who was I to tell them what to wear? What we'd come up with was a blend of 85% polypropylene and 15% wool in a high shawl-collared sweat top. The high collar protected the back of the neck from wind chill, and the fabric blend reduced water retention. I designed the sweat top with kangaroo pockets and a secure zip pocket. It was a great garment, but the prototypes were gray, and they didn't like them when they took them out of the boxes. It wasn't until they tried them and saw how functional they were that they began to accept what I had done.

The sewerman, Tony Bellingham, was the hardest to please. He had a difficult job in the toughest conditions, and he was very resistant to change. I had arranged to add 10% nylon to the all cotton rugby shirt to reduce water retention and increase flexibility, but Tony really liked his all-cotton shirts. I told him, "Try it, see if you like it," and after he'd given the new gear a workout, he was satisfied. I knew, like with Pre, if we could satisfy Tony, we could satisfy anybody.

A lot of these guys were recruited directly off the rugby pitch. They had huge thighs, and we learned quickly that they could shred a garment's seams with one movement. We added diamond crotch reinforcement inside of the short and the pant, and the problem was solved.

Our apparel developer in Hong Kong, Gary Peck, was going to be busy meeting the deadline. He had to source wool for fabrication in Asia, polypropylene pellets from Italy, cotton, nylon, molded plastic zippers, and specialty buttons. He had to have the garments fabricated, embroidered, packaged and shipped to Australia, a country with tight quota restrictions, and had to get it all done in under twelve months. He did.

On the footwear side, I combined a tumbled leather moccasin and a protective heel. A little clunky looking, but they were amazingly comfortable. Avoiding traditional siping for traction on the outsole, we used Bowerman's wide waffle in a natural and synthetic gum rubber blend. The Aussies thought it slipped a bit too much, especially bowman Donny McCracken, so I went to work on a specialty product for him. Starting with a mesh upper wrestling shoe that laced above the ankle, I removed the outsole, then wrapped, glued, and stitched a 100% gum rubber outsole in a grooved wave pattern. This proved to be a winner, and requests came in for more. But the shoe never had a name and would never be mass-produced.

As much as we worked on the details—fit adjustments, non-corroding rubber rugby buttons, nylon zips, and double reinforcements, nothing seemed more important to the Australians than color. They were used to dark green with gold. Admittedly, as clean as they kept the boats, grease could easily rub into fabric somewhere on the boat, and dark green hid the stains better. But I took a performance view, and I was more concerned with the heat of the sun on the water and the potential danger of a man going overboard. I drew up a line list of coordinated product of predominantly white, with gold saddle shoulders cut for high visibility should a man go overboard. White did a much better job of reflecting the sun as well. Green appeared only on the embroidered letters and numbers. I argued my points to the syndicate and convinced them. Now the question would be whether the crew would wear it.

All growth companies will experience growing pains, and this period was one of ours. Knight had appointed Bob Woodell as president. A little burned out, Phil was spending more time at his place in Sunriver. Not even he could have predicted Reebok's good fortune in the aerobics shoe market, nor our concurrent poor performance. At the same time, Nike was becoming many things, and our top people were both invested in their interests and seeking potential growth opportunities.

As much as Knight had put the word out to "Leave them alone," Chris and I found ourselves sitting in front of Nike footwear manager Bob Wood's office desk. Bob was a stick and ball guy, I was a running geek, and we didn't always speak the same language. Bob reached into a file drawer and pulled out a rather thin report. Proud of his MBA, Bob waved the report in his hand and said, "Some day, some day, you'll have a business plan like this." He went on to tell us of his plan to build Nike into a golf power. Chris and I gave each other a side glance in disbelief, like "Why are we supposed to be listening to this?" Bob wanted us under him rather than running our Aqua Gear Skunk Works, didn't have any interest in our boating product, but was hot for the numbers produced by the Aqua Sock. He requested more information on our business strategy.

Looking back on it now, we all should have been paying more attention to Rob's rules, especially point number 8: Dangers. His list of points under that heading—Bureaucracy, Personal Ambition, Energy Takes vs. Energy Gives, and Know Our Weaknesses—were all applicable to the situation at hand.

Down in Australia, our distributorship was owned by Beatrice Foods—another one of Moodhe's picks. The sporting goods division of Beatrice Foods was managed by the two Rose brothers, and Nike urged that the Roses be fired. Geoffrey Rose, in particular, was a problem. He was portly, disagreeable, and he owned a sock factory that was straight out of a Dickens novel. To replace them, new people were hired, including a guy by the name of Wayne Bridgeman, a former Adidas employee. The *Kookaburra* contract required product Nike had no intention of building that was needed for their more formal events. Rather than waste valuable quota with imports, we leaned on Bridgeman to ensure the needed blazers, trousers, shirts and ties were supplied and tailored if needed. Working with Bridgeman turned out to be not unlike buying a used car off a shoddy lot. You were constantly on him to keep the failed delivery of a rep tie from screwing up a much larger production effort.

October 18 was the first day of the preliminary races that would decide which of six yachts would defend the cup. I was back in the Freemantle compound with my Nikon in hand, and I nervously awaited the crew arrival as *Kookaburra II* and *III* floated next to me. There had been some complaints about the apparel I'd designed, which I understood. With such a range of body types and jobs on the boat, it was impossible to satisfy everyone. All I could think was "What will they wear?"

The gate swung open and in they came one at a time to their dockside lockers. One by one, they were wearing the gear—I was filled with excitement and relief. The Cup was to begin, and we were in it.

The preliminary races came down to a contest between Alan Bond's Australia IV and Kevin Parry's Kookaburra III. The finals of the defender selection series were held between January 14 and 20, 1987. Kookaburra III won five races, eliminating Australia IV.

As pleased as I was on my return flight to the U.S., I wondered just how durable our new product would prove to be. As *Kookaburra II* and *III* marched through the defender series, the apparel would be subjected to 72 races under often brutal conditions.

The minicams placed on the mast and stern of the competing boats beamed up-close coverage around the world. This had not escaped Bob Wood. Not a yachting fan, but himself a very competitive person, Bob acknowledged that we had "Bet on the right horse" and Nike was getting tremendous coverage.

I wasn't sure which would last longer, the *Kookaburra* product or me. I was beginning to feel that Nike management was not listening, that we were distancing ourselves from our retailers and consumers. I voiced my frustrations in front of the now 300-plus pound Strasser. I felt we were no longer honoring our promises. I argued to Rob that something had happened to the "love of work" attitude that attracted us to Nike in the first place. Bottom line, our people are our most valuable resource, and we are doing little to maximize their effectiveness.

Perhaps I should have checked my opinion that Nike had become big, fat, ugly, and not trusted, given the man I was speaking to.

I received a call from University of Washington rowing coach Bob Ernst with an invitation to visit their team practice in Seattle. Bob was one of the Olympic rowing coaches, and Seattle was the location for a pre-Olympic training camp. I headed up the freeway with line drawings and a sample from the *Kookaburra* line in hand. Ernst proved to be a great resource. We narrowed down already developed product that would work, like a fleece top and a shell jacket, and identified specific needs for racing in the boats.

Chris and I continued to attend the boat shows. Buzz Gorder, who built sales displays for Nike, had designed a booth for us. Although standing most of the day became a grind, it did put us in contact with our customers. We also got an opportunity to get away and tour the latest boats. Since my experience with the Aussies, I had reconnected with my love for sailing. And here I was owning a powerboat. I had turned my back on something that had been at my core for twenty years.

Chris and I were walking the docks of Seattle during a boat show when we came upon the broad canoe stern of a 37' sloop. "Hey, a Valiant Esprit," Chris called out, and he immediately climbed aboard. The sloop was being shown by Marine Service Center owner Jim Rard. We toured down below and Chris marveled at all "the good stuff" the boat had on it and marine architect Bob Perry's design magic. "Look at the cool bins for the cutlery and garbage," Chris said as he opened everything. "Geoff, you could do a lot worse. This is a primo boat!"

I returned to Portland, thinking of the boat beyond my budget. At the same time we were at the Seattle show, *Kookaburra III* had bested *Australia IV* in the defenders' final, and was now in the Cup Final against Dennis Conner and the *Stars & Stripes*, who had disposed of the Kiwis in the Louis Vuitton. Over a beer Chris said, "It's time to send Dennis back to the drapery

The Louis Vuitton Series always determines who challenges the holder of the America's Cup.

business!" Chris was referring to Dennis Conner and his day job in San Diego. The problem was, the man you hate to lose to was also a helluva sailor, and he had a fast boat. To our dismay, *Kookaburra III* would drop four in a row to Stars & Stripes and the Cup would go to San Diego.

So, had we really bet on the right horse? Certainly we had "Lived off the land," seizing an opportunity when it came our way. But a win by *Kookaburra III* might have changed what was to follow in the Nike corporate offices.

I drove Tracy up to Seattle to look at the Valiant Esprit, and an offer had been made on the boat, so we looked at what else was available. Nothing seemed to measure up as we walked the docks of other brokers. I looked at a French-made Elite 36, a Wauquiez, a Peterson 40 and on and on. I returned to Portland dissatisfied.

Yet another phone call came out of the blue—a woman telling me she had a client who was interested in buying our bungalow on the Willamette. I told her it wasn't available, and she said her client was serious and would make it worth our while. She said he was also interested in buying *Bogie*. That hit a chord. If I could sell *Bogie* and my first sailboat, the *Mugwump*, it would be the start on a good down payment on a bigger boat. If I sold my Mercedes 250SE Coupe, I just might have what I needed.

I decided to meet with Barry Schlesinger, the client the woman on the phone referred to. As it turned out, he had a best friend who grew up on the Willamette, and those were some of his best memories. He wanted the same for his own children. Barry loved commercial fishing, but his father, who was a successful developer in downtown Portland, had argued that unless Barry became more active in the family business, Barry risked getting left out if he didn't move to Portland and leave commercial fishing behind. "Whether or not we do the house deal, I want the boat," Barry told me. I liked his priorities.

Tracy and I were back to Seattle for a more intense boat search with the prospect that I might actually be able to afford one. To my surprise, as we walked the docks of Marine Service Center on Lake Union, there sat the Valiant Esprit. I asked Jim Rard about it and he informed me that the buyer failed to qualify and it was available. I inquired more, talked price and made an offer. The offer was countered, but something interesting happened. The owner knew me. A couple of years behind me at South Eugene High, John Coker had dated my sister Claudia and supposedly we had met. John owned shingle factories in Creswell and Forks, was going through a divorce with his wife Tina, who taught at North Eugene, and needed to sell the boat. In my offer, I stipulated that closing would coincide with the closing of my house sale in Lake Oswego. Had John Coker not known me, this offer never would have flown.

On April 27, Barry and Hazel bought our bungalow and the next day, I owned *Exuberance*. We would rename her after my daughter Kaili, Hawaiian for "Goddess of the sea."

Knight's "Leave them alone" message didn't hold and before we knew it, we were suffering with top heavy management. Jim Gorman was moved over as a footwear V.P., and since Jim had already been helpful, that assist was welcome. But then a guy with a dress shoe background by the name of Gary Wells was brought in and made a V.P., as was a former Sperry Topsider executive named John Barsorian.

As if it wasn't enough to have three V.P.'s crowding us, Nike Board member Chuck Robinson was brought in to oversee our effort. Chris and I sat through a meeting with Robinson but the closest we ever got to the topic of Aqua Gear was his strong belief that we should have a manufacturing exchange across the U.S./Mexico border. But Robinson had introduced Knight to our Japanese partners at Nissho-Iwai, and he was John

Jaqua's brother-in-law. With those kind of connections to Nike we had to listen to whatever he said.

In October of 1987, stock markets around the world crashed. Nike's stock dropped from a high of just over $21 per share in late September to a low of $13.20 in early December. Perhaps worse than the drop in stock value was the drop in sales. In 1986, sales were $1 billion, and in 1987 they plummeted to $860 million. This led to massive layoffs at Nike. Kevin Parry's net worth dropped so much he had to sell all three *Kookaburras*.

Phil Knight told me "The worst part of being in business is when your friends have to leave."

Throughout 1988, it was a struggle to keep the Aqua Gear line alive. I don't know how the books were kept, but the upper management alone must have had us over budget. Chris and I were excited when Nike hired Greg Thompson from North Face. We finally believed we had an advocate within apparel who would run interference for us in upper management meetings. We were wrong. We learned that we would be told one thing, and behind closed doors, Greg changed position.

Inside the predominately female apparel department, Thompson had other problems and women came to me with their complaints. I could not tolerate the chaos. When I ran the issues "up the flagpole," my position was not supported. Nelson and Harry Carsh sat me down—Nelson was one of my closest friends and Carsh was an accountant turned V.P. and one of the millionaires within Nike. Carsh was the deliverer of the bad news: "Tom Clarke doesn't think you're a team player. Take a few weeks off and think about it."

I was in shock. Tom Clarke was Nike's Marketing VP, and if he thought I wasn't a team player, I was in trouble. When I tried to rebut with a few successes that required team play, topped with the Aqua Sock, Harry sarcastically cut me down with, 'If you

hadn't thought of it, sooner or later, somebody else would have."
I took the full two weeks off. In a management meeting that I
didn't attend, the decision was made. Boating product was
doomed. Only the Aqua Sock would survive. Talk about stabbed
in the back. But Chris Van Dyke called before I retired in disgust.
"Geoff, get out here. Let's go to lunch."

Someone must have listened to at least some of what I said.
Greg Thompson was gone.

With the Aqua gear line heading for closeouts, I had a new
assignment. I was to join a small team in what was called "APE
Apparel." A small product think tank, APE stood for Advanced
Product Engineering. My new teammates were former Patagonia
developer Jamie Martin and two great guys I really liked, Rick
MacDonald and Bill Deiter. Bill was a Rhode Island School of
Design grad, grew up on a Midwest farm, and teethed himself
on fixing farm equipment. Bill could fix anything. His huge round
eyes were filled with curiosity. Rick, a former runner from the
Boston area, had a thin face, a thin neck, a big Adam's apple,
and long hair flowing down past his shoulders. When he ran, he
reminded me of the Road Runner, beep-beep.

The U.S. Olympic Rowing Team arrived in Seoul, South Korea,
for the Olympics, outfitted in Aqua Socks, custom competition
uniforms, the Tillicum Hood sweatshirt and the Williwaw shell
jacket. All but the competition pieces were from the boating line.
We embroidered the Olympic rings on the jacket and when the
team returned from a successful games, Zandbergen and Ernst
communicated to me that this was the first time the stylish French
and Italian teams had ever asked the Americans to trade
uniforms. That compliment was the dying salute to the line.

I thought about what we could have been. Nike's
promotional style and our constant innovation would have
propelled Nike to the top of a lifestyle industry. By the year
2000, I felt Nike would realize a half-billion dollar business.
Instead, it was over.

Kirk Richardson and I went for a run along the trails behind Creekside. A former 800 meter runner, the tall Richardson married Derderian's former wife Charlotte. They both knew the 800 distance well, as Charlotte was often a national finalist in her day. Kirk was also an avid rock climber and mountaineer. His dad was in the 10th Mountain Division with Bowerman. Kirk had launched an outdoor product line for Nike called ACG, which stood for All-Conditions Gear. But I wondered if Kirk would be "left alone." Reflecting back on Knight's words, I wondered if "left alone" was resented, and my undoing. Still I congratulated Kirk on his launch of products. And wished him success.

Rob Strasser's wife, Julie, and her sister were busy writing *Swoosh*, a book about Nike's history. The interviews were mostly complete when I rode down to Eugene with them. We visited the old Nike history locations. I told accompanying stories as they taped my voice and furiously jotted notes. One interview remained—Philip Knight.

Just prior to Knight's interview for *Swoosh*, Strasser left Nike. Some felt it was Knight's reluctance to name Rob president. Peter Moore followed Rob five months later, and they formed Sports, Inc., a consulting company. Their first client would be Adidas U.S.A. Rob and Peter went from consulting for Adidas to full-time positions and struck a deal. Jim Gorman was soon to follow.

Knight refused the interview. Phil put a high value on loyalty, and he told me that what hurt wasn't Strasser leaving Nike to go out on his own as a consultant. What hurt was the jump to Adidas, because "For a long time, Rob was my closest friend." Strasser, who once said, "The final battle will be in soccer on the fields of Germany" would now be fighting that battle for Adidas.

Three guys I really liked—Strasser, Gorman, and Moore—were now the enemy. *Swoosh* became two books in one—the genesis and the early days of Nike, and *The Rob Strasser Story* with benchmarks along the way of what Adidas was doing as Nike went through its mercurial growth. I did join the Strassers at their downtown Portland penthouse to celebrate the book release. There was "Rolling Thunder," the sleeves of his white dress shirt rolled up, his tie loosened, sweating profusely. Beads rolled down his face as he smiled through the reddish beard—all atop his 300 plus pounds.

It was the last time I'd see Rob Strasser.

CHAPTER 24: NIKE WORLD HEADQUARTERS

In July 1990, Nike moved into its new, 70-acre Murray Boulevard headquarters. With leases scattered all over Portland and primarily Beaverton, Nike was not a model of efficiency. I raced between meetings and buildings, grabbing quick lunches and trying to attend every one of Tracy and Kaili's soccer games. I was also going through a divorce. Call it selfish, but I had finally gotten up the nerve to voice how miserable I was at home, and I was leaving. No small decision, I worried daily about the impact on Tracy and Kaili. I moved to the boat as a live-aboard and put myself on a restrictive $400-a-month budget. I scrounged for coins some days to buy a gallon of gas to get me from Jantzen Beach to Nike and back. I knew I would have less. I might as well start now.

Soon after the Nike campus was built on Murray Boulevard I was walking in from the south parking lot with Mark Parker, Nike's V.P. for Research, Design, and Development. "Any concerns?" Mark asked.

I said, "Yes. This isn't real. Our consumer doesn't work or live in a place like this. And that berm. We can't see them. They can't see us."

Thompson Vaivoda & Associates, Nike's architects, designed a 20' berm to surround the campus. People driving by cannot see in until they arrive at one of three entrances. A footbridge linking the wood chip Jeff Johnson Jogging Trail extends over each entrance. The rest of the world is walled off, outside.

Knight put Howard Slusher in charge of the massive project that would accommodate 3000 employees around a man-made lake with water diverted from Tryon Creek. The creek meanders diagonally from the Southwest to Northeast corner. Nutria, ducks, and blue heron inhabit the creek and the lake is a favorite of what have become resident Canadian geese. They're smart—life couldn't be much better for them.

The planners and architects thought of everything—the jogging trail, a full gym, tennis courts, a great cafeteria, and a brew pub that doubles as an espresso stand in the morning. You can get your hair cut, use an ATM, drop your dry cleaning or shoes off for repair and never leave the campus.

Parker and I approached the lobby of the Michael Jordan Building, where I now worked on the fourth floor with the footwear designers. Mark said, "If you don't like it, why don't you see what you can do about it. Get back to me."

I came to the conclusion that Nike suffered from filtered information from the consumer. My job would be to remove that filter. Get the designers, developers, marketing managers and sports marketing staff out of their comfortable digs and face-to-face with the consumer.

It's not that Nike was completely out of touch with our customers. We were doing focus groups. I attended them. The problem with focus groups is you don't know much about the people in those groups. It was like a blind taste test, and I questioned the value of the feedback.

Something I learned from Bowerman is this: all good design solves a problem. If focus groups weren't the right strategy to solve the problem, what was? The answer I came up with was rooted in how we had approached the shoe business in the very beginning. We put our shoes on the best runners we could get because we knew if we could satisfy the most demanding customers, we could lead the market instead of following it. Common sense led me to the idea of meeting with athletes, rather than randomly chosen members of the public.

I called the solution I came up with Design Resource Meetings. They would be aimed at individual categories. I would start logically with my connections in the runners category. The list was impressive: Nike's first employee, the now retired Jeff Johnson. Jeff Galloway had already published his first book and owned Phidippedes, a specialty running retail store in Atlanta. Laurel James founded the successful Super Jock'n'Jill store in Seattle. Mark Allen was the world's top triathlete. Donald Quarrie was the retired dean of the

Mark Allen was the Ironman Triathlon World Champion six times from 1989 to 1995. In 1997 Outside magazine named him "The World's Fittest Man."

sprints. The list went on. We would spend a day and a half alone, going over the entire line, marketing and advertising. I would make a feedback list on a flip chart and coach the group to speak up— state your position and back it up, this is your chance. Then the Nike team would arrive either at a coastal or mountain location. We'd take breaks and do the activity we were discussing, and we'd have fun.

I ran the idea by Mark Parker, and he said, "Do it, and report to Notar." (John Notar was Nike's V.P. for U.S. Apparel.)

While I was preparing to get ready for the first meeting, Knight called and said, "The University of Oregon wants to honor Bill Bowerman before it's too late. I'm putting you in charge at our end. It's a surprise. Bill's not to know about it." I thought, "Oh shit, this won't be easy." I was going to need a lot of help.

I called Bob Newland, still a fixture in the Eugene lab. "Bob, I've got a tough one and we've got to keep this from Bill. Any ideas?"

Bob took to calling me every morning while I worked on this event. Each conversation started with, "Bob Newland here."

"Geoff Hollister here."

"Well hello, Geoff Hollister here."

It was our little game, and always the same prior to the sharing of the latest news. One of my earliest inspirers remained so.

I also tried calling Barbara. Bill answered the phone. I couldn't say, "I want to talk to your wife." So I made something up and tried to figure out when Bill might be gone, perhaps feeding his prized herd of bulls on the lower 40.

I came up with a shopping list, and Knight said, "We'll do it in the Bo Jackson Gym." Howard Slusher bristled at the idea, "Not on my shiny wood floor? You can't be serious." The floor would have to be carpeted, chairs and tables brought up the elevators, a stage built, and the banquet served from the adjacent racquetball courts. I came up with a speakers list that included former Oregon football coach Len Casanova, former UCLA track coach Jim Bush, Phil Knight, Bob Woodell, and Olympians Otis Davis, Kenny Moore, and Mac Wilkins. I thought of producing a documentary and Knight agreed to a budget for a 19-minute piece. Nike film and video was overloaded, but recommended an outside director. We went to work with over 50 interviews that I scripted. Again, Barbara was the toughest, as Bill was always around. Bob Newland came to my rescue and kept Bill at bay.

On May 3, 1991, athletes, university officials and "Men of Oregon" from around the country drove into Nike to our address, One Bowerman Drive, to honor "The Man." We held everyone on the second floor with cocktails while I was running around upstairs, busy with a sound check, the lighting, and trying to speed up the serving. Not easy. The doors to the racquetball courts are only so wide. The first tray of filled water glasses ended up on the floor because the tray wouldn't fit through the door.

Our guests start wandering up, checking the archival display cases, sitting next to old teammates. There was happy, constant banter. Knight and I were worried—if Bowerman finds out, he won't come, but Newland and Dr. McHolick did a great job diverting and delivering him.

When the Bowermans entered, everyone stood. On their way to the front of the room, people reached out to shake Bill's hand or pat him on the back. There were many, like Otis Davis, whom Bowerman hadn't seen in years. Phil Knight was already up front, absolutely beaming, and the Bowermans took their seats next to him. There was a slightly nervous smile on Bowerman's face as Hayward Field announcer Wendy Ray approached the mike, resplendent in his tuxedo. Wendy introduced each speaker as Bill squirmed in his chair, but if you knew him as I did, you knew underneath how Bill was enjoying the moment.

We all about fell out of our chairs as Otis Davis spoke. Perhaps you have to be a gold medalist to get away with it, but Otis addressed Bowerman with the forbidden word: "Coach." "The secret was in how he prepared you," Otis said. "I started with the high jump, then the 100, then the 220. Coach wanted to move me up to the 440. I asked how far that was. When he told me, I walked it. I came back and told him that's too far. I had a little hamstring problem and Coach said I needed a massage and he'd do it. So I lay down and he starts working this analgesic balm up my leg. He keeps workin' it and workin' it a little higher, and he's reaching some parts I'm rather proud of." Bowerman is red, but laughing at the same time as we are in hysterics. Otis continues, "Whew, I tell you, I ran that turn just as fast as I could. The sooner I finish, the sooner I can get this stuff off me!"

The lights went down after the final speaker. Wendy Ray directed everyone's attention to the screen. The 19-minute documentary played, perhaps leaving Bill in his least comfortable state. He preferred working without praise or commendation, and right then, he'd probably just as soon slip out the back door. But there he sat as athlete friends and of course, Barbara, all paid tribute. When the lights came back up, those blue eyes were visibly moist.

There was one last surprise. Bowerman was a big fan of saunas, and my last trick for the night was the mock cedar sauna I had built on the stage. Two chairs sat empty. Wendy Ray requested that Bowerman come to the stage and sit on one of the two chairs. Then Wendy began to alphabetically announce Bill's athletes, who lined up stage right. As the photographer positioned himself for the first shot of Bill sitting in the sauna with one of his athletes, Woodell waved me over, "Hollister, you aren't going to have every athlete go up? This won't work." I told Bob that it would go faster than he thought.

A few words would be exchanged as each athlete sat, either with an arm around Bill or Bill's around the athlete. Smiles all around as the flash goes off. Woodell signaled me again—a big smile this time, "Geoff, you were right. I was wrong. This is great!"

The room cleared, and I walked down to the second level of the Bo Jackson, where Knight found me. He literally lifted me off the ground, and he said "We did it, Geoff, we did it. We actually had the bastard in tears!"

I walked out to the cooler evening air and down the Walk of Fame. Each building on the Nike campus is connected with covered walkways, and along these walkways there is a plaque every few feet. Each plaque has a relief in bronze of an athlete who excelled representing Nike within their sport, and a short text telling a career highlight. The best of the best, the ones who, in Knight's eyes are the most intense, have buildings named after them—Michael Jordan, Steve Prefontaine, Alberto Salazar, John McEnroe, Mike Schmidt, Dan Fouts, and Joan Benoit Samuelson. More would come. Knight's choices are revealing. It's not the notoriety or how celebrated the athlete is in the public eye. These were the most competitive of the competitive.

Passing Prefontaine Hall, I recalled dedicating the building with a short remembrance during the campus opening party. The Prefontaine family, Knight, Hall of Famer Mike Schmidt and golfer Peter Jacobson were there in front of the large bronze statue of Pre, in full stride, one foot planted and the other reaching for the next step. I said, "If there is a spirit at Nike, it resides here in Prefontaine Hall."

The dinner for that event was held in a large tent in the south parking lot. I sat with the Prefontaines, as the great athletes and coaches milled about, hugging each other and laughing. The portable johns that night were not mere Porta-potties. They were first class trailers brought in, each one a nicely appointed restroom. When the need came, I stepped up to a urinal. Jim Valvano stepped up next to me, looking up as he unzipped. With his nasal East Coast voice, Jimmy boasted, "Hey Lefty, someday Nike's going to name this building after me."

I continued to work on the Design Resource Meetings, but I made sure I found time to get out to Lake Oswego High School and coach Tracy and his teammates in cross country. I stuck to Bowerman's successful hard/light schedule and kept the weekly mileage to 40. Tracy was responding, staying healthy, and mentally up for competition. His earlier frustration of missing varsity by one spot was long gone. Now 6'2" and powerful, Tracy was undefeated, setting course records at home, Canby, and Aloha.

On a beautiful clear day in Eugene, I watched Tracy compete in the Oregon State high school cross country championships. Held at Lane Community College, the course had a series of up and down hills, a long straight flat, a loop around two large duck ponds, a shorter up and down loop, then a final 300 on the track. Mom and Dad were there as Tracy ran with the leaders. His stride was long and controlled. He started to move on the hill during the second loop, opened a 10-yard gap and was on his own. I could tell prior to his reaching the final 300 that this was his day. No one could catch him. Afterwards, Tracy was buried in big hugs from his grandparents. The hard work had been worth it.

My old freshman coach at Oregon, Charlie Bowles found me in the crowd. Now coaching at Willamette University, Charlie had a huge smile and gave me a big hug, "He did it, he did it!" I was pleased of course, but I didn't understand why he was so elated. Turns out Charlie was head track coach at Lake Oswego before he moved on to the University of Oregon. Charlie still followed the school's track and cross country teams, and Tracy had just became the Lakers' first cross country state champion.

Back on the Nike campus, I jogged the wood chip trail. On the North side I saw a familiar figure ahead. It was Knight. I pulled up along side to say "Hello."

Phil answered, "Hey, great job with Tracy."
I told him, "I didn't do the running."
Phil added, "Well, you did something right."
Coming from Phil, that meant so much to me. We all traveled a lot, and our kids paid the price.

The Lake Oswego house was put on the market, Carol and I agreed to have one attorney draw up the divorce papers, and her store, Sportlife, was closing, but through all this, Tracy was consumed with running. We built a strong training base with fartlek runs on the Tryon Creek Park trails. Strength work continued with our version of the old Eugene 30th Street Drill—an 800 timed on the track, a hilly 4-5 mile run to another school track, a timed 800, then a run back to Lake Oswego High School and a final timed 800. This will make you tough, and it showed at the Centennial Invitational.

With 300 meters to go under the lights, Tracy's top challenge in the state for the 1500 title ran by my location. Jesuit's Seth Wetzel was breathing hard. He held a commanding lead by the time Tracy passed me. Tracy's face looked relaxed and I yelled, "He's dying Tracy—go get him!" It seemed too late, but Tracy responded. On the final turn, you could see the gap closing. Down the home stretch, Wetzel's posture was becoming more upright, as Tracy closed. Right at the tape, Tracy lunged, sprawling on the red synthetic track. The announcer announced the same time, with Tracy's momentum giving him the win. Only one runner in the country had run faster this season.

The phone calls started coming in from around the country, from coaches and athletes I'd worked with. They'd read the race results in *Track & Field News*, and they all wanted to know the same thing—is this the same Tracy Hollister? That little mop-haired boy I used to know in Eugene?

Now Tracy had a decision to make— where to go to school? Dellinger was in contact, and Sam Bell called. Now at Indiana, Sam had coached Bob Kennedy to multiple NCAA titles. I knew Sam could do the job, and Indiana deserved a look. Tracy was flown out for a visit. Bob Kennedy took Tracy for a run "up a hill." When they finished Tracy looked at Bob and said, "What hill?"

Bob Kennedy currently holds the American Record in the 5000. (12:58:21), and at one time, also held the American Records for the 3000. (7:30:84) and for two miles (8:11:59).

No hills, no mountains, and Indiana was a long way from home.

But Tracy liked Kennedy and Sam Bell, and that made the decision confusing. I suggested we drive to Eugene and he could talk with Bowerman, "Maybe he'll shed some light."

Tom Bowerman had the living room packed with friends discussing the preservation of waterways, so Bill led us back to the bedroom. I had never been in this part of the house. My eyes had to wander, taking it in. Bill's 10th Mountain Division trunk was in one corner, a bathroom in the other.

"Sit down Tracy." Bill settled on the edge of the bed.

"So why do you want to go to Oregon?" I had not prepared Tracy, and I honestly didn't think Bill would open with the same question asked of me nearly 30 years earlier. But he did. And as the conversation continued, an exact mirror. How many times had Bill done this over the years? He was unchanged, still the master.

Bill then walked us outside. In what I later realized was an act of genius on Bill's part, he asked Tracy to remove his shoes and socks and roll up his pant legs. "Stand here," he said. Bill got on his knees, his long fingers going over Tracy's feet and tendons. "Good." There was no further explanation. He simply touched him.

I pulled out my camera, and as Bill and Tracy sat with a bale of hay on the tailgate of Bill's little Suzuki pickup, I took their picture. On the way home, Tracy was abuzz, "He checked out my feet! How many runners in the country have had that done by Bowerman?"

Tracy signed with Oregon.

His senior year, with a lap to go in the State High School Final for the 1500, Tracy was boxed in, freeing Wetzel and Parkrose's Ben Andrews up front. Tracy had to break free after the bell. As he exploded out of his lane, Tracy's elbow hit Springfield's Andrew Hunt's head, and with Tracy's size, Hunt almost went over backwards. The race was on. Although Tracy ran the fastest final 400, it was Andrews and Wetzel by one tenth of a second.

When the gun went off with the best high school milers from five Western states at the starting line for the Prefontaine Classic, Tracy ran in front wire-to-wire. No contact, no boxing in. He ran it the way Pre would have—let the pack worry the whole way if anyone had enough speed to catch him. I knew Pre would have been happy, "That little kid of two is growing up!"

Dellinger red-shirted Tracy his freshman year. Carol and I had put him in school a year early due to his social maturity, and Bill wanted him to catch up physically. Tracy had matured, but Bill kept him on low mileage. He responded by winning the

AAU Cross Country Nationals for 18-19 year olds with a course record. In the spring he finished 4th in the PAC-10 1500 behind Kip Keino's son Martin. Then came the National Junior Championships, where he made the national team with Cal Berkley's Richie Boulet.

Running can be a tricky endeavor. I've always coached young runners about "the building blocks." You can have all the talent in the world, and maturity alone will bring improvement. But you can't afford to step backwards. Tracy followed a great year with a stress fracture while on a winter vacation run with none other than 1970's track star Ian Stewart and his club on icy roads in the midlands of England. They ran at a 5-minute pace for 10 miles. Tracy should have red-shirted, as advised by Dellinger, but tried to race in the spring with no base training.

After a promising sophomore cross country season, barely losing to Colorado's Adam Goucher and Alan Culpepper in a home meet, Tracy bumped his mileage. Hitting 100 miles, he left his competitiveness on some trail outside Eugene. I was furious, as I knew he had made a big mistake. Worse, he kept it a secret, failing to share it with either Dellinger or me.

And then things got even worse. While running on the beach at Mom and Dad's house, Tracy hit something sharp, slicing right through his Aqua Sock. The fatty pad of his left forefoot required eight stitches to close the gash. A second season was over.

I tried my hand at dating. I have advice for those who go through a divorce. The grass is not always greener. Dating was like finding the pieces to a complicated puzzle. It seemed some parts were missing. Some of those parts belonged to me.

Prefontaine Hall was filled with Ekins (that's Nike spelled backwards). Nike asked me to speak of Nike's heritage to this group, which was managing Nike's Running Tech Reps from around the world. At the end, a young participant introduced herself. "My name is Wendy Young. I work in our Hong Kong office and really enjoyed your talk."

The next day, she walked up to me in front of the Bo Jackson Fitness Center and repeated the message. I was dating someone at the time and really didn't think that much of it, but I appreciated the feedback. If she took the time to come up to me twice, I must not have said anything too stupid.

My Design Resource Meeting program received a green light from Mark Parker, but it drew some concern from the vice president of Nike marketing. Andy Mooney was English, and he was initially based out of the Exeter factory. Mooney rose through the ranks, coveting power and control. He put a red light on any new spike shoe development for the '92 Barcelona Olympics. When I heard this, I responded "What has to happen? Have a shoe disintegrate in front of a global audience?"

A year later that's exactly what happened. Coming off the final turn in the Olympic 400 meters, Quincy Watts' spike delaminated, separating the plate from the upper. Watts' power and superiority over the rest of the field still ensured a gold medal, but Nike looked bad. You roll out your best product each Olympic year, and we took our eye off the ball.

I don't know that my remarks reached Mooney's ears, but there he sat behind his desk. He asked pointed, direct questions as to why I was conducting the resource meetings. His thick, almost Scottish accent filled the room. I must have provided answers that eliminated the threat. His red light turned to green, and he let me go forward.

I had written an internal memo about Nike's inability to manufacture team uniforms, and for this I got called into the office of Stephen Gomez, the head of Nike apparel. Making team uniforms was such a natural, but instead Nike was chasing fashion. Tracy's Lake Oswego team sported the same colors as my Athletics West designs, and the Lake Oswego coach wanted the uniform, but could not get it. In my memo, I said that Tracy had worn Nike from the time I sewed black swooshes on his white baby booties. Now he had the opportunity to have exposure on the pages of *The Oregonian*, yet he might have to wear a competing brand.

Gomez was an ally of Tom Clarke's. They were actually housemates, along with a whole crew of mid-level Nike employees. He was visibly shaken by my memo about missed business and failed to provide an answer as to how to rectify the problem. I always believed that apparel had the potential to be as big as Nike footwear. I questioned if it would happen with the majority of people we put in charge of apparel. Once, when Gomez was touted as a guy who had really built the business, I said, "Imagine what we could do with someone who actually knows the business."

Sure enough, Tracy's picture was on the front page of *The Oregonian*, winning the state title with the Sub-4 brand on his chest.

Nike interviewed and hired Steve Miller to head Nike Running Sports Marketing. A member of our coaches' board while at Cal Poly SLO, Miller had moved to Kansas State as Athletic Director. Slick, organized, and an excellent speaker, Miller was quickly elevated to head all categories in sports marketing. He called me in to his ground floor office in McEnroe. He had a big smile, the firm handshake of an NFL player (which he was with the Detroit Lions) and was full of optimism. "Would you be interested in your old job in track and field?"

I had two questions, "Are the drugs as bad as they used to be, and are the agents as bad as they used to be?"

"Worse," Miller replied.

"No thanks."

I stuck with the resource meetings. If there was ever a product that owed its existence to these meetings, it was the GTS. Included on my tennis product team were Wimbledon doubles champion

Fred Stolle and a former neighbor of my parents in Monmouth, Oregon, Jim Marr. Now retired in Sun City, Jim complained about Nike prices, saying that he and many of his friends who competed in tournaments bought Dunlop shoes. He recommended a canvas upper price point product.

> Fred Stolle was a Wimbledon Men's Doubles Champion in 1962 and 1964, and he was a Mixed Doubles Champion in 1961, 1964, and 1969.

The Nike group responded, "We don't do canvas." Stolle who was highly respected not only as a player but as a television analyst, jumped to Jim's defense. "You don't get what this man is saying—he is leading you to a part of the market that Nike is absent in. It's a big business."

Just as I had outlined in my plan for these meetings, we played tennis during our breaks, since it was tennis that was under discussion. In a doubles match, Stolle showed he could still play. With minimal movement at mid-court, his deft touch sent the ball to both corners of the court, then just over the net, then deep into the corner. His opponents, who were decades younger, scrambled to chase each ball. Standing like a fencer with one hand behind his back, Stolle talked a little 70-year-old trash to his doubles partner—"Step in whenever you like, dear." His partner remained baffled with his control and efficiency.

That night at dinner with our Nike staff in attendance, women sat next to our long table, recognized Stolle at the end, and presented themselves. They asked Fred to sign the front of their sweatshirts. Pleased to oblige, Fred smiled as he placed his hand on the target. He said, with his distinctive Aussie accent, "I don't suppose this area would do?" Fred signed, and the Nike staff returned to Beaverton.

Within an amazingly brief six months from concept to production, the first shipment of canvas GTSs arrived from China and sold out in white and navy. Then Nike added suede in addition to the canvas and spread the colors. A great product came at the insistence of a man in his '70's—not Nike's target consumer.

One of my worst Nike moments came during the summer basketball meeting. I had a top group of participants including Arkansas' Darnell Robinson and future NCAA Tournament MVP Miles Simon. I had coordinated everyone's flights and pick-up at Portland International. We were heading through the Vista Ridge Tunnel on the way to the Oregon Coast when I sensed that we were missing someone.

We were. I called the office, "You've got to find him. He's never been to the West Coast and can't be left out there." We arrived at the coast and United Airlines finally informed us that the passenger in question never made the flight. The missing athlete was caught on videotape the night before throwing a chair in a bowling alley fight. Instead of participating in our meeting, Allen Iverson was in jail.

By 1993, the Design Resource meetings were touching global business. I had succeeded in breaking through the berm, world-wide. I contacted Juliet Moran in Hong Kong. Juliet was Nike's Asia Pacific marketing manager and willing to ensure that I got around Hong Kong and Macau for my report. At the last minute, Juliet was asked to fly to Japan for an interview for her next job. Juliet informed me that in a staff meeting she asked if anyone would be willing to chaperone me during my visit. Wendy Young raised her hand.

Have you ever been caught by surprise? As my Nikon clicked away and I interviewed people Juliet had recommended, Wendy Young was by my side. She was from Vancouver, B.C., but came to Hong Kong seven years ago to experience her roots. Both her parents were born in Hong Kong, her dad was from Wanchai and was now a structural engineer in Vancouver BC. Her grandfather was a physician and had received both the OBE and MBE from the British government for his contribution building medical units on the frontlines during WWII. Her grandmother was flown out to India by the Flying Tigers as the Japanese closed their noose around the city on the water. Wendy's father and two brothers hiked barefoot back to old family inside China. Their parents believed their chance of survival there was much better. She had a strong, athletic build. Toughness was in Wendy's genes.

In contrast, my history seemed tame. I learned that my friend Bill Hall in Nike International had hired Wendy. Wendy Young was occasionally interrupted with meetings, but most of the time she was right alongside me. At one point in a Kowloon shopping area jammed with sporting goods stores, I looked the wrong way as we crossed the street. She grabbed my hand to avoid my being hit by a car. She didn't let go.

We rode the Star Ferry together, ate at The Peak Café, and danced well into the night. I flew back to Oregon, but Wendy and I remained in constant contact. It didn't take long before the question of marriage surfaced, but we kept it to ourselves, until a few key contacts could be made.

I was again running the wood chip trail at Nike. The same familiar figure with the same stride was in front of me. "Phil, I have a favor to ask. Would it be possible for me to get married in the Nissho Gardens on campus?"

"Anyone I know?" Phil replied.

"Yes, Wendy Young from Hong Kong."

"You have my permission," was his simple reply, and I didn't think he thought much of it. I was sitting at lunch afterwards in the Joan Benoit Samuelson Center when Phil entered the checkout line across from Bill Hall.

"Hey, did you hear who Hollister's marrying?" Phil said excitely. "Wendy Young."

Bill came and sat with me as Knight walked away with a big smile. "Is this true?" I told Bill that it was. I've told him before, but I want to say it again here, in print: hiring Wendy Young was the best decision Bill Hall ever made.

Soon after, my sister had some business on the Nike campus and ran into Phil. "What do you think of Geoff and Wendy?" she asked.

"Perfect," Phil replied.

Well, nothing is ever perfect. We had an ocean between us, and I'd been there before. I also had two growing kids. One thing I had learned from my previous relationships, I had to change this time. I could not run from the tough times in a relationship.

The date was set for August 29. The temperatures were in the high '80's when Wendy met her father in Prefontaine Hall, where she and I first met. From there, Simon, resplendent in his tux, walked her down the wood chip trail. Wendy was heating up inside her wedding dress and veil by the time they reached the wooden footbridge, where fresh water cycled from Tryon Creek through the elevated garden stonework and into the 8-acre man-made lake. The bridge symbolized so may connections—of man and woman, of continents, of race, age and backgrounds. Nelson Farris stood beside me as best man, as Simon gave me Wendy's right hand.

The ceremony was followed by a much larger reception on the Joan Benoit Samuelson patio. It was a perfect night of good food, music, and dancing under the stars. Phil Knight wasn't able to attend, but he sent Wendy and me a card. He invited us to stay at his favorite retreat in Hawaii.

That night I told our guests that "My dad always said I took the circuitous route to happiness. We had our differences." He was there in the crowd, wearing a powder blue seersucker suit. I actually spoke of the moment I threw rocks at him, upset over his decision to move our family to Eugene. I'd shared this with Wendy and Tracy, but I'd never told him what I said next. "Well Dad, it was the best decision you ever made, and we would not be here without it."

CHAPTER 25: TELL ME A STORY

Dr. Stan James called me the winter of '93. He had just had an interesting conversation with a guy who had moved to Eugene from L.A. This individual was into film and could not believe that no one had done anything on Prefontaine.

The idea was definitely worth discussing, so Stan put me in touch with Jon Lutz, and we arranged a lunch meeting at the Nike campus. Jon admitted to being a bit of a novice in documentary and especially feature film, but being a USC grad, he was well schooled in delivering the pitch. The focus of our conversation was a documentary on the life of Steve Prefontaine. If that project led to a feature, so be it. I believe Jon sought the meeting simply for my insight, but by the end he said, "You've got to talk to Phil Knight about taking an 18-month leave of absence to work on this documentary."

I spoke with Phil by phone in February. He agreed to loan me to the project, but if it resulted in a feature film project, the studio would have to pick up the tab. At the end of March, I had Jon Lutz out to my houseboat for dinner. The prospect of shooting a documentary about Pre had me pretty excited. This would be an honor to the guy whose spirit was at the very core of Nike.

Wendy and I drove to Skamania Lodge on the Columbia River two days later. Nike brought Jeff Johnson out to speak to management about the early days. "Nike, in my experience, never was a job, it was a mission," Johnson told us, "and the mission wasn't to become a player in the sports shoe industry. When Phil Knight started this company . . . it was not his ambition to have a company that was going to be a player in the sports shoe business. It was Knight's ambition . . . to be where he is today, to be dominant, to be the best in the world. Not to be a competitor, not to be an also-ran, not to make the final, but to be on the victory stand."

I shared the Pre project with Jeff in front of a big fireplace and Jeff leaned back with a smile, "Remember when we had lunch with Knight, Pre, and Moodhe, and you got pissed and left, and Pre ate your lunch?" We laughed at the old memory. It was always fun being around Pre.

I sat down with Phil in April. At this point, everything was pretty exploratory. Without a budget or production house, we were just finding our way. A critical point was obvious, if the project was about Prefontaine, despite his being in the public domain, it would be important to have the family on board. In May, I met with Ray and Elfriede to let them know what we were putting together and to ask them for their support.

We also needed a budget. I met with Wieden & Kennedy's Dan Wieden to pitch the project and get some ballpark figures on film budgets. They had shot many of Nike's commercials, and Dan's input was helpful. Jon contacted a film production company, Eugene's Westcom Communications, and began preparing a line item budget.

In July, I met with Nike's advertising manager, Joe McCarthy, to pitch the documentary. With an 18-month interview and post- production schedule, the budget came in at $250,000. He said he'd get back to me.

Less than a week later, my old Navy friend and fellow runner Jeff Galloway was in town. Westcom had already stepped up to the plate and given us a talented director in Erich Lyttle. I was still waiting to hear from Joe McCarthy, but I decided to follow Strasser's advice and "Live off the Land." Galloway knew Pre, and here he was, so on July 20, Erich and I shot the first interview for what would become the documentary *Fire on the Track*. I scripted each interview simply as a start point, but the real magic came from those who knew him. Galloway gave us this gem: "Pre inhabited races, and you were intimidated by his aura."

The following day, Joe McCarthy approved the budget. Things were picking up speed. We had a green light.

It was summertime, and time for a break. I decided to take *Kaili* down the Columbia River and up the Washington coast and into Puget Sound, with Wendy and Tracy as part of the crew.

It takes roughly 40 hours to reach Sequim Bay from Astoria, Oregon. Twelve of those hours are spent in the relative calm of the Straits passing Neah Bay and Clallam Bay with the majestic Olympics overhead, looking much like Norway. The lights of Victoria loom to the north, and a close passage to Port Angeles signals a return to civilization with the sounds of mills and timber exportation. Ferries cross the 20 miles of water to Victoria Harbor. A long, low, six and a half mile sand spit grows every year from the confluence of the Dungeness River with the changing salt water tides. Dungeness Light marks the East end. After rounding the point, the water calms and shallows, exposing a second spit running east to west, protecting a generous bay. This is Sequim, native for "Peaceful Waters."

Wendy and I went ashore for a run and found ourselves on West Sequim Bay Road. Wendy asked if I'd ever thought of retiring here. "Someday," I said.

"Well, I'm thinking about it now," Wendy replied. She's not someone who wastes time when she's going after something she wants, and in short order, we had walked five available waterfront lots. The one she liked best had older, well-kept homes on each side, and sat within viewing distance of the marina. She bought it.

I entered the Michael Jordan lobby one August afternoon and saw Jaakko Tuominen giving another man a tour. Even with his back turned, I knew immediately who he was. If you ran against him when he was at his best, that's the side you usually saw. I tapped the second man on the shoulder and he turned. It was the great Kenyan runner, Kip Keino. We both lit up with big smiles, hugging each other and saying, "Can you believe it? Can you believe it?" The joy was not just about two old friends seeing each other after a long absence. It was about our sons. Both were following in our footsteps—they had become competitive runners, they'd met in several races in the Pac-10 conference, and now they were friends. Just as my generation of runners saw a lot of Kip's backside, that was the view Tracy would often have of Martin Keino. I called the film crew, and we interviewed Kip for *Fire on the Track* that afternoon.

In September, I had the film crew out to the Bowermans' home, and we interviewed Bill, Kenny Moore, and me. It was a good day of shooting, but it was the last day we were all on the same page as far as making a film about Pre went. At the same time we were proceeding on the documentary, Jon Lutz was working the feature film possibility with his contacts, and those contacts led back to Disney. It quickly became apparent that Kenny Moore was trying to develop a deal for a feature film through Warner Brothers. It was exciting to imagine a Hollywood film about Pre, but I was concerned about what happens to the truth when Hollywood does a biopic. I'd been telling Pre's story to high school and college athletes and to Nike employees for years, and I wanted to stay focused on *Fire on the Track*, where I had the best chance of getting Pre's story right.

In November, Finland's Lasse Viren flew into town. With Jaakko Tuominen and film producer Irby Smith, we drove to Coos Bay to visit Ray and Elfriede Prefontaine. Lasse was finally making good on his promise to come to Oregon. He was only 19 years late. Ray opened the door at 921 Elrod, smiled, and asked, "What took you so long?" Elfriede moved quickly, fretting over having the coffee just right, Jaakko translated, Lasse got to see Pre's bedroom, and we took pictures.

The following day, Erich had the camera rolling as we interviewed Lasse in front of the Finnish flag at the entrance to

Nike. Lasse tried his best at English, but we also shot it in Finnish, and then shot Jaakko's translation in English. I was finally back at work on the documentary, and it felt good.

Erich Lyttle and I flew to Atlanta with a cameraman to interview Pre's good friend and competitor Dave Wottle. Dave had wonderful personal stories of traveling with Pre. We went to interview Dick Buerkle, who was a tougher interview. Tape was in the camera, sound was rolling, we had spent over 30 minutes getting the lighting right, and Dick broke down in tears. An emotional Buerkle said, "I haven't had to think about this for nearly 20 years and it just hit me."

I knew how he felt. Doing these interviews was going to bring up a lot of emotions—pride in Pre's accomplishments, joy that we had been there to share in them, and a big dose of sorrow that we lost him so young. But if I could get on film a sense of the man, of who Pre really was, it would all be worth it.

Dick had learned of Pre's death with Don Kardong just after touching down in Seattle on their return from competing in China. It was on Dick's flight home to Atlanta that he wrote "An Ode to S. Roland." Then he separated himself from his grief and moved on to live his life. It was what we all had to do, each of us in our own way. On camera, Buerkle got past his tears enough to reflect, "What made me so sad was that he's me. Maybe he's more cocky and I'm less cocky, or he's different than me. But there's more of him that's like me than not like me—the 20 mile runs, the hard intervals. He always made it tough. We're brothers that way. He always made the tempo sweet."

We flew on to England and interviewed many who had known Pre, including Dave Bedford, Brendan Foster, and Ian Stewart. Stewart was a former Special Forces expert who had been trained as a military assassin, and he had a steadiness that was almost alarming. It may have been his military training that gave him that extra bit of mental toughness it took to beat as tough a competitor as Pre. Reflecting on the 5000 meter race he ran against Pre in Munich, where he edged out

Pre for the bronze, he said, "Pre deserved the medal. I didn't. Not the way I ran."

In Oslo we interviewed Arne and Knut Kvalheim, in Amsterdam it was Jos Hermans, and in Belgium it was Emiel Puttemans. It was my first meeting of this kind gentleman. Like Keino, Pre, and Foster, Puttemans was so versatile as a runner. He struggled with English and the interview, but his, "He liked to push the pace, push the pace, then swish," was a classic.

They had all been so inspired by Pre, and the interviews were a joy to do. I'd never met Stewart, Puttemans, or Bedford before, and they couldn't have been more different from one another. Bedford was a hard drinking, hard training animal of an athlete. Stewart was just as hard-working an athlete, but he was less affable and kept his distance. Puttemans was a gentle soul, a gardener, and he tended to people the way he tended to his shrubs and flowers. What struck me at the time was that Pre really liked all three of these guys. I could see why. Twenty years later they all still had the work ethic that Pre had, and they were all characters.

No one was more of a character though, than one of the last interviews I did for the documentary. Dana Carvey ran track in high school and had been a fan of Pre's ever since. We did the interview in a little studio behind his house. Carvey sat on a stool, and I sat on the floor—a good thing, because he had me literally rolling with laughter half the time. Carvey was still a runner, and he could impersonate the head bobs, the strides, and the arm movements of many famous runners. But he was a serious student of the sport, and when we got into a dispute over the exact times for Pre's great distance double, Carvey sent his brother off for "the book." He proved me wrong—Carvey had the correct times down to a tenth of a second.

I did a total of fifty-five interviews for the project. Once they were completed, Erich and I went into the Westcom Studio in Eugene and began piecing the story elements together. Westcom was owned by the Chambers family, who also owned the local ABC affiliate. That gave us access to all of the Chambers' archival footage of Prefontaine. In addition, we transferred all the cross country footage I had shot of Prefontaine and acquired as many still photos as we could find, from the Prefontaine family personal collection to the famous Brian Lanker photo that led author Ken Kesey to observe "Pre's eyes were those of a predator. The eyes of an eagle."

On a Monday in June, I received my customary phone call from Bob Newland. "Quite a nice little all-comers meet we had," he said, referring to the recent Prefontaine Classic in his normal, cheerful manner. I updated him on the film project and we said our goodbyes. It was the last time we'd talk.

Bob Newland was soon in the hospital. He had much earlier shared some prostate issues with me, but he remained silent about his 15-month bout with liver cancer. Apparently Bob had resigned himself to his fate. I don't know that he even told Bowerman. The man who inspired me so much and so often over decades died on June 23. Dad was in the Newport, Oregon hospital at the time and laid on his bed in tears over the news of his long-time friend's death. But no one was more broken than Bowerman, who sat at the end of the hospital hall. Tears flowed down the face of the man I always saw as a rock.

Editing proved to be a long and tedious process. Buried in the confined darkness, you became a mole, snipping away a few seconds here, a minute or two there. Even though the interviews were conducted independently of one another, it was amazing to see how one concluding statement led to the opening remark in another interview. Where bridges were needed to make the story flow, Ken Kesey went to work on his narrative. Kesey loved the sport and had been a collegiate wrestler himself, so he understood the physical side of Pre's life as a runner. But more than that, there

Kesey, during his collegiate wrestling career, held the University of Oregon record for most pins.

was something quintessentially Oregonian about both men. They played by their own rules, and neither one of them cared much what other people thought. They dared to dream big, and because they were so gifted, they had the power to make those dreams real. Like Phil Knight, each was, in his own way, truly one of "the Men of Oregon."

Through all of the work on the documentary I was constantly distracted by the intrusion of Hollywood. Through lawyers, injunctions, and a lot of backstabbing, behind the scenes maneuvering, the whole idea of making a feature film about Pre created conflict in the community of people who had known him. Greed drove people to do things to each other that were disgraceful and an insult to the spirit I was trying to capture in *Fire on the Track*.

All of us, from Bill Bowerman on down, are highly competitive people. We took that competitiveness into the business world, and that drive was certainly a huge part of why Nike was so successful. But Nike's approach to business—my approach to business—was always about the people involved. It was about the relationships you formed on and off the track. It was about taking special care of those who had that special gift, the ability to give something extra in the heat of competition and pull through for the PR, the win, the new world record. It was about loyalty. My loyalty was to Pre's memory and the Prefontaine family, and I never let anyone get in the way of that.

Because we were all so competitive, I guess it comes as no real surprise that a bunch of outsiders were able to drive a wedge between us. I allied myself with the Disney camp, but others fell in with the Warner Brothers group. Both films would eventually get made. Disney released *Prefontaine* in January of 1997, and Warner's *Without Limits* came out in September of 1998. But it's with some considerable pride that I assert that *Fire on the Track* is a better film than either of the Hollywood versions of Pre's life.

The beauty of documentary is in taking advantage of the voices, the storytellers, while you have them. In only a few years, some of those voices would be gone. You have to capture the moment. With Erich's masterful editing and Kesey's raspy, folksy voice woven through the interviews, our documentary got at the spirit of Pre and the spirit of times in which he lived.

Some of the mysteries of Pre's life continued to play out. I was asked after the completion of *Fire on the Track* to participate in a 5k run inside the Oregon State penitentiary. I was fit at the time and agreed to do it.

Entering a prison is a sobering experience. You get a preparatory lecture first, then you remove all your valuables. Any symbols of personal identity are left behind. I was given a bright orange bib to put over my shoulders and told that this was so the guards in the towers could identify me.

As you walked well-marked through the halls, large barred gates slammed behind you, prisoners walked in groups, looking at you and talking among themselves. I wondered what brought Pre here. Why did he start the jogging club?

It was dark when I arrived at the appointed time in the prison parking lot. By the time I walked out to the prison grounds where the run would be held, it was daylight. There were still around 200 members in the jogging club. Some were lifers. When I toed the line for the start, I had never seen so many tattoos. The run wound past the shop and the weight room, through the gates that sectioned off areas, along the tall walls and under the watchful eyes of prison guards, rifles in hand.

I did well and won the Masters. Other runners came up, shook my hand and thanked me for coming. One inmate appeared with a plate of donuts and cookies, and it reminded me of Dellinger's earlier story of his appearance at the prison. He had taken a donut from the plate. A guard observed him, came over, pointed at the inmate, and asked Bill, "You know what he's in for?" Bill looked blankly. "Poisoned his mother."

I was munching on a cookie when a tall figure tapped me on the shoulder, "Geoff?" I turned and looked up. "I'm David Buck."

David Buck was Pre's teammate on more than one team as young kids in Coos Bay. He could play any position. His father was a dentist. I asked him why he was here. David explained to me that he was on a street in Portland and shot and killed a man in a drug deal gone wrong. I asked him if he was ever going to get out. "Hopefully in six years. I'd like to see my son grow up."

Sitting in the stands at Hayward Field at the Prefontaine Classic in 1995, a man tapped me on the shoulder, "Geoff Hollister?" I said, "Yes," and he responded, "You might want to talk to my son." I moved up a row.

"I was the tow truck driver that responded to the call for the Prefontaine accident." He told me that after that event, he quit his job, moved to Alaska and became a commercial fisherman. It's hard to describe what I was feeling. I'd spent a lot of time dwelling in Pre's world while I was working on the film projects, but the moment of his death had always been elusive. Here was a guy who could shed some light on something I'd been wondering about for years.

He told me that the night of the accident he was ordered by the police to lift the car so Pre's body could be removed. Reports indicated that Pre had not worn a seatbelt. Reports also indicated that he did not suffer one broken bone. Yet the tow truck operator recalled that when he lifted the car, Pre's body went up with it. I struggled with how that could happen if he wasn't strapped in.

The day after Pre died, Eugene Police Chief Allen seemed almost proud to announce Pre's alcohol level and added, "Steve Prefontaine might have been a hero to kids, but he wasn't to us." I wondered about the alcohol level, as I had been close to Pre his last few hours. He was so busy talking, he hardly had time to eat or drink anything. With his parents,

Bowerman, and his high school coach, Walt McClure, all at the house, this wasn't a binge party. I knew he had lost considerable fluid in his 5000 effort hours earlier and he had eaten little.

What I didn't know was how the accident scene was handled. Officer Rex Ballinger's accident report was riddled with mistakes, from getting the license plate number wrong to reporting tire skids on the pavement that simply were not there. Sergeant Richard Lovell, the same officer with whom Pre had once had an angry exchange in the downtown mall over Pre's unleashed dog, was one of the first to arrive, and his dislike for Pre is well known. The county medical examiner was never called. A Dr. Jacobsen had come down from his home above Skyline and asked to at least make an attempt at CPR. The police simply said it was too late. They transported Pre's body to England's Funeral Home, where the mortician was asked to draw the blood. The mortician countered that he did not do that. The police ordered him to do it anyway.

Dr. Ed Wilson, the county medical examiner at the time, is still upset today over what transpired. He made it his mission that the public would vote on a policy change in Lane County: in the future with any non-natural death, the body must be taken to Sacred Heart hospital for testing. The vote passed.

I have always been concerned about DUI and the use of seat belts. A vehicle is a big, dangerous weapon. But I am also convinced that Pre could be alive today. The Alvarados, who lived in the house closest to the accident scene, confirmed there was a second car at the scene of the accident, yet it drove away. The police, who had already decided this was a single car accident, left the Alvarado's account out of their report. Bill Alvarado tried to chase the car down but failed. He returned to the accident a few minutes later and said that Pre was still breathing. The driver of the other car, Karl Bylund, passed a police polygraph test, saying that he left to go get help, as his father is a doctor. He never returned. Pre struggled to breathe for at least five minutes. If that driver had returned to the scene, he and Bill Alvarado could have lifted the car off of Pre. They could have saved him.

Someone painted 5-30-75 R.I.P. on what has become known as "Pre's Rock." It has been a destination ever since. The Oregon State Penitentiary donated a granite marker with Brian Lanker's famous head shot facing the road in this quiet, isolated spot. The property was owned by the Oregon Department of Transportation. Years later, Neil Goldschmidt called me and informed me that ODOT was considering auctioning it off to reduce inventory. Would I be interested in taking the issue to Phil Knight? I did. But before Knight could move, an acquaintance of Pre's, Cliff Shirley, stepped up to make the purchase and donate it to Eugene City Parks. Shirley made the first payment, was showered with attention by the Eugene media for his commendable gesture, then defaulted.

The director of ODOT called and informed me of the situation. I again took it to Knight. He did not hesitate for a second, saying "I want this to remain anonymous." However, the press searched the public record and announced Phil's gift to the city anyway.

As for his quick action, Phil only said, "It was the right thing to do."

CHAPTER 26: THE BIG BLOW

With the feature script in rewrite and production on hold, I took the opportunity to bring *Kaili* down the Washington coast. If I left the boat in Washington waters through the winter, I risked paying Washington State sales tax. Bill Dieter had sailed with me before and with two of his mountain climbing buddies we departed under blue skies. Everything went fine through the calm waters of the Straits. Once we rounded Tatoosh and headed south, the rollers increased in height, approaching 20-feet. From swell to swell, the horizon to the west and the sight of land to the east was lost. My crew might have climbed numerous mountains, but to them, the swells must have seemed like Everest, and they turned green.

I watched my crew for a while, calculated what was left in the 40-hour transit to Astoria, and decided to turn back. I would not be able to stay at the helm the complete trip. We returned to Sequim.

Late November and early December produced a two-week high pressure system that left me optimistic for another attempt to head south. On December 8, I departed under clear skies with Tracy and Oregon teammate Alex Reich as crew. It was a perfect transit through the Straits. As we approached Tatoosh, the sky was filling with angel hair clouds, and a halo surrounded the moon. I knew from experience this could mean a storm was approaching. We headed south with increasing seas and a building Southwest wind, so we reduced sail.

The northwest tip of Washington's coast juts out with the rock ledge of Cape Flattery tucked in behind Tatoosh Island. You can imagine them once connected. Further south, additional islands continue west of the coast for miles. Once rounding the northwest tip, it's best to head due south, distancing yourself from the tricky currents and rocks.

The swells built and Alex became silent in the starboard bunk, strapped in safely with lee cloths. He was seasick, and I was not turning back. Tracy and I would alternate four-hour watches.

We motor sailed through the night with reduced headsail and the Westerbeke running a steady 1800 RPMs. The 20-foot swells were not a problem. *Kaili* rode them smoothly. Morning gray light from the east arrived with increasing wind from the south. The velocity against the southern flow of the Japanese current created a swell with a solid drop on the back end. I could envision the front end of the keel exposed as the bow launched forward, dropping all nine tons flat at the bottom of the trough. Salt spray flew evenly; the boat would stop, then lurch forward. Over and over, we repeated. To see ahead, it was best to stand behind the helm. Your heels absorbed the shock with each landing. With each successive wave, I thought of Bowerman. His message of focus was ever present. One wave. The next wave. Man the helm. Focus.

Tracy and I cut our watches to two hours, as four was becoming a challenge. Alex was taking care of himself. I asked how he was doing. "I'm fine. I can hear you guys talk, so I'm confident you know what you are doing." I was not as confident.

We launched off a steep shelf of water, the boat moved sideways at the bottom, levitating Alex in midair over the lee cloth, then dropping him on the deck. At the same moment, the gimbaled stove elevated off its hinges and dropped to the deck. Not a good sign.

The life raft had begun sliding from side to side. With Tracy at the helm, I took some line and put some additional lashes over our 6-man life raft to hold it on deck in its canister.

Through all the pounding and wind whistling through the shrouds, Tracy impressed me with his resilience. I hated to wake him after only two hours. I wondered if he had even slept, as I had not. He'd bounce up out of the companionway with a smile and a joke. Perhaps this was his effort to change my expression.

The invisible sun went down with angel hair wisps of salt spray blowing north off the wave crests. Soon after I took the midnight watch, the diesel abruptly stopped. I pointed the boat further out to sea in an attempt to continue boat speed. Tracy returned to the helm as I checked our GPS position. We were 66 miles northwest of the Columbia Bar. It was hard to hold our heading with the pounding and now quartering the oncoming swells. I took a quick look in the engine bay. Just the thought of attempting to fix anything left me nauseous, and I knew I could not leave Tracy on his own. I closed the engine cover and resumed my watch. We were 35 miles west of Grays Harbor, and nearly three days had passed since we left Sequim. I had never gone into Grays Harbor and didn't carry that chart. We continued to switch watches until we had some calm. Finally, the wind reduced around noon and I lifted the cover off the engine bay.

To my surprise, a protective moisture blanket that was glued to the front of the fuel tank had dislodged with all the pounding and moisture. With the V-drive engine mount, the blanket dropped into the alternator and water pump belts, stopping the engine. In 20 minutes, I backed off the belts, freed the blanket and had us up and running again. The GPS verified that we had been kicked back up the coast 22 miles and set shoreward 25 degrees. My training as a navigator taught me to go out, not in. We corrected 25 degrees for set and drift and headed further out.

I turned the helm over to Tracy and pointed south to Astoria. "We are heading here and should track a straight line to the north jetty." As we regained hull speed, a freighter was heading east astern of us out of Grays Harbor. I tried hailing him on the VHF radio to relay a message that we were okay, but would be late on arrival. There was no answer. Yet, I could hear the NOAA weather report. Winds were expected to hit 100 mph late Tuesday night. It was imperative we sail the straightest line to the Columbia entrance.

We remained on starboard tack. After watch, my heels felt numb and thick and I was extremely tired from lack of sleep and food. With early morning light, I saw something strange on the foredeck. The chain locker was open. The anchor was still secured on deck, but the hatch screws had pulled loose. I immediately called Tracy back to the helm and moved cautiously forward on the upper rail with my harness snapped into the port jackline. Thirty feet of anchor chain was pounding and slapping the starboard rail. The diesel was still running at 1800 RPM as I pulled the chain up. Thank God we never tacked over. The chain and rope could have wrapped the prop, yanked the engine off the mounts and put a hole in the boat. With everything back on deck, I lashed the locker lid down with rope and returned to the cockpit.

The incident reminded me of Chris Van Dyke's story of his dad crewing with him on his Valiant 40. Dick Van Dyke accidentally let a jib sheet wander over the side. Close to the entry of the Straits of Juan de Fuca, the sheet wrapped the prop, pulled the diesel off its mounts and started an electrical fire. With no wind, they went in and out with the tide until the weather changed.

I also thought of the scene of Peter O'Toole in *Lawrence of Arabia* where he is riding his camel through a desert storm. Stride after stride, just as we rode wave after wave after wave. But mostly, I thought of Bowerman. As monotonous as it was, each wave was its own danger. Focus, focus.

A halo of light appeared as backdrop in the dark for an even brighter flashing light at the horizon. We were closing in on Cape Disappointment as our 40-hour transit had extended to nearly four days.

Tracy had the helm and announced a wind shift. He was already using it, and as I came to the helm, we turned into the wind and hoisted the main. We left the furled headsail at 50% as a warmer northeast wind pushed us across the Columbia Bar.

There was not a ship to be seen. Normally, they were in tight passage in a restricted channel. A sandy beach marks the south side; a narrower north passage provides small boat passage to Ilwaco. You have to follow those markers carefully, as mud flats rise at low tide all along the north and under the bridge that links Oregon to Washington.

I went below to the nav station and checked the chart for the straight five-mile course to the fuel dock and marina. The radar rotated its bright green outline of the shore and placed us in the middle of the channel. I checked the course one more time. Then there was a loud "Bang!" on deck. It sounded like a shotgun blast, as Tracy yelled through the howling wind, "Dad, I've lost helm!"

I moved low alongside him as the bow of the boat was swinging north. The bang we heard came when the wind put so much tension on the lines running through the main traveler car that it exploded. Now, with the main traveler car gone, the boom was bouncing frantically up and down, which could be deadly. A quick look at the wind gauge registered what I estimated at 87 mph. Then just as quickly, nothing. I suspected that we'd lost our instruments at the top of the mast, but there was no way I could go up to find out. The wind still blew, and you had to yell to be heard. I thought we were home when we crossed the Columbia Bar, but it wasn't so. We were being tested.

I told Tracy to complete the 360, throttle up to 2000 rpm, and I went forward. I kept my head low and grabbed the main sheet like I was trying to tame a wild stallion. The metal traveler bounced up and down, no longer attached to its track in front of the dodger. I raced to the mast and dropped the main, working to get two sail ties over the bucking boom. I pulled a loop of line through a deck grab rail on the cabin top, hurriedly tied a double half hitch, and returned to the cockpit. It was 2 a.m. Tracy was beat and asked to go below to nap.

Back on the helm, rain was so horizontal it peppered what was exposed of my face tucked under my hooded foul weather suit. My eyes were narrow slits as the rain stung. The wind was directly on our nose, coming from 125 magnetic. You could feel the hull lift. I felt as though I was flying the boat. The bow, over 30 feet in front of me felt light, extremely light. Just slightly out of the nose of the wind, the bow started turning north. I had lost helm. The wind was simply so strong that it was lifting our nine- ton boat out of the water even though all the sails were down. I throttled up to 2200 rpm and completed the 360 back into the horizontal wind and rain.

Down below, the boat was wet as the wind drove water through the smallest opening. Tracy and I removed our foul weather gear every trip below. There was barely a dry spot in the boat.

Normally, *Kaili* could make the final leg in under an hour. As we approached the marina entrance, I called Tracy to the cockpit. This night, it took us 2 hours 45 minutes to cover just 5 miles.

The water flattened within the marina. We tied up at the fuel dock. I felt like kissing it. I was staggering because my legs were still at sea. For the first time in some hours my hands were free, and I pulled out Wendy's cell phone and called home to inform her we were in.

It was only now that I realized that my nightmare trip was not our secret. When we were overdue, she alerted the Coast Guard. "They've been searching for you for two days. Your family is frantic, and I've been trying to hold them together. It's been in the news."

I told Wendy where we were and to please call the Coast Guard "But ask them not to come to the boat. We need sleep more than anything right now." As for Tracy and Alex, sleep meant the Red Lion Motel at the top of the marina ramp, and they checked in.

That is when I fell into the deepest sleep.

"Rap, rap, rap," on the starboard side of my solid sloop. I awoke in daylight to the Coast Guard. They wanted to complete their report and know what happened. Wendy had given them names of former crew like Bill Hall. Bill and others confirmed that I was conservative and always stayed in visual contact with the coastline. "Not this time. I went out as far as 40 miles." I was informed that the search was approximately 20 miles and in.

I took everything that was wet and hung it out to dry as the sun actually was out. The boys were in their room watching of all things, *Waterworld*. I climbed into the shower, with no sensation in my heels. They felt two inches thick. I turned the shower on and screamed. I had worn the same cotton briefs for four days. The briefs had gotten soaked with everything else. With the constant lurching left then right, the wet cotton had removed a layer of skin from my penis. The hot water proved quite a shock.

My sisters called. Laura was livid. "You scared the hell out of Mom and Dad. They not only saw losing you, but Tracy, too." Claudia wasn't much happier. With clean, dry clothes, the boys accompanied me to the boat to clean things up, while my ex-wife Carol drove out to pick us up. We'd leave the boat for a week in a slip provided by the harbormaster. As we maneuvered through the many boats, the fishermen looked up and stared at us. I was thinking they must be saying, "So those are the sorry bastards who were out there."

It was a somewhat quiet ride back to Portland. Carol did inform us that "our being lost at sea had made the news in Portland and Eugene." My error in judgment was now public.

My mind on the return to Portland focused on the dream I had in my deep sleep at the fuel dock. It was in full color, and it was about Pre. "Why at that time?" I thought, as it had been years since the last one. In the dream, Pre was going out for a run. I asked him to wait, and I'd join him. Typically impatient, he said, "No, I've got to go now." I hustled and joined him as we ran down a lane lined with tall elephant bark Eucalyptus trees. The rest of the dream was all about our running together.

Had we met disaster 40 miles offshore, Tracy and Alex might have joined us on that run.

Another thought surfaced. Pre always backed himself into a corner with bold predictions, then fought his way out. I always wondered how he did it. All the races, the media, and yes, the women. Perhaps for the first time in my life, I put myself in that corner. Somehow I fought my way out. Pre and Bowerman were there.

I showed up at Nike for lunch and was not prepared for the response. Outside the Joan Benoit Samuelson Building, I ran into fabric developer Mary Ellen Smith. With a big smile came a heartfelt hug. Mary Ellen grew up sailing around Boston. Inside, surprisingly, Bob Wood ran up, "You eating with anyone?—I want to know what happened." This was a total shock. A guy I assumed had a complete dislike for me actually cared. He cared like hell. From that moment on, Bob Wood and I had a new respect for each other.

Bob returned to his office, and Knight walked up with a big smile on his face. "I only have one question. Were you scared?"

I smiled, and said, "Yeah, a little bit." The truth is, I didn't have the luxury of being scared when I was out there.

I returned to my office and called Galloway, sharing the Navy training that most likely saved us. E-mails and calls began coming in. I had been unaware of the weather in Portland. We were out at sea in balmy, windy conditions while Portland experienced a severe ice storm, freezing the ground and the trees. People envisioned us on the boat frozen to the shroud, like in an old Cape Horn movie.

I called the Bowermans and spoke with Barbara about how Bill's lessons were invaluable to me. She responded, "You and Tracy have always been close, and this experience will bond you even closer the rest of your life."

Nike's sales meetings were taking place in Hawaii when the word traveled that our boat was lost at sea in a big storm. Nelson was preparing himself to have to speak at my service. So was Kent Davenport. The word spread that we had made it safely, and my sailing buddy Van Dyke e-mailed me, "Shit oh dear, what were you doing? Tell me what happened and how did you make it." I wrote him back, "How many days do you go to the office and have total control of the outcome? Despite our troubles, this was a time when we had our fate in our own hands. It doesn't happen very often."

I was embarrassed by how public my mistakes had become, but I was well satisfied with how seaworthy the boat was and how well she handled the weather. The boat made up for my own inadequacies. Tracy, Alex and I gave our maximum effort, and our survival came down to how we dealt with the conditions we'd placed ourselves in. We didn't give in to fear, and whatever mistakes we made, we did the right things to correct them.

Talking with Wendy, perhaps the biggest surprise was Nike President Tom Clarke, another guy I didn't always see eye-to-eye with. He called Wendy from Hawaii when things were looking bleak. He wanted her to know that he and the company were there for her. The gesture left me in tears. Nike moves like this huge battleship through the water but just for a moment, it stopped to recognize the potential loss of a teammate.

Although I was moved to tears, I was delighted to quote Winston Churchill, "The reports of my demise have been highly exaggerated."

CHAPTER 27: THE UNEXPECTED CHAPTER

"Here, you might want to keep these."

The words sounded like they were coming from inside a nearby closet. I was flat on my back on a gurney, covered with a white blanket. Out of focus, my eyes looked down to a stack of gruesome color photos. My eyes gradually came into focus. What I was looking at was a tumor. I had rectal cancer.

Thanks to a referral from my friend Steve Bukeida, I had a great oncologist, Dr. Keith Hansen. Dr. Hansen is a take-no-prisoners kind of guy. The key to survival is early detection. Then you have a chance. It was determined by Dr. Hansen that I was a full-blown stage 3 plus. At stage 4, it's pretty well guaranteed that the cancer has penetrated the rectal wall and migrated.

It takes a while for the reality of cancer to settle in. The 2004 Olympics were coming up in Athens. Thanks to Steve Simmons, a Nike consultant, many NCAA track coaches and a few Athletic Directors had raised money to send Wendy and me to the XXVIII Olympiad as a retirement thank you gift. Our tickets were booked, we had an apartment in Athens, and a sailboat chartered for a cruise afterwards. I asked Dr. Hansen if I could go, delaying the start of my treatment until I returned.

Dr. Hansen got hot immediately and started yelling. "Can't you see?" he boomed. "I'm trying to save your rectum!"

It was like so many moments I had with Bill Bowerman. You argued with these men at your own peril. Athens would have to wait.

I started simultaneous chemotherapy and radiation treatment on August 2, less than two weeks before the Athens Olympics began. A cute little Italian radiologist named Claire Bartuccio asked me questions in her office. Then she said, "Let's see if I can find this tumor." She snapped on some latex gloves and asked me to drop my pants and bend over the exam table. I thought "You've got to be kidding. I bet there are a few women out there who would love the opportunity to do this to some guy—any guy!" But wait, this is me.

Thank God for small fingers.

I decided I would rather be in Sequim for the treatments instead of Portland. Radiation and chemo had shrunk my tumors and stopped them from migrating, so now Dr. Hansen was recommending surgery, and a surgeon he respected, Dr. Patrick Lee. Dr. Lee installed a portacath in my chest for infusions. The chemo drug 5-FU would be infused in me five days a week through a pump I strapped onto my side. You could hear it ticking. It was with you when you showered and when you slept.

The only thing I didn't like about Dr. Lee—he has big fingers.

There was a long stitch line centered on my abdomen. I was on morphine, and the world was dreamy and confused. The nurses want you up and walking as soon as possible, but I could barely lift myself up. This was October and with my first operation I could see that recovery was going to be a long process.

Dad had passed away the previous April. Mom had Alzheimer's, a kind of living death, and I chose not to tell her about my cancer. I was relieved neither of them knew.

When your parents die, it's like placing bookends on your own life. How long did they live? What were their habits? Did you do anything better? At age 58, I had run nearly every day.

It is like having a cup of coffee. I was addicted. Wendy is a great cook, creating a healthy, balanced diet. I had never smoked. I felt I was the most unlikely candidate for cancer. It would visit others but not me. I was wrong.

I thought back to Bowerman's, "You can only do two things well at the same time." At my doctor's urging, I took myself off the five non-profit boards I sat on to reduce my stress level. I focused on my treatment and writing this book.

Bowerman lived life on his own terms. If you wanted to really challenge him, you simply told him, as one shoemaker did, "you cannot do it." Bill went on to design and build shoes that changed an industry. He became a millionaire while the shoemaker is still making shoes.

Bowerman always put the athlete first in his decision making—that was his compass, and I learned to make it mine as well. He was guided by common sense and a love of work. If you could add a little humor and mischief to the soup, it made for a better day. If he saw someone heading off in the wrong direction, he set an ambush. If that failed, he took a more direct approach. He was secretive about his personal life, and it was a long time before I understood why. He didn't want you to know that he had already made most of the mistakes you were making. That secrecy, combined with his taciturn nature, made him pretty inscrutable. He expected you to accept his methods without a lot of questions, and that frequently left people around him with some hurt feelings.

I remembered one of my last, and perhaps favorite, meetings with Bill in the house on the hill. We were sitting in the kitchen. He had stoked the fire in the woodstove. Bill cut his toast in half and covered it with peanut butter and jam. He gave me half, even though I had already had breakfast. I was warm with the comfort of the moment. Bill then shared something I will never forget. "I did a lot of things in my life. If I offended anyone, I'm sorry." This was an incredible admission from a man who was never wrong, who never admitted a mistake. I had been the target of his ire more than once, but I knew his message was meant for more than just me.

If there is one moment that should prompt anyone to get a colonoscopy at age 50, this is it. In preparation for my radiation treatment, the doctors and technicians must pinpoint the tumor location. So here I am, face down on the radiation table. Again, I am told to drop my pants to my knees. A lab technician then has me get on my hands and knees, pulls out a metal wire slightly narrower than a coat hanger and sticks it—yep, you know where. Then a metal washer, not unlike you would have in your shop, was placed over the wire and pressed up close against my buttocks. Next, a female lab technician approached me in this compromising position with a digital camera and started snapping pictures.

The photos from Iraq's Abu Ghraib Prison had just hit the American newsstands, and I resembled one of those prisoners. I simply lacked the dog leash. Unless you are into such kinky stuff, save yourself the embarrassment. Get that colonoscopy.

Cancer was the last battle I ever thought I would have to fight. I have had a lot of titles, but I never thought "cancer survivor" would be one of them. So far, I am just that. I remain resilient, focused and confident. I've been coached well in the past. I listen to my doctors today. Being an athlete helps—it teaches you to deal with disappointment and rejection.

Dr. Lee determined during a follow-up appointment that my rectal wall was not healing properly. The wall itself had hardened, most likely a result of radiation. One option was to do nothing. I could just remain as I was. But I was intent on returning to normal and eventually having the ostomy bag removed. To do that, I had to return to the hospital for another major surgery.

You never know what has happened until you awake from the anesthesia. As I came to, I saw myself in an unusual room. It was quite large. I could see what seemed like a football scoreboard behind my head detailing all my vital signs. I learned that I was in what was nicknamed "The Gene Hackman Suite." This was the same room the actor was in following his heart attack while on vacation on the Oregon coast.

Dr. Lee informed me that six hours into the surgery, my heart took off, racing up to 210 beats a minute, while my blood pressure dropped to 60 over 50. They had not completed the surgery, so they zipped me up as quickly as possible and rushed me to intensive care.

Let's say it was the morphine, but when Dr. Lee informed me that they simply stuffed a purple latex glove up my bottom end to reduce the drainage, I said, "Hey, that's great. Purple and white were my South Eugene school colors!"

I would remain in the "Hackman Suite" for five days to get my heart back to normal. The nurses were the best I have ever had. I couldn't believe how one of them could change me and the bed without assistance. I felt hopeless as the nurse coached me, "Now grab the rail with your right hand and pull yourself to the left." I told her how little I felt I was helping.

"If I could," she answered, "I'd take your spirit and bottle it."

As much as I realized the severity of my situation, I never once shed a tear over my condition. I simply focused and, like an athlete, thought about Bowerman's date pace/goal pace. Here's where I am today. Here's where I want to be. What I do today is preparation for whatever comes next.

I did shed a tear for others. After I got my cancer diagnosis, the first call I made was to Steve Bukeida. I'd known Steve almost forty years, going back to when he joined the U of O track team my sophomore year. For the last twenty-three of those years, Steve had been battling non-Hodgkin's lymphoma, and I had stayed in touch with him through all of that. Throughout my cancer journey, no one understood the test of will better than Steve.

Now we were members of the same club. We regularly got together for breakfast. It lifted my spirit to engage in discussions as far ranging as which quarterback the Ducks would start on Saturday to a full-on attack of the George W. Bush White House. Laughter was a big part of what we shared. I remember Steve saying, "They got the cork shoved so tight in Cheney, it affected his smile."

Steve came up to visit me on the Olympic Peninsula. He was really getting into bird watching and had joined a club. This was a perfect match for his catch-and-release fly fishing addiction. On a drive down our road, he looked into a tree over an estuary and exclaimed, "Hey, Geoff, there's a bald eagle!"

We turned around and drove back so he could get a better look. There, proudly perched on a crag in the top of a tall conifer, sat a blue heron. We burst out laughing. Now, every time I see a blue heron, I call it "a Bukeida eagle."

Steve's medical issues ran much deeper than mine, and Dr. Hansen's treatments required a far more aggressive approach. He was in and out of the hospital for a number of procedures, including a stem cell transplant. The donor was known only as a female in her 20s.

His wife, Michelle, called me and brought me up to date. She said Steve had a tough night, "We almost lost him." The staff had made some mistakes on his food and fluids, and he had weakened. I was in tears with the news.

I entered Steve's room the next day. He was asleep, so I sat and waited. He had lost his hair and his face was puffy. He often complained of his "raccoon eyes." He awakened and acknowledged my presence. "Hey! How long have you been here?"

"Not long." The door opened with a nurse checking Steve for vitals and another with a breakfast tray. He was encouraged to eat and then the therapist was in to take him for a walk. "If I can get up a few flights of stairs," he said, "I can get out of here."

Steve slowly managed a flight of stairs. I walked behind him with the therapist at his side. It was like being an athlete again—just slower and harder. Back in his room, Steve continued to bitch and fight. I finally said, "Steve—the good news is you're alive. You want to hear the bad news?"

"What?"

"You've got a vagina!"

"Damn you, Hollister," he said, but he finally started laughing.

When I returned North to the Peninsula, we were on the phone regularly. We supported each other and covered the usual range of topics, which now extended into being grandparents. Michelle had two sons, Matt and Scott, and Matt was now a dad. Steve loved it.

One morning the phone rang early. It was Michelle Bukeida on the other end. "We lost Steve last night."

"What?"

Michelle explained that Steve didn't feel well, was dizzy and vomiting. She knew that this was worse than previous episodes and called for an ambulance. Steve's heart kept stopping on the way to the hospital as the medics struggled to keep it going. Keith Hansen arrived at the hospital and said they tried everything. "But a virus attacked Steve's heart and his organs just started shutting down."

I can still call his number and listen to the voice of my close friend and biggest supporter. Michelle never changed the voicemail recording. "Hello. You've reached the Bukeida household ... "

It's hard to accept a loss and you wonder about the luck of the draw. Steve Bukeida fought cancer for more than twenty years before an infection took him. He used to joke that "maybe he could buy himself another year," but I always told him he'd live a long time. All that time we had together, and he went so fast at the end that I never got a chance to say good-bye.

With my father, it was different. I had a chance to tell him about the plaque that was put up in his honor at Canby High and the Bowerman track renovation there. I don't know which way is worse—a death you see coming and have time to prepare for or one that comes quickly. I just know I've spoken at a lot more memorial services for people I cared about than I ever expected to. You have to get yourself focused so you can speak without breaking down, and you have to bring some humor with you. Humor honors the person you've lost.

Jaakko Tuominen had become a Nike employee, moved his family to the United States, and was working at the Nike campus. After work one day there was a voicemail waiting from Jarrko, Jaakko's son. It was unusual because Jarrko never called. I responded, and Jarrko informed me that his mom and dad were driving to a birthday party for an 85-year-old friend. Jaakko had a hard time breathing in the passenger seat. Kati was a registered nurse when they lived in Finland. She turned the car around and sped to the hospital. As Jaakko struggled, she pounded on his chest with her right fist, yelling, "Jaakko, don't leave me now! Don't leave me now!"

"So how's he doing?"

"He didn't make it."

As I am now in tears, remembering this moment, so was I then. You can't prepare yourself for the sudden loss of someone so close. At the memorial, I prepared myself to speak. I knew that if I stuck to the script and avoided eye contact with the audience, I could get through it.

The story I ended with was this: Once, Jaakko and Kati took care of our yellow lab puppy, Sam. They jumped at the chance, as Sam had already outgrown their little terrier mutt, Baggio. Sam could send Baggio into a helicopter spin at the end of a towel, lifting all four legs off the floor. Another of Sam's favorite things to do was chasing balls.

One morning, Kati and Jaakko were on the back deck of their home that bordered a fairway at the Rock Creek Golf Course. Sam was laying on the deck as Jaakko drank his coffee, eyeing a foursome teeing off. Two balls dropped in front of him on the groomed fairway. Sam raised his head. Two more balls dropped and Sam was off in a flash.

Jaakko knew this was not good and raced after Sam with nothing but his bathrobe on. Jaakko told me, "Sam was on a mission to collect every ball on the golf course as I'm running after him. The golf balls were going one way," Jaakko said, "and mine were going the other!"

A loss like that is so hard, but that image left everyone, including the minister, rolling on the floor.

I had retired from Nike in 2001. I plunged myself into the design and construction of our new home in Sequim, Washington, on the Olympic Peninsula. Painting, setting the cabinets, doing tile work and laying floor coverings were all part of the process. I finished just prior to being diagnosed with cancer.

Retirement did not mean that I quit working. I continued to consult for Nike. I spoke to young athletes across the country, I represented the Bowerman Track Renovation Project, and I served as chairman of a non-profit board for Wings of America. Wings of America uses running to inspire and motivate native American youth. Through Wings, I had gotten to know James Nells and Sam Horsechief, coaches at Sequoia High School in Tahlequah, Oklahoma. They submitted a successful grant request to the Bowerman Track Renovation Project, and they wanted me to attend the dedication just prior to Thanksgiving. I found myself in Tahlequah, home of the Cherokee Nation, where I met with Chief Brad Smith, Wings founder Will Channing, and Wings executive director Edison Eskeets.

A few months earlier, James Nells had called me and informed me that his top runner, Konrad Holmes, the captain of their cross country team, had been diagnosed with brain cancer. James told me that Konrad was a big Prefontaine fan, so I had Tom Jordan send Konrad an autographed copy of his book *Pre*. Bob Speltz of Nike community affairs sent Konrad a Nike black leather jacket, and apparel developer Bob Smith sent a new Prefontaine T-shirt.

I went to visit Konrad, and met him at the school. He had lost his hair and steroid treatments had puffed his face up, but Konrad was holding on. It was all about attitude.

James told me that when Konrad was informed by his doctors that he could not run anymore, he called a team meeting that included his younger brother. He said, "I can't do this anymore, but you can." Sequoia High School went on to win their first state title.

Konrad was graduated early, as the faculty didn't think he'd make it to June. Lance Armstrong wrote a letter to Konrad, and there was Konrad in November again watching his former teammates at the state meet. He sported purple hair, his Prefontaine T-shirt and the black leather jacket. The team successfully defended their title.

Konrad continued his own fight. Then James Nells told him of my diagnosis—I had joined Konrad's club. I started receiving cards and messages from Konrad.

I couldn't believe it. This guy shouldn't be alive, and he's taken the time to write to me?

Konrad continued to go to his team's meets and cheered them on. A card and a series of photos from Konrad arrived in the mail. I especially loved the one of Konrad sitting with his bulldog Tumbo. I took a second photo and put it in my wallet next to the photos of Tracy and Kaili. Whenever I feel a little down, I pull out Konrad's photo—what an incredible-looking young guy.

Konrad attended his team's next state cross country championship. Amazingly, the team defended their title again, and the girls team finished second. This was the last time Konrad would leave home. His notes continued to arrive. The messages became shorter. Prior to Thanksgiving, he simply wrote on a card with an illustration of a turkey, "Geoff, eat lots of good food. Konrad."

Wings executive director Edison Eskeets flew up to Portland to visit me. We spoke on a number of Wings topics. At the end, Edison informed me, "We no longer have Konrad with us."

As much as you prepare yourself, you are not ready for what is inevitable. Konrad Homes died two days after he wrote his short Thanksgiving message.

Prior to the first event of the 2000 Prefontaine Classic, white-haired former athletes appeared at the northwest corner of Hayward Field's Stevenson Track. A large plaque was raised. Behind "The 1940's," a small group marched out and around the north turn. A larger group followed behind "The 1950's" that included Otis Davis, Phil Knight, Bill Dellinger, Jim Bailey and Jim Grelle. Photographers jogged ahead and panned the participants. I took my place in "The 1960's." Ray Prefontaine, sitting on a golf cart, joined "The 1970's" to represent Pre. These were "The Men of Oregon," Bill Bowerman's boys, all grown up, many retired from their profession. The west grandstands were filled, and spectators were on their feet as we circled the track. We were all filled with a sense of community.

Prior to the mile run, the venerable and retired Hayward Field announcer took the microphone. Wendy Ray called everyone's attention to the two rows of athletes on the west infield near the start line. Again, Ray Prefontaine stood in for his son Steve. Wendy proceeded to announce the name of every sub-4-minute miler and 1500 meter equivalent coached by Bill Bowerman—16 in all.

I reflected on this gathering years later when Barbara Bowerman was interviewed by *The Oregonian*. She mentioned that at the realization that Bill had quietly passed away in his sleep, she did not weep. She simply sat down and reflected on the life she shared with this remarkable man. Then she went on to say, "But when I read the headline in the paper the next morning, I thought of all the young men he coached. Then I cried."

I have thought often of what it all means. Life thrusts you into a competitive environment. How do you prepare for the realities and the unknown? Hopefully, you have a mentor, a Bowerman who pushes you at that critical time. A time when someone has a belief in your future more than you do. It's not about how long you live but how you contribute. It's about doing your best and doing the right thing. It's about recovering from your mistakes and not giving up. It's about the baton pass to a new generation. It's about the realization that you can not go it alone. It takes a team.

In the end, you are somewhere in the middle, part of a never-ending process. The future will never remember what was in your bank account or what kind of a car you drove. The future will remember that wild ride of life where you believed in others and left a gift behind for someone else to dream the impossible. That gift was your own life. It does not matter whether it was long or short. What did you leave behind?